the
ANIME CAFÉ

50 Iconic Treats, Snacks, and Drinks from Your Favorite Anime

NADINE ESTERO

Illustrations by
JANA PAYNOR

ROCK
POINT

First published in 2024 by Rock Point, an imprint of The Quarto Group,
142 West 36th Street, 4th Floor, New York, NY 10018, USA
(212) 779-4972 www.Quarto.com

Rock Point titles are also available at discount for retail, wholesale, promotional
and bulk purchase. For details, contact the Special Sales Manager by email
at specialsales@quarto.com or by mail at The Quarto Group, Attn: Special Sales
Manager, 100 Cummings Center Suite, 265D, Beverly, MA 01915, USA.

Library of Congress Control Number: 2024933384

10 9 8 7 6 5 4 3 2

ISBN: 978-1-63106-991-8
Digital edition published in 2024
eISBN: 978-0-7603-8766-5

Publisher: Rage Kindelsperger
Creative Director: Laura Drew
Editorial Director: Erin Canning
Managing Editor: Cara Donaldson
Editor: Leah Jenness
Interior Design: Evelin Kasikov
Cover and Interior Illustrations: Jana Paynor

Printed in China

This book is dedicated to every anime foodie who has drooled over these meals on the screen! A special thank-you to those who continue to support my work. Let's eat good together!

AUTHOR'S NOTE

Anime cafés are establishments that immerse fans in their favorite anime, servings dishes straight from episodes or inspired to look like characters and items from the anime.

I created this book with recipes worthy of being in an anime café, so anime fans can enjoy the anime café experience anywhere.

Choose recipes from any section depending on your preference that day. Recipes in the Bar section might be great on the weekend. Take Outdoor food on picnics or hikes. Modern recipes are great when you want to make something fancy. Cute foods make great gifts. If you're having a tough day, try a Comfort recipe. Classic recipes are great to make anytime!

Classic Café

Comfort Café

Cute Café

Modern Café

Outdoor Café

Bar Café

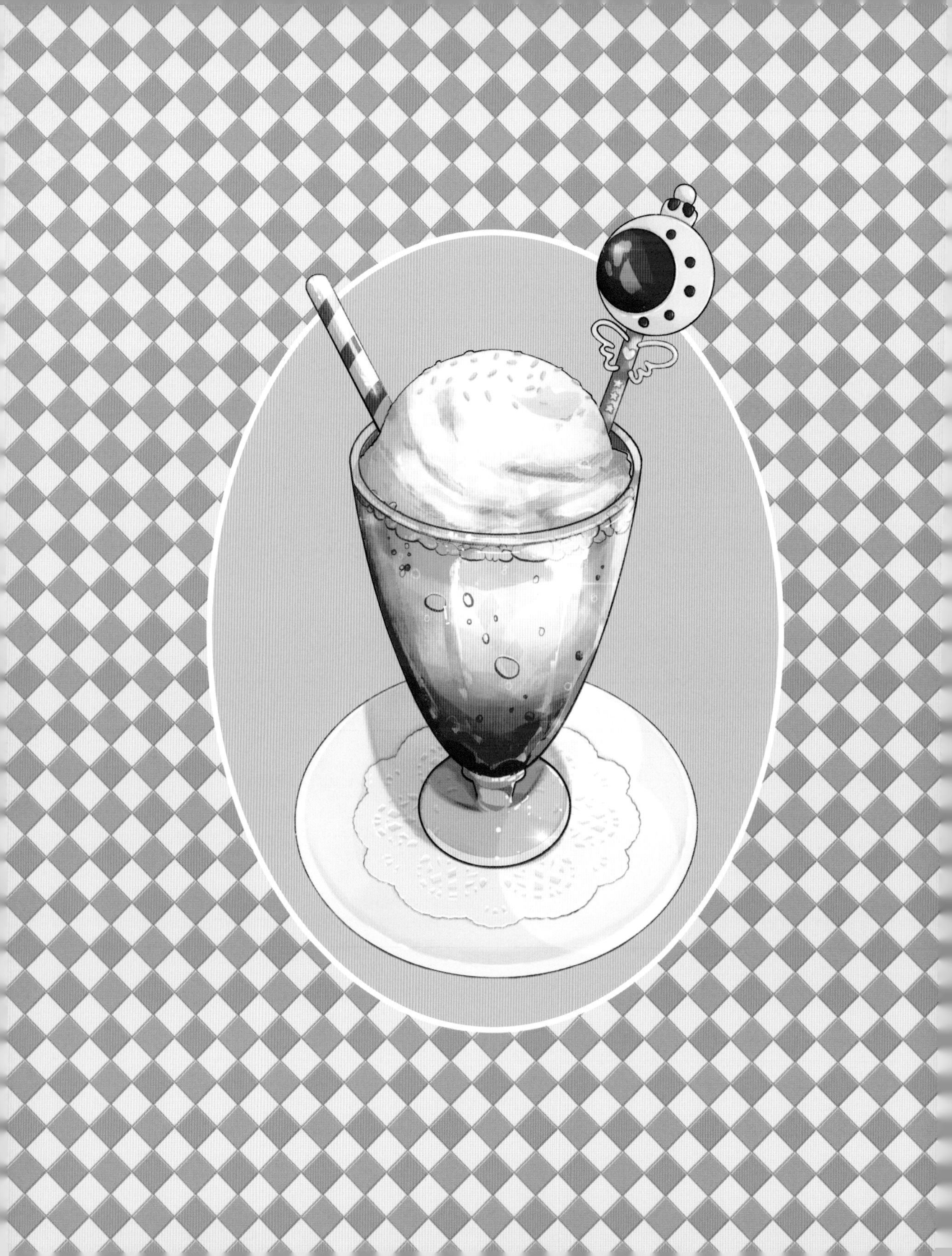

Classic

Café

MONT BLANC CUPCAKE

ANIME

TOMO-CHAN IS A GIRL!

EPISODE 13

"To Stay by Your Side . . ."

When Tomo and her high school friends eat at a café, Tomo updates them on the progression of her relationship with her childhood crush, Jun. Over their treats, they devise a plan for Tomo's first date with Jun. Most Japanese bakeries feature Mont Blanc cupcakes, especially in the fall. They're deliciously savory and sweet. With this recipe, you can enjoy a Mont Blanc all year round.

YIELD	PREP TIME	COOL TIME	COOK TIME
12	**40**	**45**	**1**
cupcakes	minutes	minutes	hour

SPECIAL TOOLS

12-cup muffin pan

12 cupcake liners

VANILLA SPONGE CUPCAKES

2 large eggs

⅓ cup (65 g) granulated sugar

½ cup (65 g) cake flour

1 pinch salt

1 tablespoon milk, at room temperature

1 tablespoon unsalted butter, melted

1 teaspoon vanilla extract

CANDIED CHESTNUTS AND CHESTNUT PUREE

1 cup (100 g) granulated sugar

¼ teaspoon salt

42 roasted peeled chestnuts (see Note on page 11)

2 tablespoons unsalted butter, melted

1 pinch salt

VANILLA WHIPPED CREAM

¾ cup (180 ml) heavy whipping cream

1 teaspoon vanilla extract

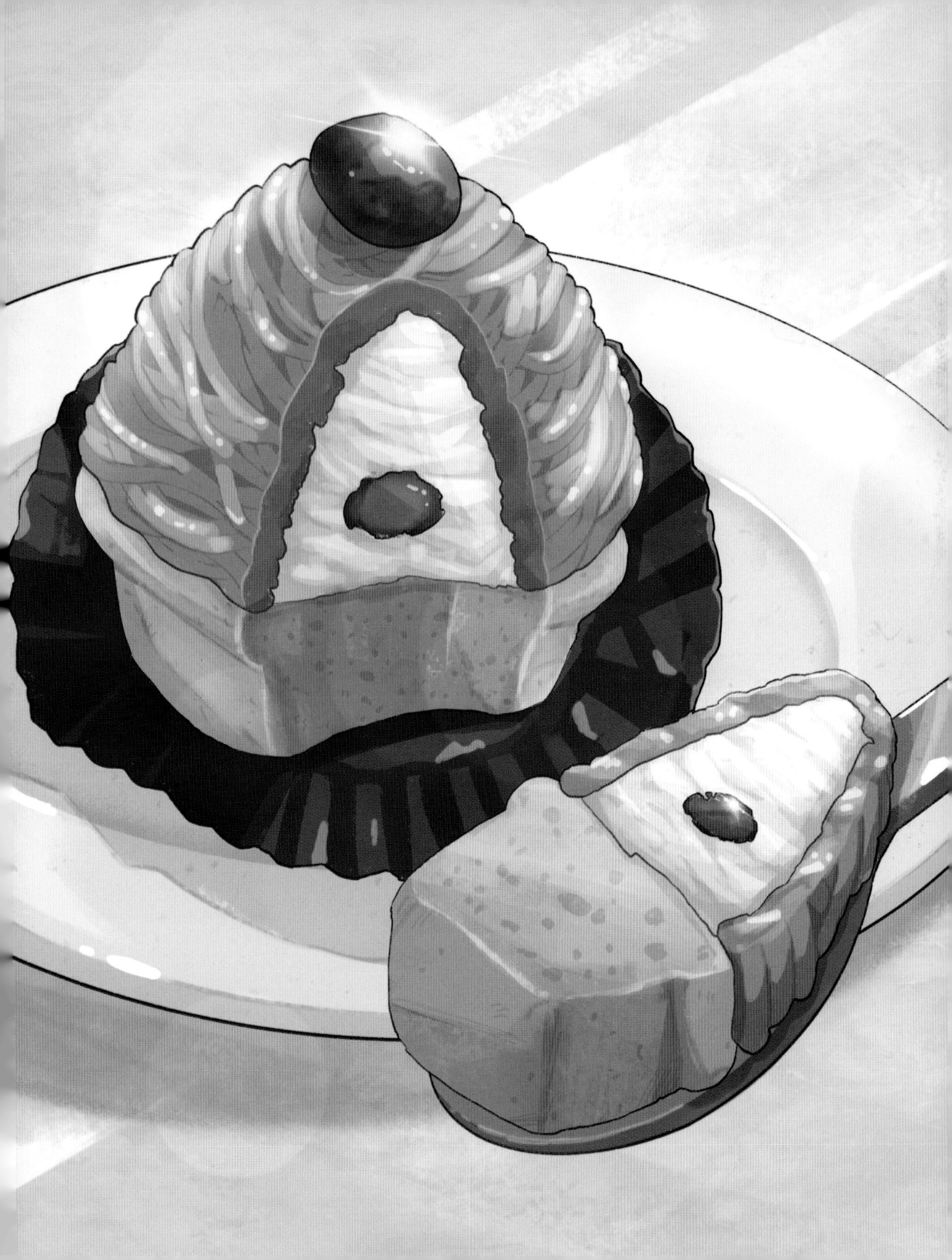

STEPS

1 **To make the vanilla sponge cupcakes:** Preheat the oven to 350°F (175°C). Line a muffin pan with cupcake liners and line a baking sheet with parchment paper.

2 In a medium heatproof bowl, using a wire whisk, whisk together the eggs and ⅓ cup (65 g) sugar. Prepare a double boiler by bringing at least 1½ inches (4 cm) of water to boil in a saucepan. Once the water boils, reduce the heat to medium and place the bowl with the egg-sugar mixture on top, making sure the bottom of the bowl is not touching the water. Heat the mixture, whisking constantly, until it reaches 100°F (38°C) measuring with a candy thermometer. Remove from the heat.

3 Using a hand mixer with a whisk attachment, beat the mixture on high speed until the volume has tripled, the color has lightened, and ribbons appear in the batter, about 10 minutes. Mix on low speed for 1 minute more to get rid of large air bubbles.

4 In a small bowl, sift together the cake flour and salt. Using a rubber spatula, fold the dry mixture into the batter. In a separate small bowl combine the milk, melted butter, and vanilla. Add the mixture to the batter, one-third of the mixture at a time, folding with the spatula until just combined and making sure to scrape the bottom of the small bowl for any loose liquids. Pour the batter into the prepared muffin pan, filling each cup about 80 percent full. Gently tap the muffin pan on a flat surface to get rid of large air bubbles and transfer to the oven immediately.

5 Bake for 20 to 25 minutes, until when you touch the top you hear sounds of bubbles popping and the cupcake springs back to its original height. Remove the pan from the oven and turn the cupcakes over onto the prepared baking sheet. Leave the cupcakes upside down for 10 minutes to achieve a flat top, then flip them upright and let cool to room temperature.

6 **To make the candied chestnuts and chestnut puree:** In a medium pot, combine the 1 cup (200 g) sugar and salt with 2 cups (480 ml) of water. Heat over medium-high until boiling. Once boiling, reduce the heat to medium-low, carefully add the chestnuts, and simmer slowly for 45 minutes. After 45 minutes, remove from the heat and let cool to room temperature.

7 Once cooled, reserve 12 candied chestnuts and ¼ cup (60 ml) of the simmered sugar syrup for decoration. Place the rest of the candied chestnuts along with the melted butter, 3 tablespoons of the simmered sugar syrup, and ¼ cup plus 2 tablespoons (90 ml) of water, and a pinch of salt into a food processor. Blend until smooth, scraping the sides as needed. Set a fine-mesh sieve over a medium bowl and pass the mixture through to create a lump-free chestnut paste for easy piping. Transfer the chestnut paste to a piping bag fitted with a small piping tip or a multi-hole piping tip (such as a Wilton #233 tip).

8 **To make the vanilla whipped cream:**
In a medium bowl, combine the whipping cream and vanilla. Using a handheld electric mixer with the whisk attachment on low speed, and gradually increasing to medium-high, whip the mixture until stiff peaks form, about 3 minutes. Transfer the whipped cream to a piping bag and cut a 1-inch (2.5 cm) hole at the tip when ready to decorate.

9 **To assemble:** Cut the reserved 12 candied chestnuts in half using a small knife and set aside. Dip a pastry brush into the reserved simmered sugar syrup and dab it onto the cooled cupcake tops. Squeeze a tablespoon of vanilla whipped cream onto the center of each cupcake and place a halved candied chestnut, cut side down, on top of the whipped cream.

10 Cover the chestnut with more whipped cream, creating a triangular mound about 2 inches (5 cm) in height. Cover the whipped cream with the chestnut puree by piping it neatly, starting from the base of the whipped-cream mount and rotating upward to the top of the whipped cream to cover it entirely. Top each cupcake with the remaining halves of the candied chestnuts, cut sides down.

11 Serve immediately for the best taste, or refrigerate until ready to serve for up to a day.

NOTE

Prepackaged roasted chestnuts are used here for hassle-free baking, but you can make this even faster by purchasing candied chestnuts in jars and chestnut paste in cans from your local grocer or online markets—just make sure they are made in France. I've spoken with a few bakeries to ask how they make their Mont Blanc, and they told me that the chestnuts and chestnut paste are imported.

"The three of us can just eat together."

—Misuzu Gundo

VALENTINE'S CHOCOLATE CAKE

ANIME

HORIMIYA: THE MISSING PIECES

EPISODE 6

"Sleepover"

Valentine's Day is celebrated widely in anime. Celebrating it usually consists of gifting homemade chocolate or confections—called "obligatory chocolates"—to both friends and love interests. In terms of the latter, Hori and Miyamura exchange desserts privately. Miyamura presents Hori with this Valentine's chocolate cake. Hori eats it and exclaims, "Delicious as always!"

YIELD	PREP TIME	COOK TIME	COOL TIME
4–6 servings	40 minutes	30 minutes	45 minutes

SPECIAL TOOLS

6-inch (15 cm) round cake pan

CHOCOLATE CAKE

2 tablespoons unsalted butter, plus more for greasing

¼ cup (60 ml) milk

1 teaspoon vanilla extract

¼ cup (60 ml) boiling water

⅓ cup (33 g) unsweetened cocoa powder

½ cup (60 g) all-purpose flour

⅓ cup (65 g) granulated sugar

¾ teaspoon baking powder

¾ teaspoon baking soda

⅛ teaspoon salt

CHOCOLATE GLAZE

⅓ cup (80 ml) heavy cream

¼ cup (44 g) dark chocolate chips for baking

1 tablespoon unsalted butter

1 teaspoon vanilla extract

1 pinch salt

VANILLA WHIPPED CREAM

½ cup (120 ml) heavy whipping cream

2 teaspoons granulated sugar

1 teaspoon vanilla extract

TOPPING

Crushed pistachios

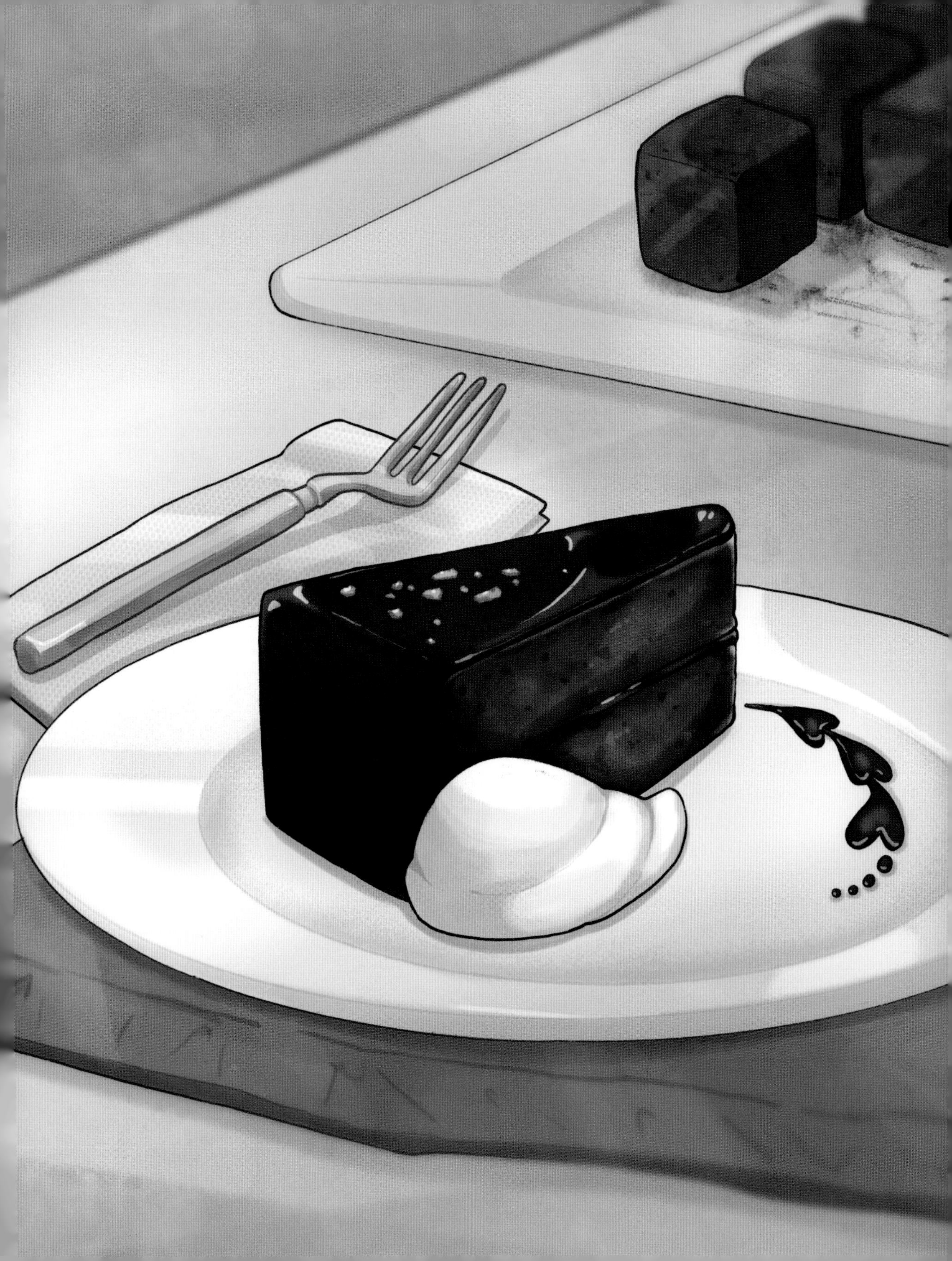

STEPS

1. **To make the chocolate cake:** Preheat the oven to 325°F (170°C). Grease the sides and bottom of a 6-inch (15 cm) round cake pan with butter or line it with parchment paper.

2. In a heatproof bowl, combine the 2 tablespoons butter and milk, then microwave in quick blasts until the butter is melted and the milk is warm, 40 to 60 seconds. Transfer to a large bowl.

3. Stir the vanilla extract into the warm milk mixture. In a small heatproof bowl, mix the boiling water with the cocoa powder. Add the cocoa mixture to the bowl of wet ingredients and combine. In a separate bowl, sift together the flour, ⅓ cup (65 g) sugar, baking powder, baking soda, and ⅛ teaspoon salt. Add the dry ingredients to the wet ingredients and stir until combined. Do not overmix.

4. Pour the cake batter into the cake pan, tapping the pan twice on a work surface to get rid of any large air bubbles, then bake for 25 to 30 minutes, until the top is flat and a toothpick inserted into the center comes out clean.

5. Immediately after baking, place a piece of parchment paper on top of the cake and carefully flip the pan onto a cooling rack to remove the cake from the pan. Let the cake cool for 10 minutes to achieve a smooth top, then flip the cake upright on the rack and let cool to room temperature, about 20 minutes. Once cooled, use a serrated knife to slice the cake in half lengthwise to create 2 layers.

6. **To make the chocolate glaze:** In a heatproof bowl microwave the heavy cream until hot, 1 to 2 minutes. In a separate heatproof bowl, add the chocolate chips, then pour the hot heavy cream over the top. Let the mixture sit for 1 minute, then stir until the chocolate melts. Add the 1 tablespoon butter, vanilla extract, and a pinch of salt, then stir until the mixture becomes smooth.

7. **To assemble:** Working quickly while the chocolate glaze is still warm (do not reheat), place the top half of the cake, cut side down, on the cooling rack and set a sheet pan underneath to catch drips. Set aside 1 tablespoon of the chocolate glaze for serving. Pour about one-third of the chocolate glaze on top and gently spread it over surface of the cake with an offset spatula or a spoon. Place the bottom half of the cake, cut side up, on top of the glazed half, making sure to center both halves. Pour the remaining chocolate glaze over the entire cake, gently spreading with an offset spatula or spoon. Let the chocolate glaze set, about 15 minutes. Transfer to a cake box or plate for serving.

8. **To make the vanilla whipped cream:** Right before serving, in a medium bowl and using a hand mixer with a whisk attachment, mix the whipping cream, 2 teaspoons sugar, and vanilla extract, starting from low speed and gradually increasing to medium-high, until medium peaks form, about 2 minutes.

9. **To serve:** Cut the cake into 4 or 6 equal slices, wiping the knife on a paper towel in between slicing to achieve clean cuts. Place a slice in the center of a dessert plate. With the reserved tablespoon of chocolate glaze, use a small spoon to create hearts on the plate. Scoop a spoon of vanilla whipped cream beside the cake. Sprinkle a pinch of crushed pistachios on top.

CLASSIC STRAWBERRY CAKE

ANIME

DEATH NOTE

EPISODE 18

"Ally"

Throughout the *Death Note* series, L is seen eating sweets ranging from small chocolates to elaborate cakes. I wanted to include this classic strawberry cake because it was so good that he asked Misa for her slice after he quickly devoured his.

YIELD	PREP TIME	COOK TIME	CHILL TIME
8	**45**	**40**	**30**
servings	minutes	minutes	minutes

SPECIAL TOOLS

7-inch (18 cm) round cake pan

Rotating cake stand (optional)

VANILLA SPONGE CAKE

2 tablespoons unsalted butter, melted, plus more for greasing

4 large eggs

⅔ cup (135 g) granulated sugar

1 cup (130 g) cake flour

1 pinch salt

2 tablespoons milk, at room temperature

1 teaspoon vanilla extract

WHIPPED CREAM

2½ cups (600 ml) heavy whipping cream

1 tablespoon granulated sugar

1 teaspoon vanilla extract

2 drops pink food coloring

¼ teaspoon strawberry extract, or to taste

SIMPLE SYRUP

¼ cup (50 g) granulated sugar

FOR ASSEMBLY

5 medium strawberries, hulled and sliced ¼ inch (6 mm) thick

8 small strawberries, hulled

STEPS

1. **To make the vanilla sponge cake:** Preheat the oven to 350°F (180°C). Grease the sides and bottom of the 7-inch (18 cm) round cake pan with butter or line it with parchment paper.

2. Prepare a double boiler by bringing at least 1½ inches (4 cm) of water to a boil in a saucepan. Find a heatproof bowl that will fit on top of the saucepan without touching the water. In this bowl, whisk together the eggs and the ⅔ cup (135 g) sugar. Once the water is boiling, place the bowl over the double boiler, and continue whisking constantly until the mixture reaches 100°F (38°C), measuring with a candy thermometer. Remove the bowl from the heat, then, using a hand mixer with a whisk attachment, mix on high speed until the volume has tripled, the mixture has turned lighter, and ribbons are left in the batter while mixing, about 10 minutes. Whisk on low speed for 1 minute more to get rid of large air bubbles.

3. In a small bowl, sift together the cake flour and salt, then use a spatula to fold the dry mixture into the batter. In another small bowl combine the milk, melted butter, and vanilla extract. Add this mixture to the batter, one-third of the mixture at a time, folding with the spatula until just combined and making sure to scrape the bottom of the small bowl for any loose liquids. Transfer the batter to the prepared cake pan and immediately place in the oven.

4. Bake for 25 to 30 minutes, until when you press gently on the cake's surface, you hear sounds of bubbles popping and the cake springs back to its original height. Immediately after baking, place a piece of parchment paper on top of the cake and carefully flip the pan over to remove the cake and set on a cooling rack for 10 minutes to achieve a smooth top. Flip it back to its original position and let cool to room temperature.

5. **Meanwhile, make the whipped cream:** Using a hand mixer with a whisk attachment on low speed, in a medium bowl, whip the whipping cream with the 1 tablespoon sugar and vanilla. Gradually increase the speed to medium-high until soft peaks form, about 2 minutes. Transfer one-third of the soft whipped cream to a separate bowl.

6. Continue to whip the rest of the cream on medium-high speed until stiff peaks form, about 1 minute more. Transfer half of the stiff whipped cream to a separate bowl.

7. Add the pink food coloring and strawberry extract to the remaining stiff whipped cream. Mix until well combined and the color has distributed.

8. **To make the simple syrup:** In a small saucepan over medium heat, bring ¼ cup (60 ml) water and the ¼ cup (50 g) sugar to a boil. Reduce to a simmer, stirring occasionally, until the sugar has dissolved, 4 to 5 minutes. Remove from the heat and let cool.

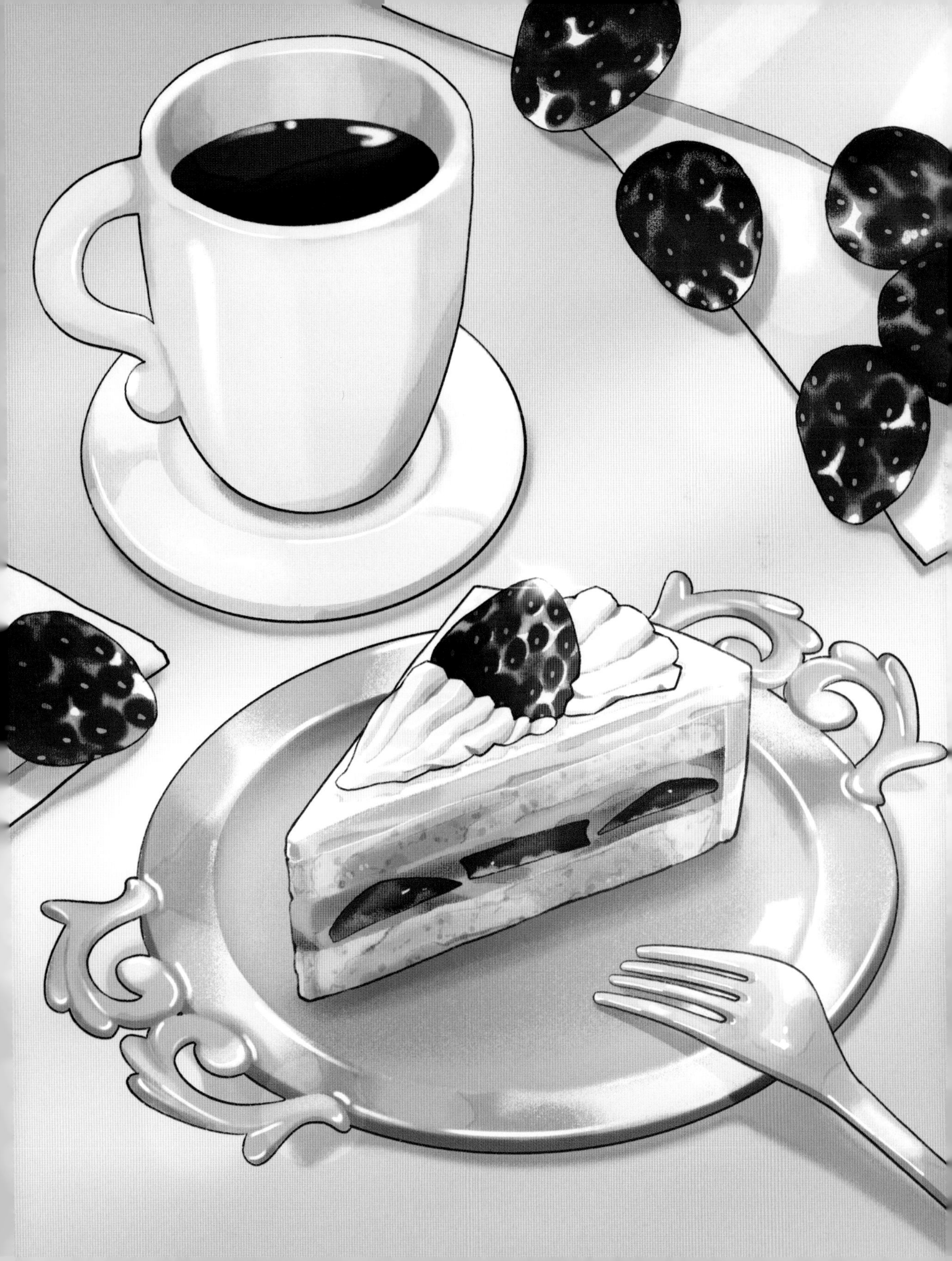

9. **To assemble:** Slice the cooled vanilla sponge cake in half lengthwise to create 2 layers. Using a pastry brush, lightly dab the simple syrup onto the cut sides of both cake halves. Place a teaspoon of the soft whipping cream from step 5 on the center of a serving plate or a rotating cake stand, if using, to prevent the cake from slipping while decorating. Place the top half of the cake, cut side down, onto the cake stand.

10. Spread a ¼-inch (6 mm) layer of the strawberry whipped cream from step 7 over the top of the cake on the stand and smooth it out with an offset spatula. Layer on the sliced strawberries to cover the cake, then cover them with another ¼-inch (6 mm) layer of the strawberry whipped cream and smooth out.

11. Set the bottom half of the cake, cut side down, on top of the strawberry whipped cream. Cover the sides and top of the cake with a thin layer of regular stiff whipped cream from step 6, using a clean offset spatula to smooth the cream into all the crevices. Refrigerate the cake for 30 minutes, or until it is chilled and the outer layer of the whipped cream has hardened.

12. Remove the cake from the refrigerator. Using an offset spatula, cover the entire cake with an even layer of the soft whipped cream from step 5. Place the remaining soft whipped cream in a piping bag fitted with a star tip.

13. Hold the piping bag at a 45-degree angle and make a roughly 1-inch (2.5 cm) mound starting from the center of the cake and pulling outward to the edge. Repeat once more right behind the first mound. Repeat 7 more times radially, then place a small strawberry on top of each second mound. Cut the cake into 8 equal slices and serve.

"By the way, are you going to eat that piece of cake?"

—L

BAKED RED BEAN BUNS

ANIME

GINTAMA

SEASON 2, EPISODE 4

"Meals Should Be Balanced/ We Are All Warriors in the Battle against Fate"

Gintama is an anime favorite, having several crossover episodes with other popular animes such as *Dragon Ball*, *Bleach*, and *Death Note*, just to list a few! Yamazaki strongly believes in the superstition of eating baked red beans (*anpan* in Japanese) during stakeouts, so he buys a plastic bag filled with anpan and rushes to his stakeout position—but crashes into someone—his target!—and drops all of his anpan. In the end, Yamazaki is caught by his target—because his target knew that anpan is eaten on stakeouts and she was being watched. Anpan is the equivalent of donuts for American police officers, readily available in convenience stores and perfect for easy eating.

MAKES	PREP TIME	PROOF TIME	COOK TIME
6	20	1	1
buns	minutes	1 hour 30 minutes	1 hour 48 minutes

RED BEAN PASTE

½ cup (100 g) dried red beans (also called adzuki beans)

¼ cup (50 g) granulated sugar

⅛ teaspoon salt

FLUFFY BREAD BUNS

½ cup plus 1 tablespoon (135 ml) milk

2 tablespoons granulated sugar

1 teaspoon active dry yeast

2 cups (240 g) bread flour, plus more for dusting

¼ teaspoon salt

¼ cup (50 g) unsalted butter, at room temperature

1 teaspoon canola oil, for greasing

1 egg yolk

2 tablespoons white sesame seeds

1 tablespoon unsalted butter, melted, for brushing

STEPS

1. **To make the red bean paste:** Pour the dried red beans into a medium saucepan and cover with enough water to submerge them (about four times the amount of beans). Bring to a boil over medium-high heat and cook for 5 minutes. Drain the beans and rinse them, then rinse the saucepan with fresh water. Return the beans to the pan. Fill the saucepan with more water, enough to submerge the beans again. Bring to a boil once more over medium-high heat, then reduce the heat to medium and cover the pan with a lid. Cook the beans until soft, 1 hour and 30 minutes to 2 hours.

Stir in the ¼ cup (50 g) sugar and ⅛ teaspoon salt and cook, stirring occasionally, until the water is fully evaporated, about 30 minutes. Remove the pan from the heat. Use a masher to squish about three-quarters of the beans into a paste, leaving the rest whole to add texture. Let the beans cool to room temperature.

2   **Meanwhile, make the fluffy bread buns:** In a heatproof bowl, microwave the milk for 40 to 60 seconds until warm. In the bowl of a stand mixer, stir together the warm milk, sugar, and active dry yeast and mix until the yeast becomes saturated. Cover the bowl with plastic wrap and let rest until the yeast bubbles and blooms, about 5 minutes, then add the bread flour and salt to the bowl. Using the dough hook attachment, set the mixer to low and mix, gradually bringing the mixer to medium-high speed. Knead for 10 minutes, or until the dough is smooth and not sticky. Add in the unsalted butter, and continue to mix until fully incorporated, around 5 minutes. Stop the mixer and test the dough: You should be able to stretch a small piece of the dough into a layer thin enough to see light through it without the dough ripping. If you can do this without any tears, continue to the next step. If not, continue to knead the dough for another 2 minutes before testing it again. Repeat until the dough passes the test.

3   When the dough is ready, remove it from the bowl and hand-knead it into a ball. Lightly oil the bowl before returning the dough ball to it. Cover the bowl with plastic wrap and proof at room temperature until the ball doubles in size and holds its shape when poked in the center, about 1 hour.

If the dough returns to its original shape, then it is not ready and must be proofed further. Keep testing it every 5 minutes. Be careful not to over-proof, as that will result in collapsed buns.

4   Line a baking tray with parchment paper. Punch down the dough and transfer it to a lightly floured work surface. Knead the dough by hand for 2 minutes to get rid of large air bubbles, then shape it into a log. Divide the dough into 6 equal pieces (about 80 g each). Wrap all but one in plastic wrap. Working with one piece at a time, roll the dough into a smooth ball, then use your hands or a rolling pin to flatten it into a roughly 3½-inch (9 cm) circle, leaving a small mound of dough in the center. Place a ball of red bean paste in the center of the flattened dough, then wrap the dough around it, pinching together the opposite edges of the dough and repeating until the bean paste is covered. Pinch the seams together, then turn the bun seam-side down and roll into a neat ball before transferring it to the prepared baking tray. Repeat for the rest of the dough pieces, spacing the buns at least 2 inches (5 cm) apart on the baking tray. Cover the buns with a tea towel or cloth, and let them rise until doubled in size, about 30 minutes. Meanwhile, preheat the oven to 350°F (180°C).

5   When the buns have risen, beat the egg yolk. Using a pastry brush, brush the tops of the buns with the beaten yolk and sprinkle each with a pinch of white sesame seeds. Bake until the buns are golden brown, 18 to 20 minutes. Remove from the heat and brush the tops with melted butter. Serve hot or at room temperature.

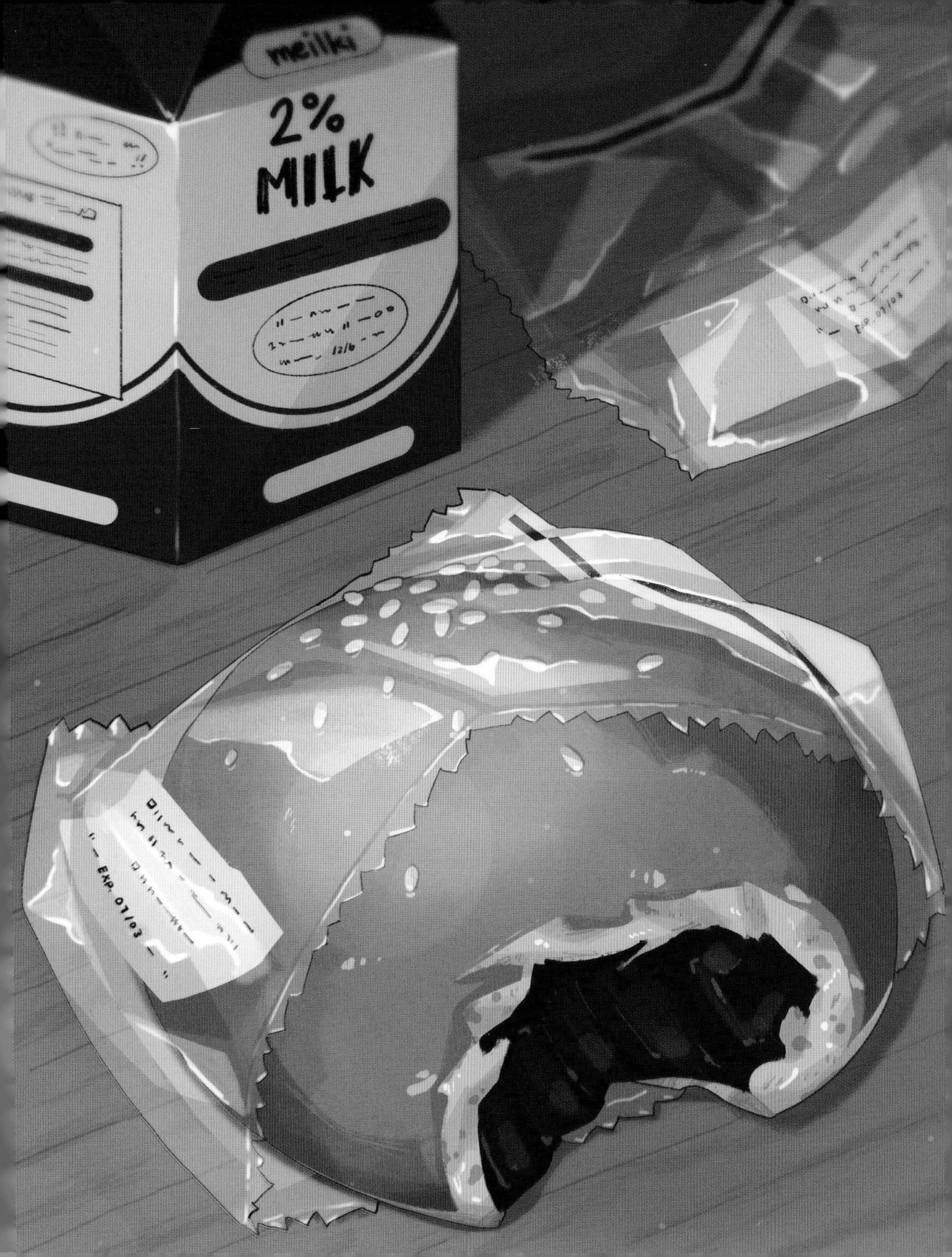
2%
MILK
EXP. 07/03

CELESTIAL STRAWBERRY FLOAT

ANIME

SAILOR MOON R

EPISODE 30

"Magic of Darkness: Esmeraude's Invasion"

Usagi and her friends arrive at Maxi-5 Bakery's grand opening event offering all-you-can-eat cakes. The display case shows a variety of sweets and drinks, including this pink strawberry float. Usagi's friends worry about the calories, but Usagi assures everyone that the drink will replenish their energy. Later, Usagi eats right at the dessert bar, rather than bringing the plates to her table. This pink strawberry float has a beautiful aesthetic that ties in with *Sailor Moon*. I've also added Sailor Moon's iconic weapon from this season, the Moon Scepter.

YIELD	PREP TIME	COOK TIME	DECORATE TIME
2	**5**	**5**	**20**
servings	minutes	minutes	minutes

THE MOON SCEPTER

2 red hard candies (such as Jolly Rancher)

2 strawberry Pocky biscuit sticks

¼ cup (40 g) white chocolate melts

1 drop yellow gel food coloring

1 drop red gel food coloring

STRAWBERRY FLOAT

2 cans (12 ounces, or 355 ml, each) strawberry soda

2 cups (300 g) vanilla ice cream

Yellow sprinkles

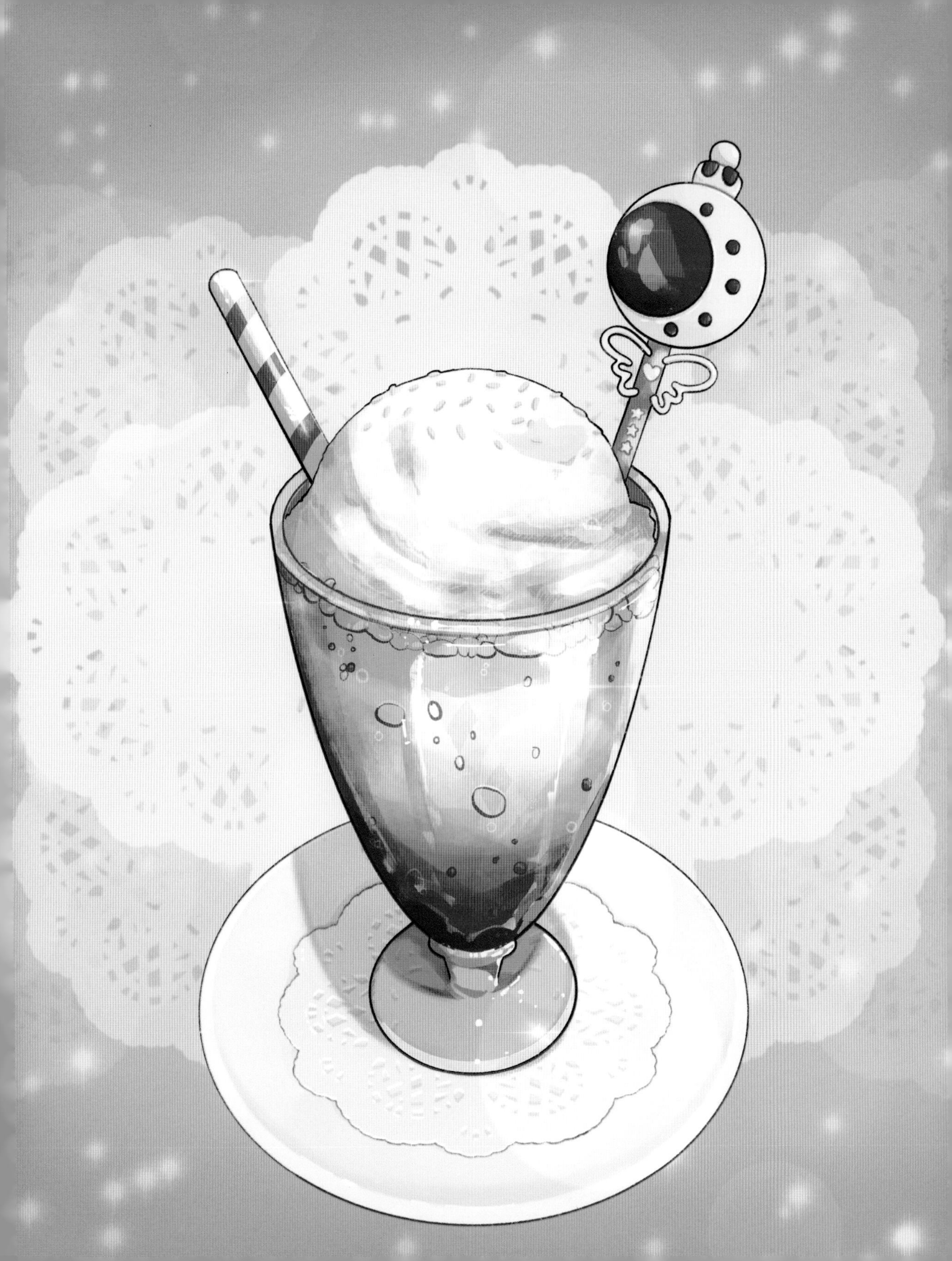

STEPS

1. **To make the Moon Scepter:** Preheat the oven to 350°F (180°C). Line a baking tray with parchment paper.

2. Place the red hard candies in a resealable plastic bag and set the bag on a cutting board. Using a meat mallet or a rolling pin, crush the candy into small pieces. Remove the crushed candy from the bag and arrange the pieces into two ½-inch (1 cm) circles on the prepared parchment. (Hint: Make extra if you have more candy, as some circles will come out better than others.) Bake until the candy fully melts, 1 to 2 minutes, watching closely to avoid burning. Remove the tray from the oven, and use a toothpick to gently perfect the shape of the circles. Let the candy circles cool to room temperature, about 10 minutes.

3. Meanwhile, place a piece of parchment paper on a cutting board or work surface and set out the strawberry Pocky vertically (strawberry-dipped ends at the top and the plain biscuit ends at the bottom). Microwave the white chocolate melts in a small bowl until melted, about 30 seconds. Pour half of the melted white chocolate in a separate small bowl. In one bowl, stir in the drop of yellow gel food coloring; in the other, stir in the drop of red gel food coloring. Quickly transfer the yellow and red chocolate to individual piping bags and cut a roughly ⅛-inch (3 mm) hole in the tip.

4. Assemble and decorate the Moon Scepters using the melted chocolate; use a clean toothpick to spread or sharpen corners of the chocolate at any point in decorating. Making one Moon Scepter at a time, place one cooled red candy circle at the top of a strawberry Pocky, leaving ¼ inch (6 mm) of space in between. Starting with the yellow chocolate, draw a crescent moon shape (a backward C), surrounding and touching the perimeter of the candy. Connect the bottom of the crescent to the tip of the Pocky. Pipe wings underneath the crescent, sketching a rounded E on the right side of the Pocky to make the right wing and a backward rounded E on the left side to make the left wing. Pipe a small heart between the wings and, just underneath that, add three stars vertically on the Pocky.

5. Using the red chocolate, pipe 5 evenly spaced small dots on top of the yellow crescent, a small square on top of the crescent, and a vertical rectangle in the center of the heart.

6. Repeat steps 4 and 5 for the second Moon Scepter. Let the designs cool and harden, about 5 minutes, before carefully peeling off the parchment paper.

7. **To make the strawberry float:** Fill a parfait or large glass about 70 percent full with strawberry soda. Add a generous scoop of vanilla ice cream on top. Decorate the ice cream with yellow sprinkles, then gently push the Moon Scepter decoration into the ice cream. Repeat for the second strawberry float. Add a straw to each and provide a dessert spoon on the side. Serve immediately.

STRAWBERRY BANANA CREPES

ANIME

JUJUTSU KAISEN

SEASON 1, EPISODE 3

"Girl of Steel"

The setting is Harajuku, the popular shopping district for fashion and cute street food in Tokyo. The food sold here is handheld on sticks or in wraps to make eating convenient with one hand. Colorful crepes are popular and served savory and sweet. In this episode, Itadori is seen with a strawberry banana crepe while waiting for friends.

YIELD	PREP TIME	COOK TIME	DECORATE TIME
4	**15**	**10**	**5**
crepes	minutes	minutes	minutes

SPECIAL TOOLS

8-inch (20 cm) pan

CREPE BATTER

1 large egg

1 tablespoon granulated sugar

½ cup (120 ml) milk

2 tablespoons unsalted butter, divided

1 teaspoon vanilla extract

⅓ cup (45 g) cake flour

1 pinch salt

MILKY CHOCOLATE SYRUP

2 tablespoons condensed milk

2 teaspoons unsweetened cocoa powder

1 pinch salt

VANILLA WHIPPED CREAM

1 cup (240 ml) heavy whipping cream

½ tablespoon granulated sugar

1 teaspoon vanilla extract

FOR ASSEMBLY AND DECORATION

8 strawberries, hulled and thinly sliced

1 banana, sliced thin

2 cups (300 g) vanilla ice cream

Chocolate sprinkles

STEPS

1. **To make the crepe batter:** In a large bowl, combine the egg and sugar and, using a wire whisk, whisk vigorously until lumps disappear, about 1 minute. In a heatproof bowl, microwave the milk and 1 tablespoon of the butter together for 40 to 60 seconds, until warm. Then stir in the vanilla extract. Stir the warm mixture into the egg and sugar. Sift in the cake flour and salt, then whisk the mixture until the flour lumps disappear. Using a fine-mesh sieve, strain the mixture into a large pouring vessel, and then set aside for at least 10 minutes, or overnight (see Note). Meanwhile make the milky chocolate syrup and vanilla whipped cream.

2. **To make the milky chocolate syrup:** In a small bowl, whisk together the milk, cocoa powder, and salt until smooth.

3. **To make the vanilla whipped cream:** In a medium bowl, combine the whipping cream, sugar, and vanilla extract. Using a hand mixer on low and gradually increasing to medium-high speed, whip the mixture until soft peaks form, about 2 minutes. Transfer the vanilla whipped cream into a piping bag fitted with a large star tip.

4. **To cook the crepes:** Heat a crepe pan or a large nonstick skillet over medium heat. Once hot, add ¼ tablespoon of the butter until melted, then reduce the heat to low. Use a folded piece of paper towel to remove excess butter. Mix the batter with a whisk to reconstitute, then pour in a quarter of the batter and swirl the pan to create a thin circle. Cook until the top of the crepe is dry to the touch and the bottom is browned, about 2 minutes. Gently flip the crepe and cook for another 5 seconds. Immediately transfer the cooked crepe from the pan to a plate. Repeat using the remaining butter and batter to make 3 more crepes.

5. **To assemble and decorate:** Set each crepe, browned side down, on the plate. Using the vanilla whipped cream, pipe a line roughly 3 inches (8 cm) long from left to right at the top edge of the crepe. At the end of the line, from the right side, pipe diagonally down to the center of the crepe to create a number 7. Arrange a quarter of the strawberries and a quarter of the banana on top of the vanilla whipped cream. Scoop ½ cup (75 g) of vanilla ice cream in the center of the crepe, then drizzle a zigzag of milky chocolate syrup over the whole crepe. To close the crepe, fold it in half vertically and then fold it again horizontally in thirds. Repeat for the other crepes. Decorate the tops with another drizzle of milky chocolate syrup and chocolate sprinkles and serve immediately.

NOTE

You can make the crepe batter and milky chocolate syrup the night before, and then refrigerate. Simply whisk the batter until smooth again before cooking.

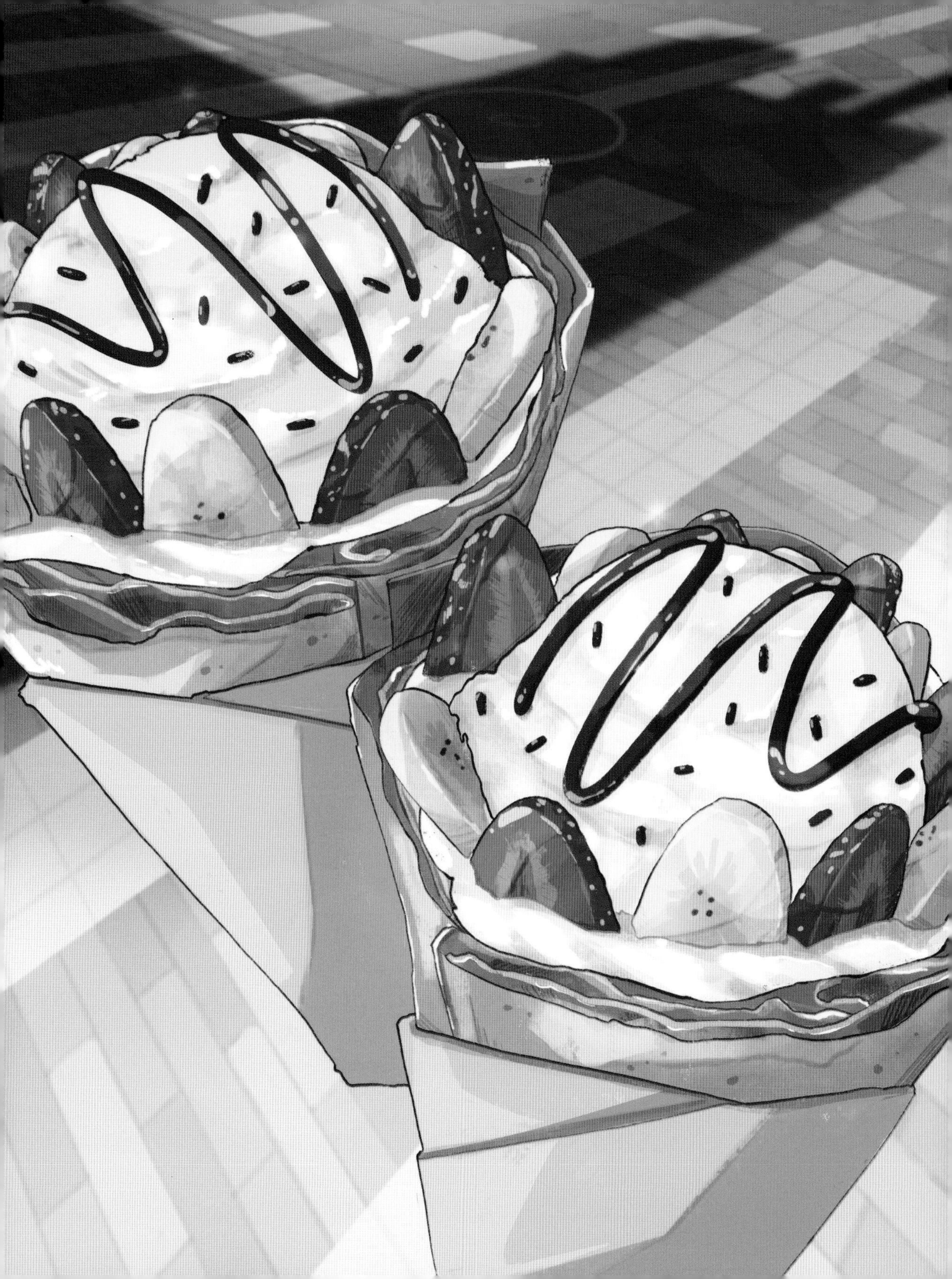

CLEAR-BONUS BLUEBERRY CHEESECAKE

MOVIE

SWORD ART ONLINE THE MOVIE: ORDINAL SCALE

Cheesecake is often mentioned in the anime, so I've decided to include it! The world of *Sword Art Online* seems to be taking data from all the players' everyday lives, so when they order dessert at a café, the AI surprises them with their favorites. The players are shocked by this. It feels relatable to real life because of all the data the internet is taking from us!

YIELD	PREP TIME	COOK TIME	SET TIME
5	**40**	**30**	**8**
servings	minutes	minutes	hours

SPECIAL TOOLS

6-inch (15 cm) springform pan

GRAHAM CRACKER CRUST

¼ cup (55 g) unsalted butter

¾ cup (90 g) graham cracker crumbs

½ tablespoon packed dark brown sugar

¼ teaspoon salt

BLUEBERRY GEL LAYER AND TOPPING

½ tablespoon unflavored gelatin

16 ounces (454 g) blueberries

¼ cup (50 g) granulated sugar

¼ teaspoon salt

CHEESECAKE

½ cup (120 ml) heavy whipping cream

8 ounces (227 g) cream cheese, at room temperature

¼ cup (60 ml) sour cream, at room temperature

¼ cup (50 g) granulated sugar

Zest and juice of ½ lemon

1 teaspoon vanilla extract

1 pinch salt

TOPPING

¼ cup (60 ml) heavy whipping cream

½ tablespoon granulated sugar

1 teaspoon vanilla extract

5 sprigs fresh mint

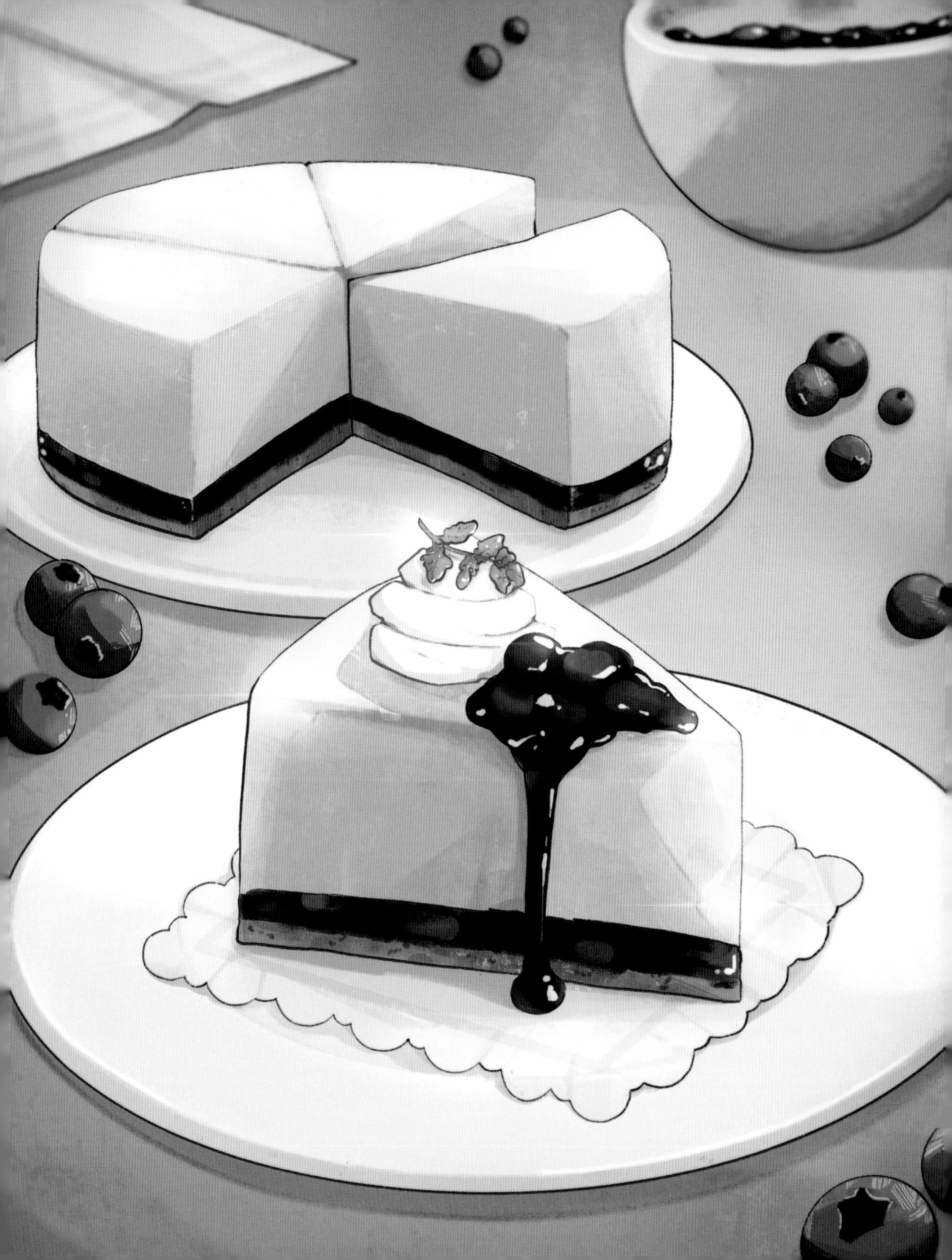

STEPS

1 **To make the graham cracker crust:** In a microwave-safe container, microwave the butter until melted, about 40 seconds. Add the graham cracker crumbs, dark brown sugar, and ¼ teaspoon salt and mix until well combined. Transfer the mixture to a 6-inch (15 cm) springform pan, pressing it tightly into the bottom of the pan. Refrigerate as you work on the other layers.

2 **To make the blueberry gel layer and topping:** In a small bowl, combine the unflavored gelatin with 2 tablespoons of water. Mix until combined and set aside. In a medium pot over medium-high heat, combine 1¼ cups (300 ml) of water with the blueberries, ¼ cup (50 g) granulated sugar, and ¼ teaspoon salt and bring to a boil. Once boiling, reduce the heat to medium and cook, stirring occasionally, for about 10 minutes. Then use a masher or the back of a fork to smash the blueberries. Continue cooking until the sauce is reduced by about a third of its original volume, about 15 minutes more (25 minutes total). Remove from the heat. Transfer ¼ cup (60 g) of the mixture to a heatproof container and refrigerate until serving.

3 Add the rehydrated gelatin to the remaining blueberry sauce in the pot. Over medium-high heat, stirring occasionally, bring the mixture to a boil, about 5 minutes. Once boiling, remove the pot from the heat. Remove the graham cracker crust from the refrigerator. Pour the blueberry gelatin over the graham cracker crust, spreading it evenly with an offset spatula or a spoon. Return the pan to the refrigerator.

4 **To make the cheesecake:** In a medium bowl, using a hand mixer, whip the ½ cup (120 ml) whipping cream on low, gradually increasing to high speed, until stiff peaks form, about 3 minutes.

5 In a separate medium bowl, using the hand mixer set to medium speed, whip the cream cheese until softened and whipped, about 2 minutes. Continuing to mix, add the sour cream, ¼ cup (50 g) granulated sugar, lemon zest and juice, vanilla extract, and pinch of salt and mix until well combined, about 3 minutes.

6 Using a rubber spatula, fold the stiff whipped cream into the cream cheese mixture, adding one-third of the whipped cream at a time until well combined and smooth. Remove the springform pan from the refrigerator. Pour the cheesecake filling on top of the blueberry gel layer and smooth the top using a clean offset spatula or spoon. Cover with plastic wrap, making sure it touches the cheesecake filling to prevent a skin from forming, then refrigerate until set, 8 hours, or overnight.

7 **To make the topping:** In a medium bowl, using a hand mixer on low and gradually increasing to medium-high speed, whip the ¼ cup (60 ml) whipping cream, ½ tablespoon granulated sugar, and vanilla until medium peaks form, about 2½ minutes. Transfer the whipped cream into a piping bag fitted with a star tip. Remove the set cheesecake from the springform pan and cut into 5 equal slices. Place a slice on a plate and pipe a small mound of whipping cream on top. Garnish with a sprig of mint. Finish by spooning on a tablespoon of reserved blueberry topping. Repeat for the remaining slices, then serve.

COFFEE AND SODA FLOATS

ANIME

RESTAURANT TO ANOTHER WORLD

SEASON 1, EPISODE 9

"Fried Seafood / Melon Soda Float"

Western Cuisine Nekoya is a restaurant that opens to other worlds on Saturdays. During this time, they serve a unique clientele, such as lizard warriors, fairies, and wizards, each with particular tastes. In this episode, royal siblings of the Land of Sand enter the restaurant after a long journey through the desert. They order cold floats to escape the heat. Shareef orders a coffee float that features sweet and bitter flavors, while Renner orders a sweet, carbonated float. Just like the siblings, you may be tempted to order one or the other, depending on your preference!

YIELD	PREP TIME	CHILL TIME
2	**10**	**15**
servings	minutes per float	minutes for the Coffee Float

SPECIAL TOOLS

Ice cream scoop

CREAM SODA FLOAT

1 cup (150 g) vanilla ice cream

1 can (12 ounces, or 355 ml) green melon soda

¼ cup (60 g) crushed ice

1 Maraschino cherry

COFFEE FLOAT

3 teaspoons instant coffee

3 teaspoons granulated sugar, or to taste

¼ cup (60 ml) boiling water

1 cup (240 ml) cold water

¼ cup (60 ml) heavy whipping cream

1 cup (150 g) vanilla ice cream

CREAM SODA FLOAT

1. Fit a piping bag with a star tip and place it, tip down, inside a tall glass to hold it upright. Scoop the vanilla ice cream into the piping bag and let the ice cream defrost in the bag until it is soft enough to squeeze through the piping tip, about 5 minutes.

2. Meanwhile, pour the green melon soda into a parfait glass. Add the crushed ice, then pipe the softened ice cream on top in a tall swirl. Garnish with the Maraschino cherry. Poke a straw through the ice cream and serve immediately, along with a dessert spoon.

COFFEE FLOAT

1. In a parfait glass, combine the instant coffee, sugar, and boiling water. Mix until combined, then pour in the cold water. Set the glass in the refrigerator until the drink is cold, about 15 minutes.

2. Meanwhile, in a small bowl, using a wire whisk, vigorously whip the whipping cream until soft peaks form, about 3 minutes.

3. Once the coffee is chilled, remove the coffee parfait glass from the refrigerator. Scoop the soft whipped cream on top. Using an ice cream scoop, make a vanilla ice cream ball. Using a spoon, gently set the ice cream ball on top of the whipped cream. Add a straw and serve immediately.

> ### It's as beautiful as ever
> ### It's as delicious as always
> ### The smooth sweetness of soft serve
> ### and the exhilarating sweetness of melon soda . . .
> ### The harmony they create is too good.
>
> —Renner

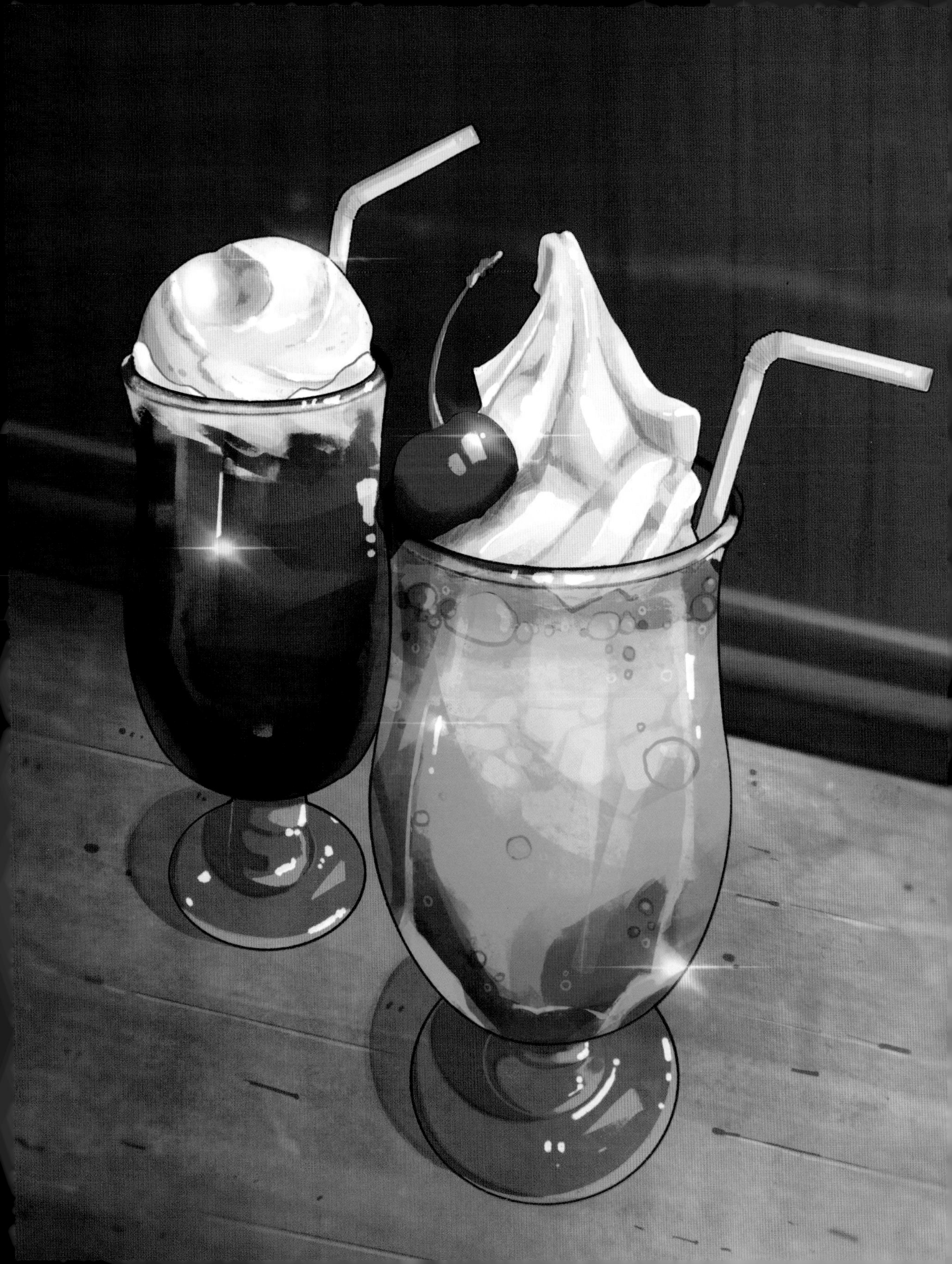

MUSCULAR CREAM PUFFS

ANIME

MASHLE: MAGIC AND MUSCLES

SEASON 1, EPISODE 5

"Mash Burnedead and the Unpopular Classmate"

Mash's addiction to cream puffs is shown in comedic ways in this anime. In this episode, Mash's friend Lance teaches him how to create potions using a Mandragora (think of Mandrake from the Harry Potter books). Mash attempts to re-create Lance's Mandragora potion using the same steps, but instead creates a cream puff! Everyone is curious. They ask him to make it again. In disbelief, they watch as he once again creates a cream puff!

YIELD	PREP TIME	COOK TIME	REST TIME
6	**40**	**1**	**1**
servings	minutes	hour	hour

JUMBO CREAM PUFFS

¼ cup plus 1 tablespoon (70 g) unsalted butter

1½ teaspoons granulated sugar

⅛ teaspoon salt

½ cup (60 g) all-purpose flour, sifted

2 large eggs

DIPLOMAT CREAM

2 egg yolks

2 tablespoons granulated sugar

1 pinch salt

2 tablespoons cornstarch

1½ cups (360 ml) milk

1 tablespoon unsalted butter

1 teaspoon vanilla extract

¼ cup (60 ml) heavy whipping cream

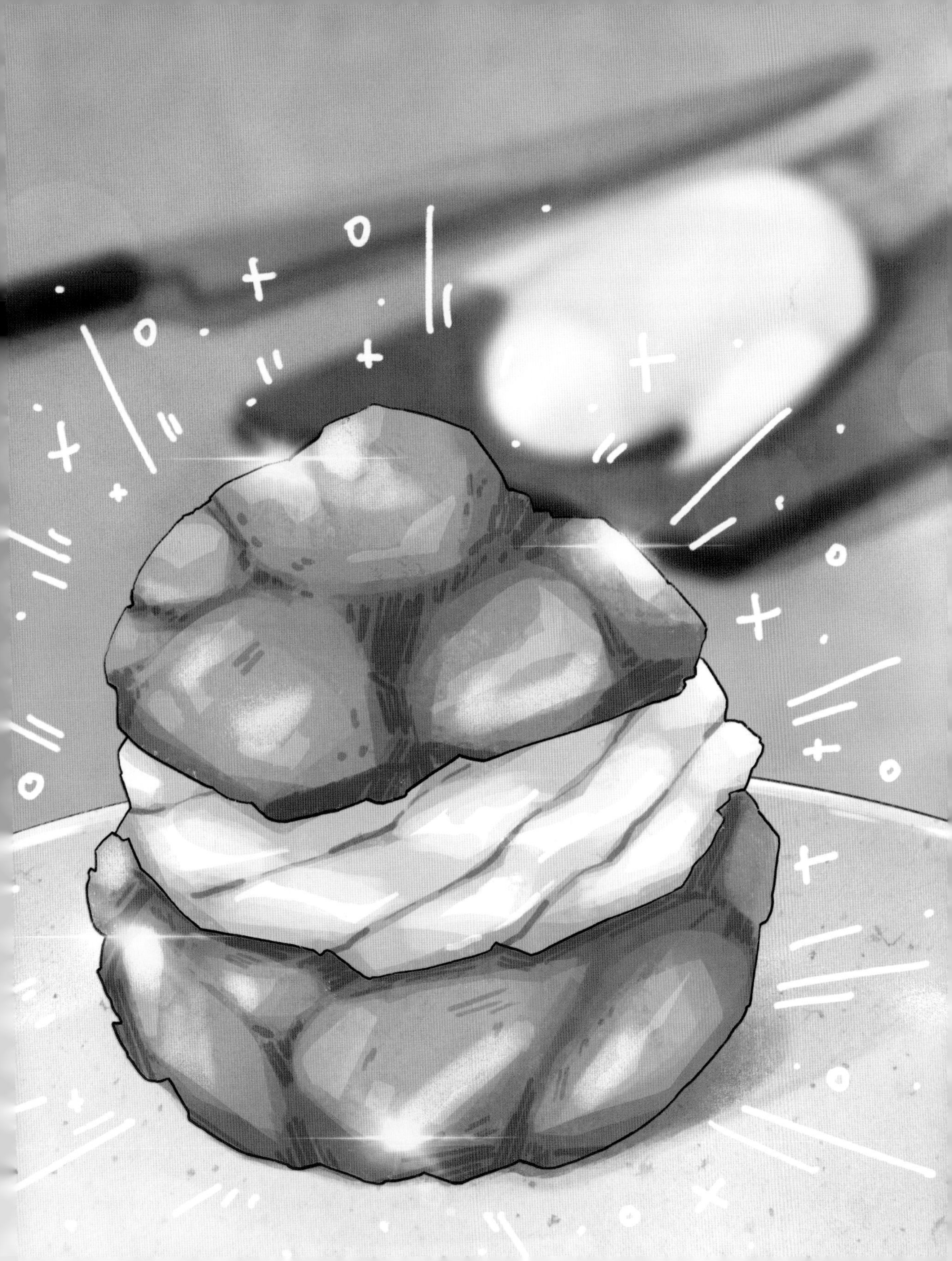

STEPS

1 **To make the jumbo cream puffs:**
Preheat the oven to 400°F (205°C).

2 In a medium pot over medium heat,
combine the butter, 1½ teaspoons sugar,
and ⅛ teaspoon salt with ½ cup (120 ml)
of water and, stirring occasionally, bring to
a boil. Once boiling, remove from the heat.
Stirring vigorously with a wooden spoon or
spatula, add the all-purpose flour. Return
the pot to the stove over low heat and
cook for 3 minutes, stirring and squishing
the mixture to dry out the dough. When
the mixture becomes a ball of dough that
leaves only a slight film in the pot, remove
the pot from the heat. Transfer the dough
to a stand mixer fitted with the paddle
attachment. (Alternatively, you may
transfer the dough to a food processor.)

3 In the stand mixer set to medium-high
speed, beat the dough to cool it down,
about 2 minutes. Meanwhile, in a small
bowl, beat the eggs. When the dough is
warm to the touch, continue beating at
medium-high speed and slowly drizzle
in the eggs until incorporated, scraping
down the sides of the bowl with a spatula
as needed. Once the mixture turns into
a smooth, shiny paste, about 2 minutes,
transfer it to a piping bag fitted with a large
round tip, or cut a ⅞-inch (2¼ cm) hole in
the tip of the bag.

4 Line a baking tray with parchment paper.
(You can pipe a small dot of batter under
each corner of the parchment paper to
prevent it from slipping off the tray.) Pipe
the cream puffs. Holding the piping tip

about ¼ inch (6 mm) over the parchment
paper, squeeze the piping bag while slowly
bringing it upward until you have a mound
that is about 3 inches (8 cm) in diameter
and 1½ inches (4 cm) tall. Repeat 5 more
times for the rest of the cream puffs,
leaving 2 inches (5 cm) between each puff.

5 Fill a small bowl with water. Dip your finger
into the water and then, with your wet
finger, gently tap down any peaks that may
have formed on top of the cream puffs.

6 Bake for 20 minutes, then reduce the heat
to 350°F (180°C) and bake for 15 minutes,
or until the puffs are golden brown and the
bottoms are dry. Leaving the tray in the
oven, turn the heat off and leave the oven
door ajar for about 30 minutes to slowly
cool the cream puffs; this will allow the
puffs to hold their shape and not deflate.

7 **Meanwhile, make the diplomat cream:**
First make the custard cream. In a small
heatproof bowl, whisk together the egg
yolks, 2 tablespoons sugar, pinch of salt,
and cornstarch until smooth. In a medium
saucepan over medium heat, bring the
milk to a rapid simmer, then remove it from
the heat. Temper the egg yolks by slowly
pouring one-third of the heated milk into
the egg yolk mixture and whisking until fully
combined. Add the remaining two-thirds
of the milk and whisk until fully combined.
Pour the mixture back into the saucepan
and turn the heat to medium. Continuously
stir the mixture until it thickens and coats
the back of a spatula, about 8 minutes.
Remove the pan from the heat, stir in the

butter and vanilla, and pour the mixture into a clean medium bowl. Cover the bowl with plastic wrap, making sure that the plastic wrap touches the surface to prevent a skin from forming. Refrigerate until set, about 30 minutes.

8. Once the custard cream is set, make the whipped cream. In the bowl of a stand mixer fitted with a whisk attachment or using a hand mixer, whisk the whipping cream on low and gradually increase to medium-high speed until stiff peaks form, about 3 minutes.

9. Remove the custard cream from the refrigerator and whisk until smooth. Add one-third of the whipped cream and whisk to loosen the custard cream. Fold in the rest of the whipped cream until incorporated. Transfer the diplomat cream to a piping bag fitted with a star tip.

10. **To assemble:** Slice the cream puffs in half lengthwise with a serrated knife. Pipe a generous amount of diplomat cream on the bottom half of the puff, then place the top half back on top of the piped cream. Repeat for the remaining puffs and diplomat cream and serve.

"I can't ignore the call of an empty stomach."

—Mash Burnedead

HEART CAPPUCCINO

ANIME

KAGUYA-SAMA: LOVE IS WAR

(SPECIAL OVA RELEASE)

Ai is a maid in the anime who has a lot of technical knowledge about various topics, such as building computers. In this scene, she explains how to make a cappuccino. She explains that it's a complicated process, going through all the steps—all to spill the drink on the ground as she shows off the end result! This recipe is adapted so you can make it without an espresso machine.

YIELD	PREP TIME	COOK TIME
1	**10**	**10**
cappuccino	minutes	minutes

SPECIAL TOOLS

French press

Handheld milk frother

Stainless steel pitcher

Paper

Writing utensil

Scissors

INGREDIENTS

⅔ cup (160 ml) milk

⅓ cup plus 1 tablespoon (95 g) boiling water

1 tablespoon finely ground coffee

1 teaspoon cocoa powder (optional)

STEPS

1. If you would like, write down and cut out a stencil of a message on a piece of paper.

2. In a small saucepan over medium heat, warm the milk until it steams and the temperature registers between 60°F and 65°F (15°C and 18°C), about 8 minutes.

3. Meanwhile, prepare the espresso. Pour the boiling water into the French press and pour the finely ground coffee on top. Steep for 3 minutes before pressing through, then transfer the espresso to a cappuccino mug.

4. When the milk is steaming, pour it into a stainless steel pitcher and froth with a handheld frother until small bubbles appear, 20 to 30 seconds. Tap the pitcher on a surface 3 times and swirl to get rid of large air bubbles.

5. To create the heart art, tilt the cappuccino mug at an angle so that the espresso almost pours over the rim of the mug. about 45 degrees. Carefully pour the milk straight into the center of the cup. As you straighten the cup, make circular motions so that the liquid continues to nearly pour out. When two-thirds of the mug is filled, pour the milk at a spot about one-third of the way to the rim until a circle forms. Continuing to pour, quickly move the pitcher so the milk cuts straight through the circle, creating a heart shape. Stop pouring.

6. If you are including a message, hover the paper stencil ½ inch (1 cm) above the drink, centering it over the middle of the heart, then sift the cocoa powder over the stencil to make your message.

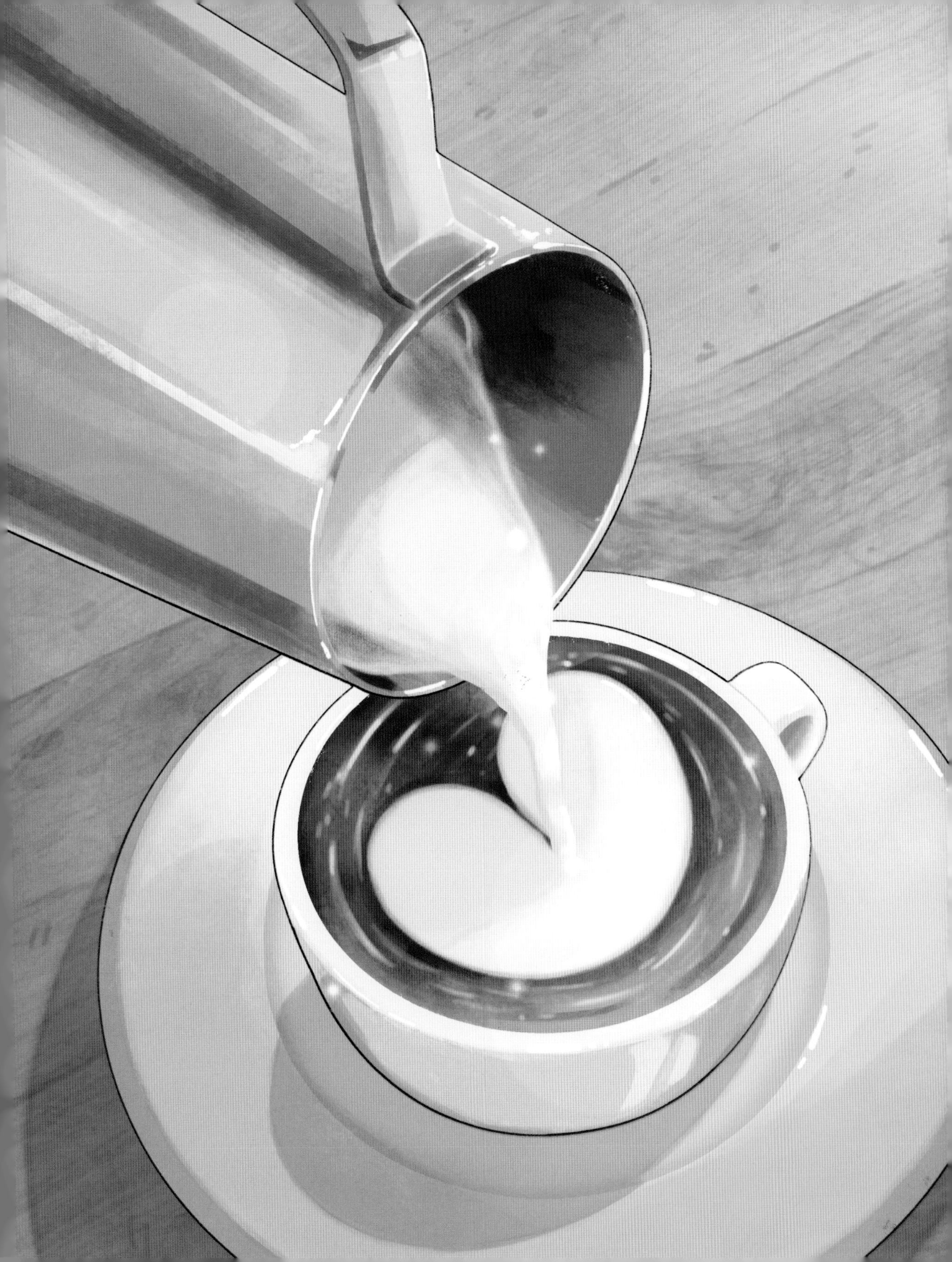

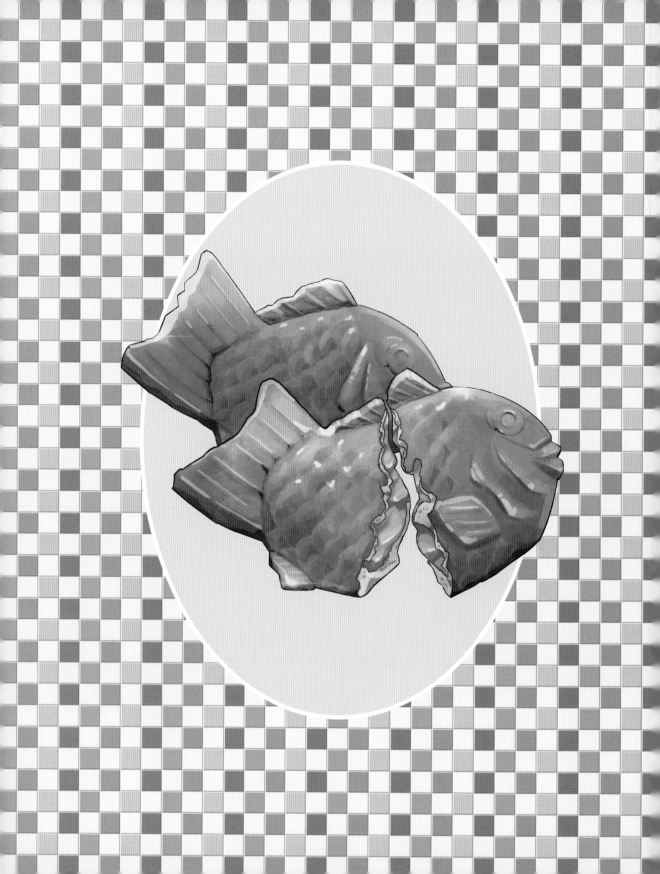

Comfort

Café

OMURICE BLESSED WITH DARK ARTS

ANIME

MISS KOBAYASHI'S DRAGON MAID

SEASON 2, EPISODE 1

"New Dragon, Ilulu! (Please Be Nice to Her Again)"

In Japan, omurice is always used as an opportunity to write messages in cafés and even at home. Usually the message or pictures are drawn with ketchup, often in the shape of hearts. In the maid café setting, omurice offers an opportunity to perform a cute "spell" as a table performance for the customers to make the omurice more delicious. Tohru calls upon the Shadow King to perform dark arts on the omurice, making it cursed with purple ketchup instead of red.

YIELD	PREP TIME	COOK TIME
2	**15**	**30**
servings	minutes	minutes

SPECIAL TOOLS

Squeeze bottle or a piping bag

SWEET PURPLE "KETCHUP"

4 purple carrots (see Note on page 44), peeled and cut into 1-inch (2.5 cm) rounds

¼ cup plus 1 tablespoon (75 ml) honey

¼ cup (60 ml) purple water from boiled carrots

2 tablespoons apple cider vinegar

1 tablespoon Worcestershire sauce

1 teaspoon garlic powder

1 teaspoon onion powder

¼ teaspoon salt

⅛ teaspoon black pepper

CHICKEN RICE

1 tablespoon unsalted butter

2 boneless, skinless chicken thighs, cut into ½-inch (1 cm) cubes

1 teaspoon garlic powder

1 pinch each salt and black pepper, plus more if needed

½ small onion, cut into small dice

1 small carrot, peeled and cut into small dice

2 cups (410 g) day-old steamed short-grain white rice

½ tablespoon soy sauce

¼ cup (60 ml) ketchup

¼ cup (34 g) frozen peas

OMELETS

3 large eggs

1 tablespoon milk

1 pinch each salt and black pepper

1 tablespoon unsalted butter, divided

FOR SERVING

4 cherry tomatoes

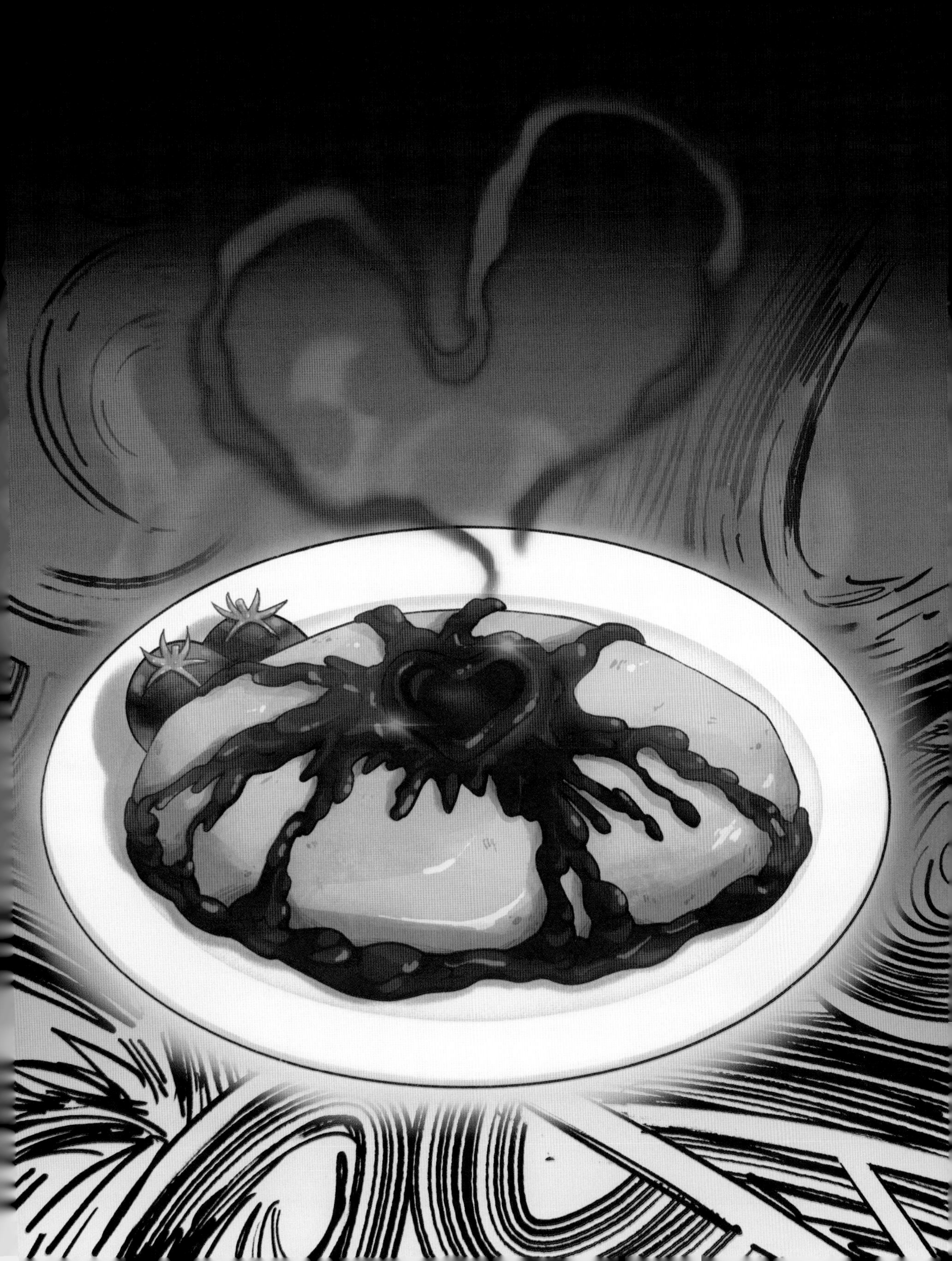

STEPS

1. **To make the sweet purple "ketchup":** In a small pot over medium-high heat, bring 2 cups (500 ml) of water to a boil. Add the carrots in and cook until a knife easily pierces through, about 12 minutes. Remove from the heat. Reserve ¼ cup (60 ml) of water for the sweet purple "ketchup." Carefully transfer the carrots to a blender with 1 tablespoon of their cooking liquid, and the rest of the ingredients. Once the mixture has cooled, about 10 minutes, pulse until smooth. Transfer to a squeeze bottle or a piping bag for decorating.

2. **To make the chicken rice:** Heat a medium skillet over medium heat, then melt the butter. Add the chicken thigh pieces and season with the garlic powder and a pinch each of salt and pepper. Cook until all sides are browned, 2 to 3 minutes per side. Remove the chicken from the pan and set aside.

3. Add the onions to the pan and cook until translucent, about 2 minutes. Add the carrots and cook, stirring occasionally, for 3 more minutes. Add the day-old rice, breaking it up with a spatula. Add the soy sauce and ketchup and continue to cook and stir until fully combined with the rice.

4. Add the chicken and all its juices back into the pan. Add the frozen peas and cook for 1 minute, or until warmed through. Taste and season with more salt and pepper, if needed. Remove from the heat and set aside.

5. **To make the omelets:** In a medium bowl, crack the eggs and whisk until combined and there are no visible egg-white lumps. Add the milk and season with a pinch each of salt and pepper.

6. Heat a separate medium nonstick skillet over medium heat. Melt ½ tablespoon of the butter, then add half of the egg mixture. Let the egg set for 30 seconds, then quickly swirl the egg with a chopstick to create ridges, about another 30 seconds. Run a spatula along the sides of the pan to detach the egg from the pan. Reduce the heat to medium-low.

7. While the egg is still custardy, divide the chicken rice in half. Place one-half on the middle of the egg lengthwise. Fold one side of the egg to the middle, then do the same with the other side, creating a blanket for the rice. Push the omurice to the edge of the pan then carefully flip it over onto a plate with the seam side down. You may refine the omurice into its iconic football-like shape by compressing it with paper towels. Place paper towels on top of the omurice and squeeze and shape as necessary. Repeat for the second omurice.

8. **To serve:** Using the sweet purple ketchup, draw a heart in the middle of each omurice, then draw lines from the edges of the heart to the perimeter of the plate. Add 2 cherry tomatoes to each plate.

NOTE

The sweet purple "ketchup" is achieved by making a sweet-and-sour blend with purple carrots for natural coloring. When picking purple carrots, make sure they are purple inside and out, as some are purple on the outside and orange on the inside.

TAIYAKI ZUNDA

ANIME

MY HERO ACADEMIA

SEASON 2, EPISODE 27

"Bizarre!
Gran Torino Appears"

Izuku "Deku" is a student at U.A. High School, a hero academy that trains students with superpowers. Deku lands an internship with Gran Torino, a retired Pro Hero, who has knowledge of Deku's given superpower, called "One for All." Gran Torino tells Deku that he uses his power inefficiently.

Gran Torino orders a new microwave to his house to heat up frozen taiyaki. As it's heating in the microwave, it fails to rotate, leaving only part of the taiyaki hot and the rest mostly cold. Deku thinks that the heat distribution of the taiyaki is a metaphor for him and how he uses his powers in specific areas of his body. He realizes that he would be more efficient if he distributes his power throughout his entire body continuously. Deku starts to master his new ability in this pivotal moment, making taiyaki a delicious and unforgettable symbol for the anime.

YIELD	PREP TIME	COOK TIME
6	**20**	**35**
servings	minutes	minutes

SPECIAL TOOLS

Mortar and pestle

Taiyaki pan

ZUNDA (MASHED EDAMAME)

½ cup (80 g) edamame pods

3 tablespoons granulated sugar

2 tablespoons milk

CRUNCHY TAIYAKI

3 tablespoons granulated sugar

1 large egg

⅔ cup (160 ml) milk

1 teaspoon vanilla extract

1 pinch salt

1 cup (120 g) all-purpose flour

¼ cup (40 g) cornstarch

1 teaspoon baking powder

1 teaspoon matcha powder

1 teaspoon canola oil, for greasing

STEPS

1. **To make the zunda:** In a medium pot over medium-high heat, bring 2 cups (480 ml) of water to a boil. Add the edamame and cook until tender, 4 to 5 minutes, then drain. Once cool enough to handle, remove the edamame beans from the outer shells. (This ensures a pleasant texture for the final product.) Grind the edamame into a paste using a mortar and pestle. Stir in the 2½ tablespoons sugar and 1 tablespoon milk.

2. **To make the crunchy taiyaki:** In a medium bowl, using a wire whisk, whisk together the 3 tablespoons sugar and egg until smooth. Add the ⅔ cup (160 ml) milk and vanilla and continue whisking. Add the pinch of salt, flour, cornstarch, and baking powder and whisk until the batter is smooth. Transfer 2 tablespoons of the batter to a small bowl and set aside. Transfer the rest of the batter to a pouring vessel. To the batter in the small bowl, stir in the matcha powder.

3. Lightly grease the taiyaki pan with canola oil, removing extra oil with a paper towel. Heat the pan over medium heat. Once warm, reduce the heat to low. Working with one side of the taiyaki pan at a time, brush 1 teaspoon of green batter at the top of the fish head to create Deku's spiky green hair, then add about 1½ tablespoons of regular batter (no coloring) to fill in the rest of the fish indentation. Use a clean pastry brush or the back of a small spoon to spread the batter to the outer edges of the indentation. Repeat for the remaining fish indentations in the pan. Once the batter sets, with small bubbles forming and the surface becomes almost dry to the touch, like a pancake, close the pan and cook for 2 minutes on each side.

4. Scoop 1 to 1½ tablespoons of zunda in the center of a fish on one side of the taiyaki and spread it gently to cover. Pour ½ tablespoon of batter on top of the zunda, to bind both sides of the taiyaki together. Repeat for the other fish indentations in the pan and close the pan.

5. Continue to cook over low heat until both sides of the taiyaki are golden brown and crisp, turning the pan as needed to cook evenly on both sides, 3 to 4 minutes per side. Serve hot.

"This taiyaki is . . . Me!"

—Izuku Midoriya "Deku"

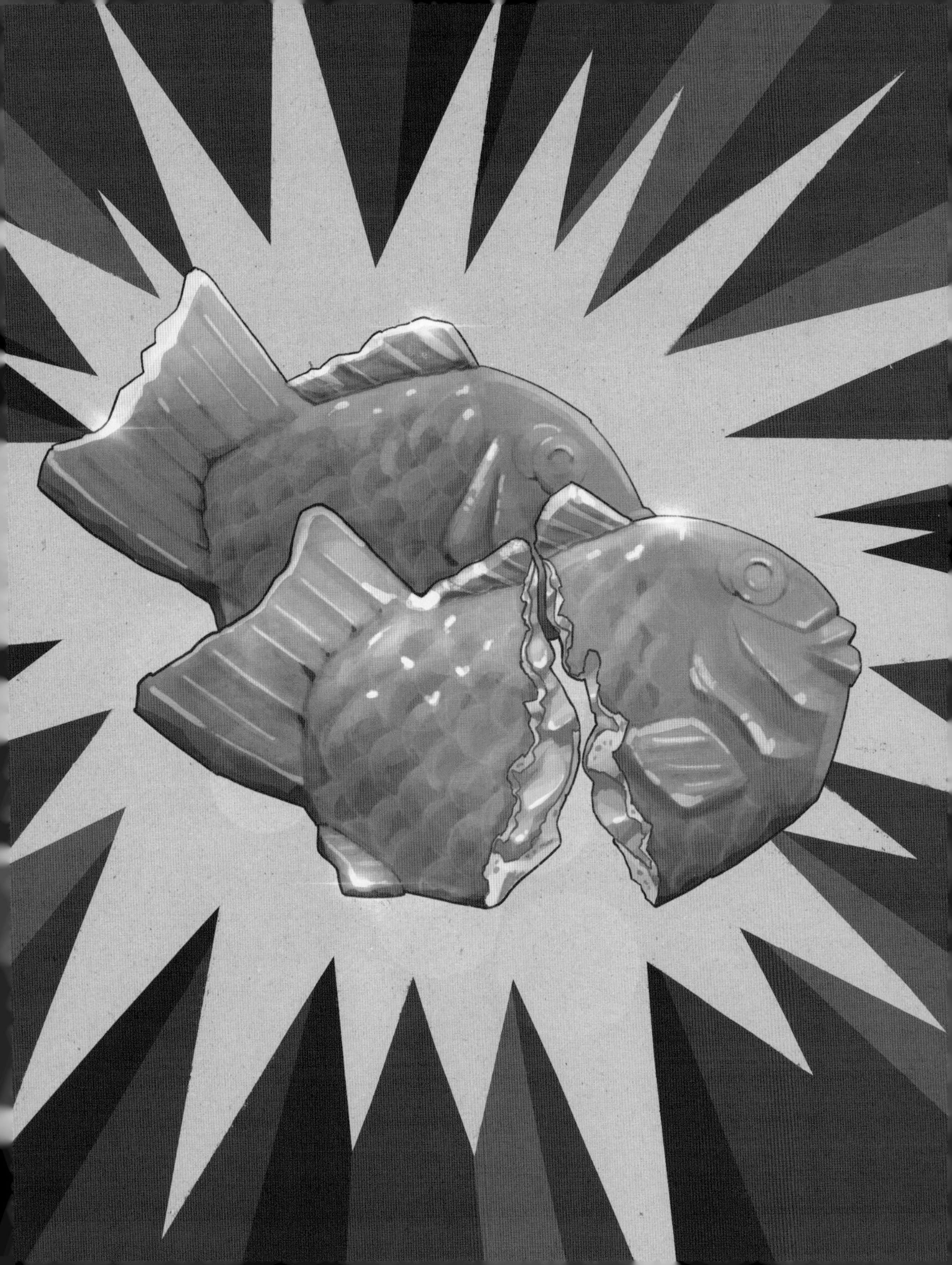

MINI PUMPKIN HERRING PIES

MOVIE

KIKI'S DELIVERY SERVICE

Kiki was called to Madame's house to deliver a pie, but it turns out it's not ready because grandma couldn't start a fire to bake it. So Kiki helps build the fire, bake the pie, and then deliver it, which is ill-received by Madame's granddaughter. I've decided to make four mini pies instead of one. This dish needs a few hands to finish; it could be a great activity to bond together with someone—and eat some delicious, warm pie as a reward.

YIELD	PREP TIME	COOK TIME	DECORATE TIME
4	**30**	**3**	**15**
servings	minutes	hours	minutes

SPECIAL TOOLS

Mortar and pestle

Masher

Four 5-inch (13 cm) circular gratin
   baking dishes

BROWN BUTTER SAGE PUMPKIN LAYER

3⅓ pounds (1.5 kg) kabocha squash

½ cup (115 g) unsalted butter

20 fresh sage leaves

1¼ teaspoons salt, divided

⅜ teaspoon black pepper, divided

½ cup (120 ml) heavy whipping cream

GARLIC CHERRY TOMATO LAYER

90 cherry tomatoes (about 53 ounces, or 1.5 kg)

1 tablespoon balsamic vinegar

2 tablespoons olive oil, divided

¼ teaspoon plus 1 pinch salt, divided

6 cloves garlic, peeled

Black pepper

LEMON SMOKED HERRING LAYER

1 can (150 to190 g) boneless smoked herring

Zest and juice of ½ lemon

DECORATIONS

1 egg

2 boxes (17.3 ounces, or 490 g, each) puff pastry,
   thawed

24 pitted black olives, sliced

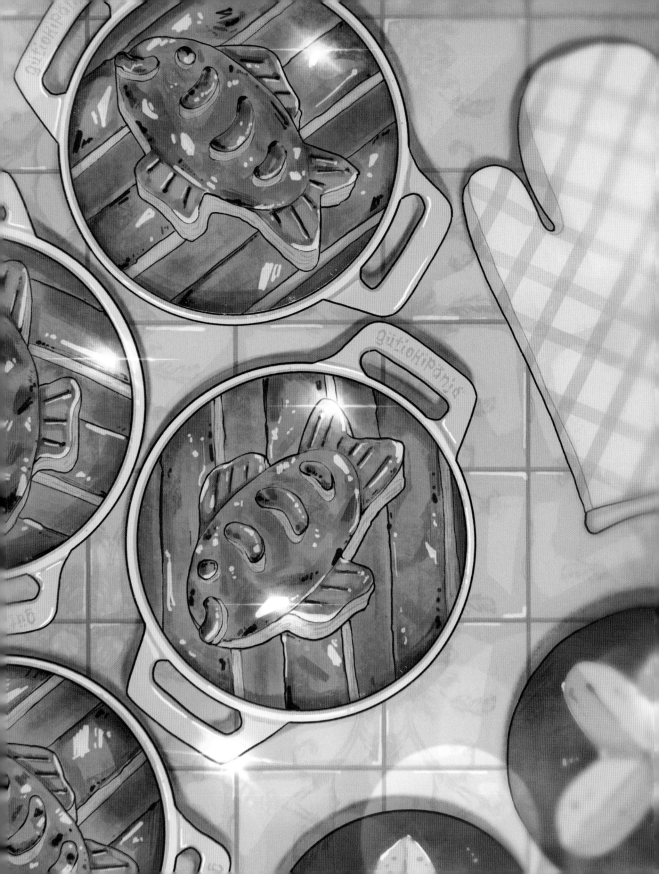

STEPS

1. **To make the pumpkin for the brown butter sage pumpkin layer:** Preheat the oven to 400°F (205°C). Line a sheet pan with parchment paper. Place the kabocha on the prepared sheet pan and bake until soft enough for a knife to cut through it, about 1 hour. Remove the kabocha from the oven and transfer to a cutting board. Avoiding the steam, carefully slice the squash in half. Using a spoon, remove the ribbing and seeds. Place the squash halves back on the sheet pan, cut sides down, and roast until the flesh is mashable, about another 1 hour and 30 minutes.

2. **Meanwhile, make the garlic cherry tomato layer:** Line another sheet pan with parchment paper. Spread the cherry tomatoes on the sheet pan and drizzle with the balsamic vinegar and 1 tablespoon of the olive oil. Sprinkle ¼ teaspoon of the salt over the top, then shake the tray to coat.

3. Create a garlic pouch by placing parchment paper big enough to cover the garlic on top of aluminum foil, then place the garlic cloves on top. Drizzle with the remaining 1 tablespoon olive oil and pinch of salt, then carefully scrunch the foil and parchment paper around the garlic. Transfer the garlic pouch to the sheet pan with the tomatoes.

4. Roast the garlic and cherry tomatoes alongside the squash for 1 hour, or until the tomatoes blister and darken slightly and the garlic is easily pierced with a knife. Remove from the oven. Carefully open the garlic pouch, then use a fork to mash the garlic. Toss the garlic with the blistered cherry tomatoes to combine. Season with pepper.

5. **Meanwhile, make the brown butter sage:** In a medium pot over medium heat, melt the butter. Add the sage and cook, stirring occasionally, until the butter browns and has a nutty smell and the sage is crispy, about 9 minutes. Remove from the heat and pour into a large heatproof bowl. Transfer the sage leaves to a mortar and pestle and grind until a paste forms. Return the sage paste to the brown butter and add ¼ teaspoon of the salt and ⅛ teaspoon of the pepper.

6. Once the squash is soft and mashable, remove it from the oven. (Leave the oven on.) Scoop the flesh into the large bowl with the sage brown butter and, using a masher, mash the squash until smooth. Add the whipping cream and the remaining 1 teaspoon salt and ¼ teaspoon pepper and mix until combined.

7. **To make the lemon smoked herring layer:** Drain the canned smoked herring. Transfer to a paper towel and pat dry. In a small bowl, using a fork, flake the smoked herring into pieces, then mix in the lemon zest and juice.

8. **To assemble the pies:** Divide the brown butter sage squash equally among the gratin baking dishes. Layer the garlic cherry tomatoes on top, about 22 tomatoes per dish or enough to cover the surface of the squash layer, then divide the lemon smoked herring equally among the dishes.

9. **To make the decorations:** In a small bowl, using a wire whisk, whisk together 1 egg and 1 tablespoon of water. Set aside. Using a rolling pin, roll the puff pastry to ¼-inch (6 mm) thickness. Set a gratin dish on the puff pastry and run a knife around

the dish to trace a circle for topping the pie. Repeat for the remaining dishes. From the remaining puff pastry, cut out twelve 6 by 1-inch (15 by 2.5 cm) strips and the fish decorations. To make a fish body, cut an oblong shape, tapered on one side, with a tail shaped like the number 3. Repeat 3 more times. Cut out the details for the fish: Cut 8 slanted and curved-edge fins, about 1 inch (2.5 cm) wide, and use a straw to punch out four ¼-inch (6 mm) circles for the eyes. For the scales, cut out twelve ½-inch (1 cm) backward Cs. For the smiles, cut four ¼-inch (6 mm) Cs. (Use the illustration as a guide.)

10 To decorate the pies, brush one of the circular pastry tops with some egg wash, then place 3 equally spaced pastry strips diagonally across it. Set the pastry on top of the dish and trim the overhang with a knife. Brush the tops of the strips with egg wash, then place the fish body on the center of the dish and brush it with egg wash. Place one fin on top of the fish and one at the bottom, on the center of the body. Set an eye on the fish head. Arrange 3 scales on the body, equally spaced between the eye and the tail. Place the curved smile under the eye. Finally, use a knife to create 3 lines on each fin and 6 lines on the tail. Brush egg wash over the whole design. Repeat with the remaining pastry tops and decorations. At this point, cover the entire baking dish with plastic wrap and refrigerate for up to a day before baking, if desired.

11 Place all the baking dishes on a baking tray and bake for 20 minutes, or until golden brown. Remove from the oven and serve hot.

"First don't panic, second don't panic, and third did I mention not to panic?"

—Jiji

APPLE RISOTTO WITH BACON

ANIME

FOOD WARS!: SHOKUGEKI NO SOMA

SEASON 1, EPISODE 16

"The Chef Who's Crossed a Thousand Leagues"

Soma's father, Joichiro, surprises him by showing up at his high school dorm, Polar Star Dormitory at Totsuki Culinary Academy. Joichiro often has cook-offs with Soma to check how far his son has grown culinarily. They have a breakfast cook-off—their 490th cooking battle—strictly using pantry items from the Polar Star Dormitory. Soma has never won a battle against his father, but this is probably the closest he's ever come to winning: the dorm judges have nothing but praise for both of them. This dish is extremely heartwarming and is the perfect mix of sweet and salty. Not sure whether you want something sweet or savory for breakfast? This is for you.

YIELD	PREP TIME	COOK TIME
2	**10**	**25**
servings	minutes	minutes

RISOTTO

½ small, crisp red apple, peeled and finely diced

½ teaspoon lemon juice

2 tablespoons unsalted butter, divided

¼ small onion, finely diced

½ cup (95 g) arborio rice

¼ cup (60 ml) white wine

Salt

STOCK

¼ cup (60 ml) apple juice

1¾ cups (430 ml) unsalted chicken broth

3 sprigs fresh thyme

Salt

TOPPINGS

2 tablespoons chopped flat-leaf parsley

4 slices bacon, cooked crisp

½ teaspoon grated Parmesan cheese

¼ teaspoon freshly cracked black pepper

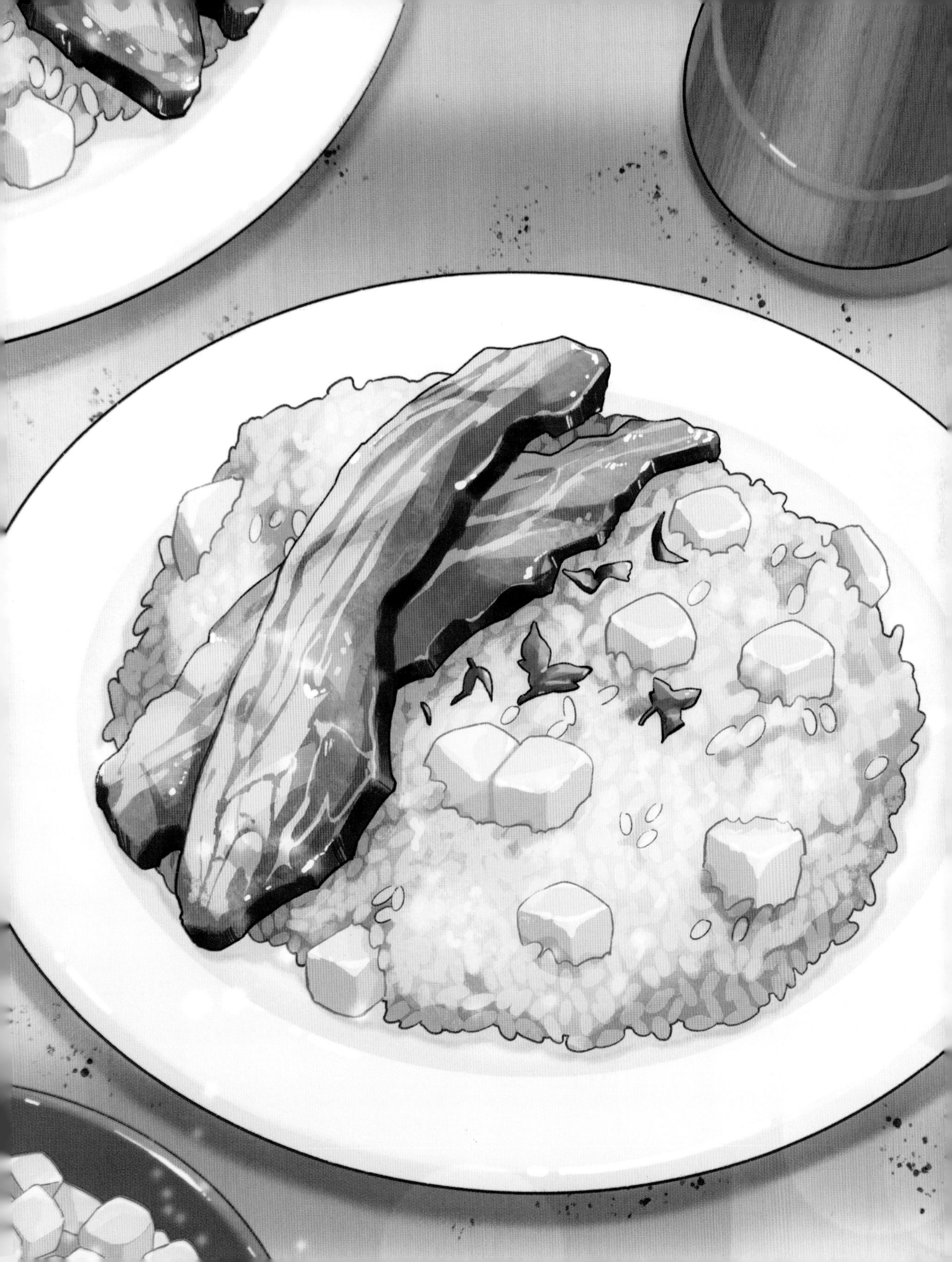

STEPS

1. **To prepare the apples for the risotto:** In a shallow bowl, to prevent browning, add the diced apple, lemon juice, and just enough water to cover them.

2. **Meanwhile, make the stock:** In a small pot, combine all the stock ingredients. Cover the pot with a lid and bring to a boil over medium heat. Reduce the heat to low and let the stock simmer.

3. **To make the risotto:** Heat a separate small pot over medium heat. Once warm, melt 1 tablespoon of the butter, then add the onion. Cook and stir until the onion is translucent and fragrant, about 1 minute, then add the arborio rice. Stir to coat the rice in the melted butter and onion and cook for 30 seconds. Once the rice is shiny from the butter, add the white wine. Cook, stirring occasionally, until 90 percent of the wine is absorbed by the rice, about 2 minutes.

4. Reduce the heat to medium low, then ladle ¼ cup (60 ml) of the simmering stock over the rice, stirring occasionally to prevent burning. Once 90 percent of the liquid has been absorbed, 2 to 3 minutes, ladle in another ¼ cup (60 ml) of the simmering stock. Repeat until three-quarters of the broth has been added and absorbed, around 18 minutes. As you ladle in the last ¼ cup (60 ml) of stock, drain the apple and add it to the pot. Reduce the heat to low and cook for 2 to 3 minutes more, until the stock has been almost absorbed, the rice is al dente, and when dropped from a spoon, the risotto's consistency is like lava—about 20 minutes total cook time.

5. Remove from the heat and stir in the remaining 1 tablespoon butter. Season with salt.

6. Divide the cooked risotto between 2 shallow bowls and sprinkle with the chopped parsley. Top with 2 slices of the cooked bacon each. Serve immediately alongside grated Parmesan and freshly cracked black pepper (just like the anime)!

"Even if the menu item is humble in the extreme, we use our creativity to transform it into a masterpiece! *That* is Yukihira cooking."

—Soma Yukihira

POTATO MOCHI

ANIME

DEMON SLAYER

SEASON 3, EPISODE 11

"A Conquered Bond: Daybreak and First Light"

Tanjiro's sword is worn down from fighting demons, so he heads to the Swordsmith Village to sharpen the blade. There, he encounters demons too powerful for him to defeat, even equipped with his sharpened sword. As time is running out to slay the demon, Tanjiro has a flashback of his friend Zenitsu, who gives him advice to unlock his potential. In this crucial flashback, Zenitsu is eating potato mochi, a Japanese dish. It is chewy, and covered with a sweet, sticky, and salty sauce. It makes a great snack or a side dish.

YIELD	PREP TIME	COOK TIME
4	**15**	**40**
skewers	minutes	minutes

SPECIAL TOOLS

4 bamboo skewers

Kitchen scissors (optional)

MITARASHI SAUCE

3 tablespoons soy sauce

3 tablespoons mirin

¼ cup (55 g) granulated sugar

POTATO MOCHI

1 small russet potato, peeled and quartered

¼ cup (40 g) potato starch

2 tablespoons salted butter

½ teaspoon salt, plus more to taste

Black pepper

2 ounces (55 g) fresh mozzarella cheese, cut into roughly
1 x 1 x ¼-inch (2.5 x 2.5 x 0.6 cm) cubes

Oil (such as vegetable or canola), for frying

1 sheet nori

STEPS

1. **To make the mitarashi sauce:** In a small pot over medium heat, combine the soy sauce, mirin, and sugar and bring to a boil. Reduce the heat to low until the sugar dissolves. Remove from the heat.

2. **To make the potato mochi:** In a medium pot, add the potato and enough water to cover the pieces by 1 inch (2.5 cm). Bring to a boil over medium-high heat, then reduce the heat to medium and cook until the potato is easy to pierce with a knife, about 20 minutes. Remove from the heat, drain, and transfer the potatoes to a medium bowl. Add the potato starch, butter, and salt, and mash together until smooth. Season with salt and pepper.

3. Divide the mashed potato into 8 equal pieces and roll them into balls. Working with one potato ball at a time, press a hole into the center of each ball and fill it with a mozzarella cube. Enclose the mozzarella in the potato, making sure to fully seal it inside the ball to prevent leaking when cooking. Shape the ball into a 1½-inch (4 cm) square that is ½ inch (1 cm) deep. (Note: This size is just a guideline, but do not shape them bigger, as they will be too heavy to stay on the stick.) Repeat for the remaining potato balls.

4. Heat a medium skillet with ¼ inch (6 mm) of oil over medium-high heat. Once the oil reaches 350°F (180°C) when measured with a thermometer, carefully add the potato cubes to the pan using tongs, working in batches as needed. Cook until golden brown, about 3 minutes per side. Transfer from the pan to a paper towel-lined plate. Let cool until safe to handle.

5. Carefully pierce 2 potato mochi with a skewer. Repeat for the remaining mochi and skewers. Generously brush all the mochi with the mitarashi sauce. Finally, use scissors or a small knife to cut eight 1-inch (2.5 cm) squares of nori. Additionally, use a small knife to cut a triangle in the center of each square to represent Zenitsu, if desired. Center a nori square on each potato mochi and serve!

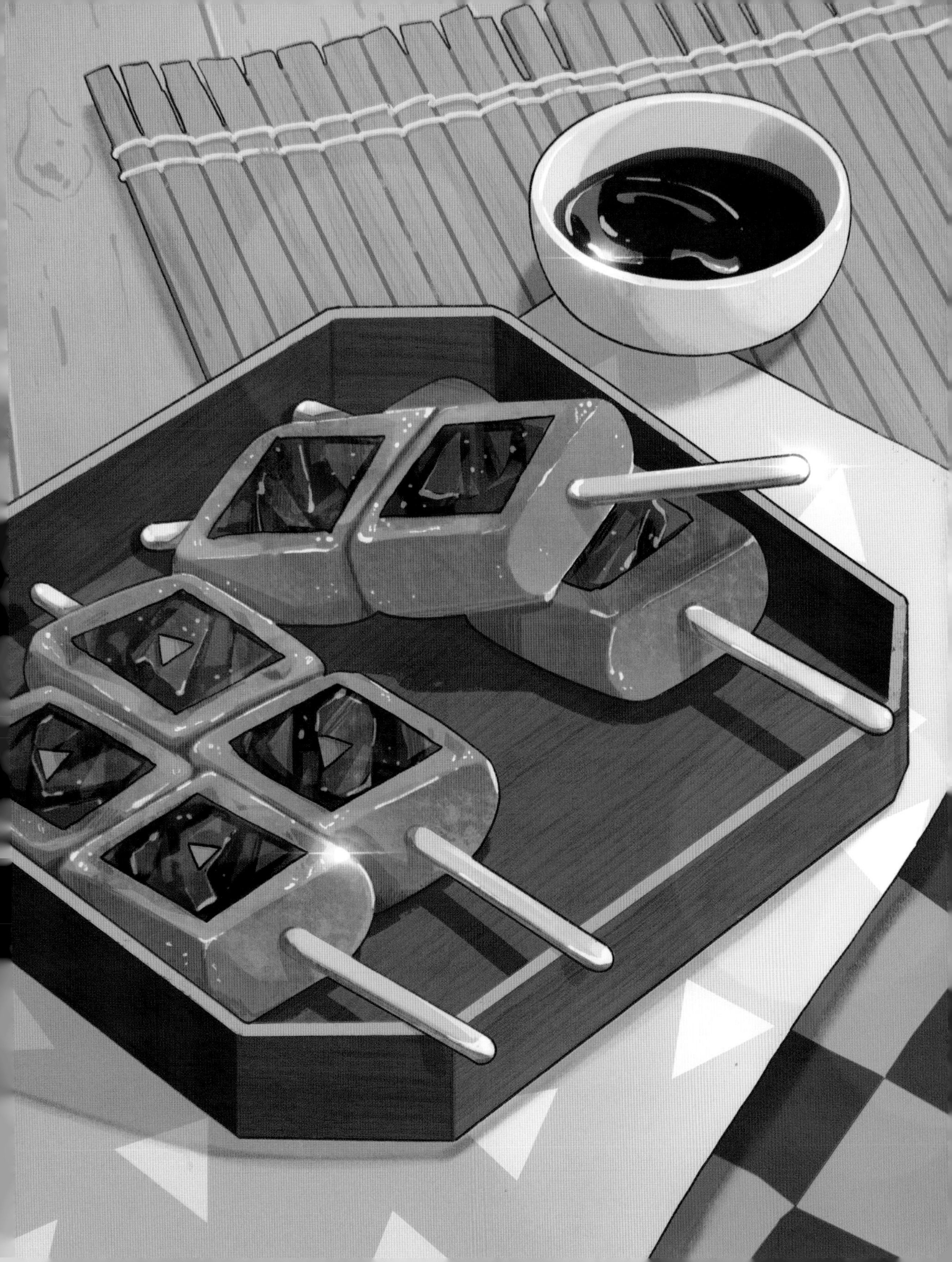

AGEDASHI TOFU

ANIME

HAIKYUU!!

SEASON 1, EPISODE 24

"Removing the 'Solitary King'"

This is the favorite dish of Iwaizumi, vice captain of the volleyball team. *Haikyuu!* meals show variety in terms of nutrition, emphasizing the importance of food in relation to recovery from practice, and tofu is packed with protein. The agedashi tofu is soft with a fried crispy exterior and served with a sweet and salty sauce.

YIELD	PREP TIME	COOK TIME
2-3	**10**	**20**
servings	minutes	minutes

FRIED TOFU

1 package (12 ounces, or 340 g) soft tofu

Canola oil, for frying

½ cup (95 g) potato starch

1 pinch salt

SAUCE

2½ tablespoons soy sauce

2½ tablespoons mirin

½ teaspoon dashi powder

½ teaspoon granulated sugar

1 tablespoon cold water

1 teaspoon potato starch

FOR SERVING

¼ cup (40 g) grated daikon radish, drained

2 green onions, green parts only, thinly sliced

¼ cup (3 g) bonito flakes

Steamed rice

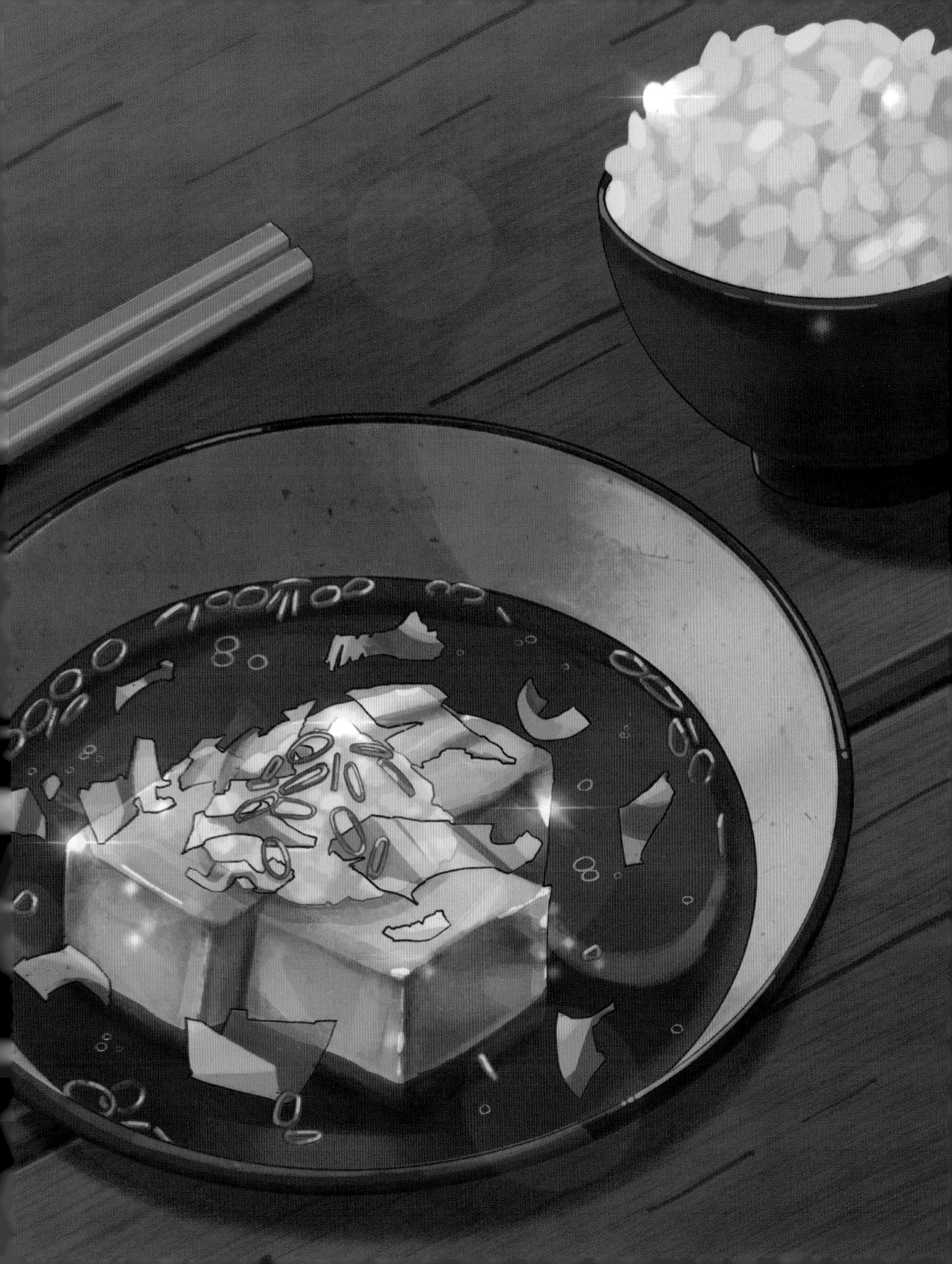

STEPS

1. **To prepare the tofu for the fried tofu:** Cut the tofu into 1½-inch (4 cm) cubes. Set the cubes on top of a few paper towels, cover with another paper towel, and, taking care not to break the tofu, lightly press down (see Note). Leave the tofu to drain while you make the sauce.

2. **To make the sauce:** In a medium saucepan over medium heat, combine 1¼ cups (300 ml) of water with the soy sauce, mirin, dashi powder, and sugar and bring to a boil. In a small bowl, make a slurry by mixing the cold water and 1 teaspoon potato starch together until smooth. Slowly pour the slurry into the saucepan and, using a wire whisk, whisk for 1 minute until combined. Reduce the heat to low to keep warm.

3. **To make the fried tofu:** Fill a small saucepan with 1½ inches (4 cm) of oil over medium high heat. Pour the ½ cup (95 g) potato starch onto a plate and prepare a frying rack by placing a wire rack on top of a baking pan, to catch excess oil. Once the oil reaches 350°F (180°C) when measured with a thermometer, working with one cube of tofu at a time, coat the tofu on all sides in the potato starch and shake off the excess. Slowly lower the piece into the cooking oil and cook until the tofu is crispy and lightly browned, 2 to 3 minutes. Remove the tofu from the oil and transfer to the prepared frying rack. Repeat with the remaining tofu.

4. To serve, place the tofu in a bowl and pour the sauce on top. Top the dish with a ball of grated daikon radish and sprinkle with the green onion and bonito flakes. Serve hot with steamed rice.

NOTE

Pressing tofu squeezes out extra moisture and results in sturdier pieces of tofu that don't fall apart during cooking and are chewier to eat. To press tofu, remove the block of tofu from its packaging. On a plate or cutting board, set a layer of paper towels or a clean kitchen towel. Place the tofu on the towel(s) and top with another layer of towel(s). Set something heavy, such as a pan, on top and let the tofu sit for 30 minutes.

> **"Right after a match, like now, your muscles are at their limits, so you've got to repair them by eating . . . So eat. Eat a proper meal."**
>
> —Keishin Ukai

POTATO CHIP FRIED RICE

MOVIE

WEATHERING WITH YOU

High school student Hodaka runs away from his island home in Kozushima and moves to busy Tokyo for a lifestyle change. He starts working for a magazine. In the office, he meets Natsumi, the niece of the owner. This fried rice is inspired by the iconic scene where Natsumi cooks for Hodaka. It's a heartfelt moment in which Natsumi helps Hodaka feel comfortable in his new environment. Famously, this dish uses pantry ingredients, making it approachable—but with the irresistible (and addictive) seasoning of salty seaweed potato chips (which act a bit like furikake here). The anime specifically uses brands that exist in real life, so look for them to get the authentic taste!

YIELD	PREP TIME	COOK TIME
2	**15**	**10**
servings	minutes	minutes

POTATO CHIP FRIED RICE

1 bag (1.83 ounces, or 52 g) Koikeya Salt & Seaweed Potato Chips

2 tablespoons cooking oil (such as vegetable or canola), divided

¼ small onion, diced

2 cups (380 g) day-old steamed jasmine rice (see Notes on page 62)

3 egg yolks, beaten

¼ cup (22 g) chopped pea shoots

3 teaspoons sesame oil

2 teaspoons soy sauce

1 pinch salt

TOPPINGS

2 egg yolks (see Notes on page 62)

12 pea shoots

STEPS

1 **To make the potato chip fried rice:**
Open the bag of Koikeya Salt & Seaweed Potato Chips and set aside 5 chips to reserve for the topping. Close the bag and, using a rolling pin, crush the contents into a fine seasoning powder. (Alternatively, you may grind the chips using a mortar and pestle.)

2 Heat a medium skillet over medium heat. Once hot, add 1 tablespoon of the cooking oil. Add the onion and cook until translucent, about 2 minutes, then add the jasmine rice. Separate any clumps of rice using a spatula. Cook until the rice is glossy and warmed through, about 3 minutes.

3 Push the rice to one side of the pan, then add the remaining 1 tablespoon cooking oil to the other side. Add the beaten egg yolks and scramble before combining with the rice. Stir in the chopped pea shoots and cook until vibrant in color and slightly wilted, about 1 minute. Add the sesame oil, soy sauce, 2 tablespoons of crushed potato chips, and salt and mix until combined. Remove from the heat and transfer to shallow serving bowls.

4 Use a spoon to shape the rice into mounds, then gently press down in the center of each mound to create a divot about ½ inch (1 cm) deep. Set an egg yolk into each divot, then arrange 6 pea shoots in a circle around each yolk. Lastly, arrange the reserved potato chips around the edges of each dish. Serve hot!

NOTES

Use day-old jasmine rice because it is dry enough to prevent the fried rice from becoming sticky. If you cook the rice on the same day, follow the package directions, then spread it out in a layer on a small sheet pan. Let cool, only up to 1 hour, then place the sheet pan in the freezer for 2 hours, or until the rice is frozen. Now it is ready to use!

This recipe calls for a raw egg yolk, which may contain salmonella (1 in 20,000 pasteurized eggs contain it) and make you ill. Make sure you only use pasteurized eggs and understand the risk of eating raw egg yolks.

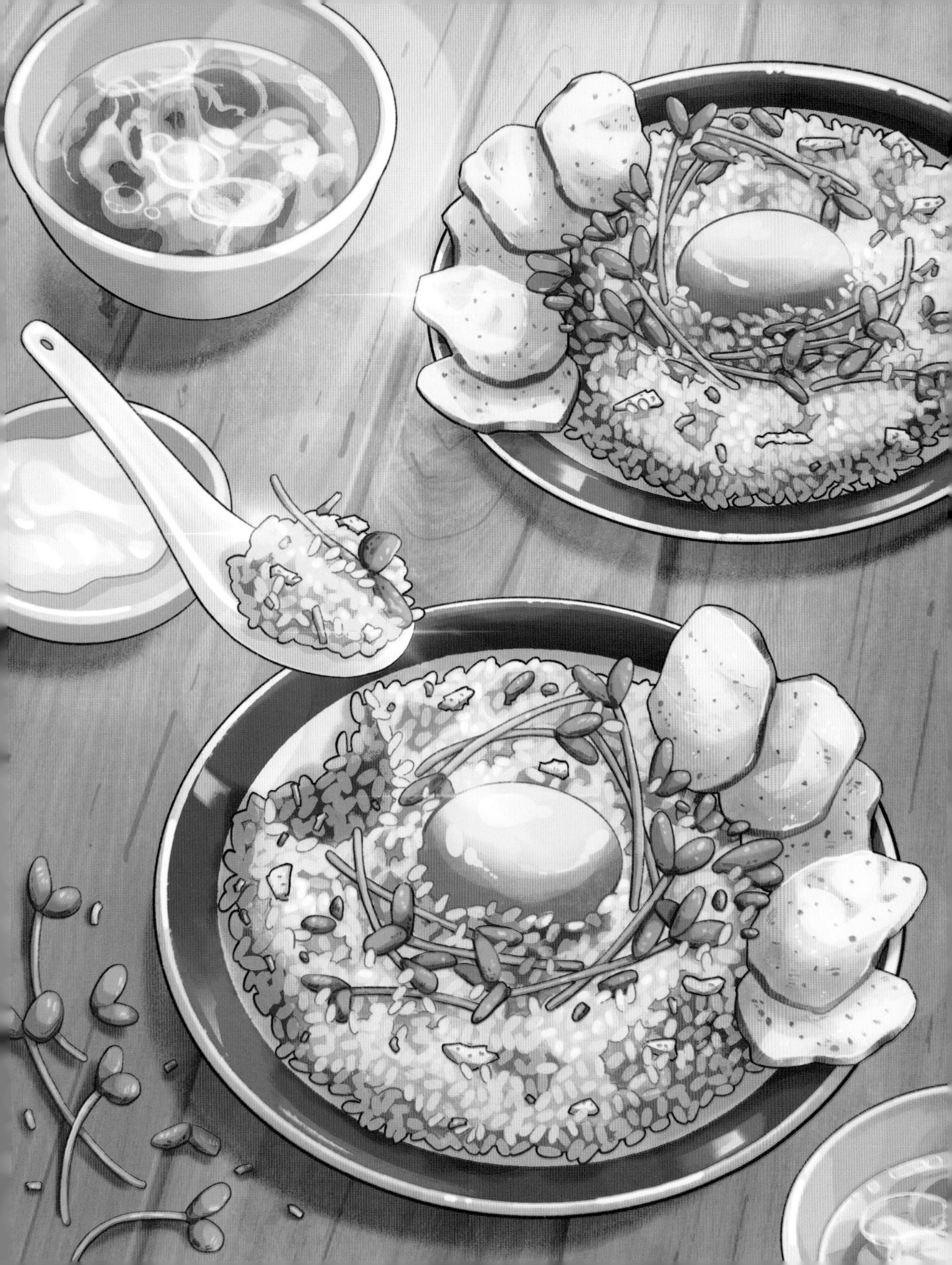

HONEY MILK

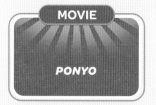

MOVIE

PONYO

Another favorite film from Studio Ghibli, *Ponyo* is the story of Ponyo, a goldfish princess, who is rescued by five-year-old Sosuke. After Ponyo transforms into a little girl, she gets her first taste of human food when Sosuke invites her to his house, and his mother makes them this warming honey milk.

YIELD	PREP TIME	COOK TIME
2	**5**	**5**
servings	minutes	minutes

INGREDIENTS

2 cups (480 ml) boiling water

1 cup (240 ml) milk (or dairy-free alternative)

2 tablespoons honey

STEPS

1. Carefully divide the boiling water between two mugs. Divide the milk between the mugs.

2. Spoon 1 tablespoon of honey into one of the drinks and stir, leaving the spoon in the mug. Repeat for the second drink with a separate spoon.

3. Serve immediately. Just before all the honey melts into the drinks, taste the honey-covered spoons, just like Ponyo!

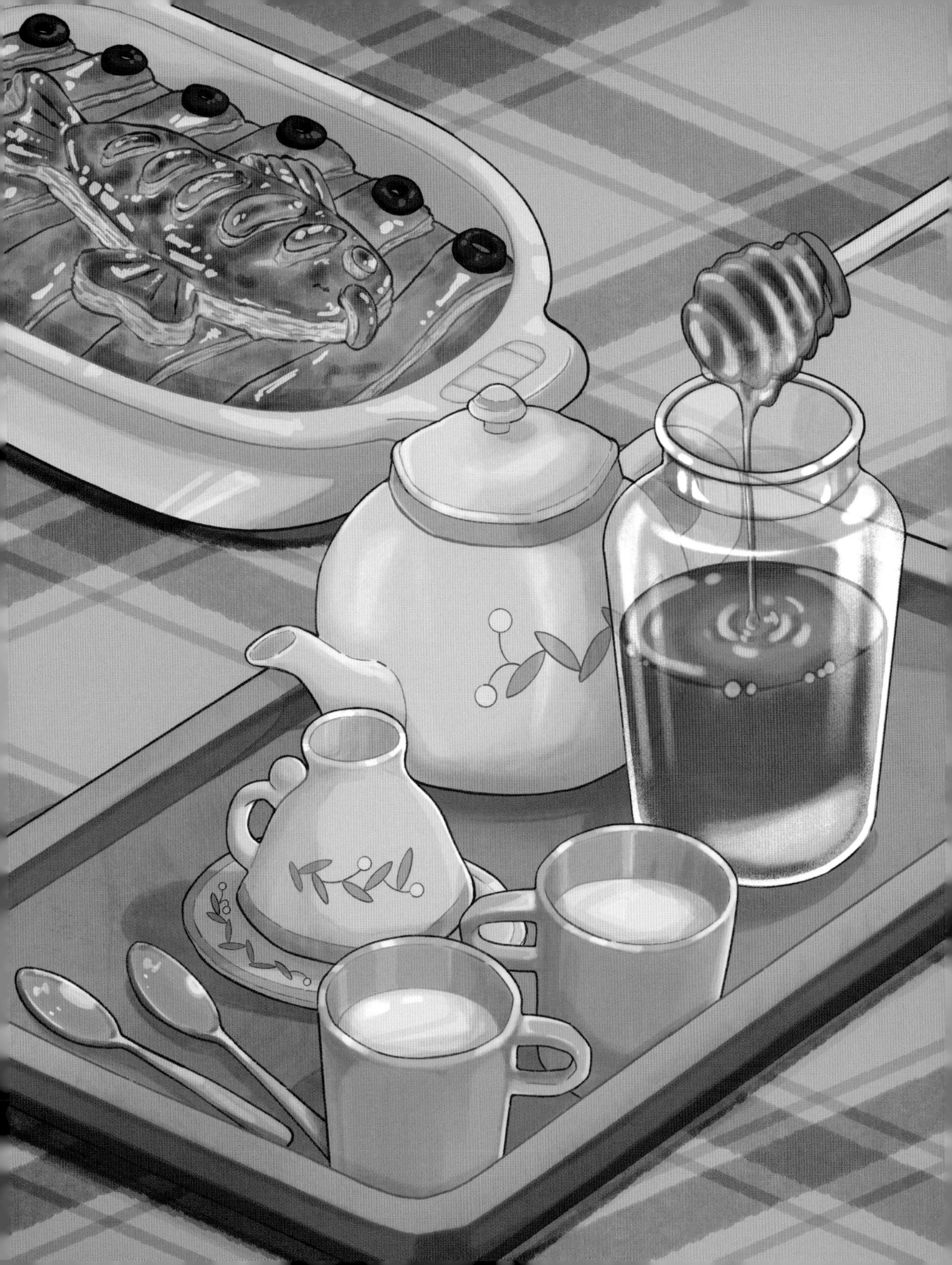

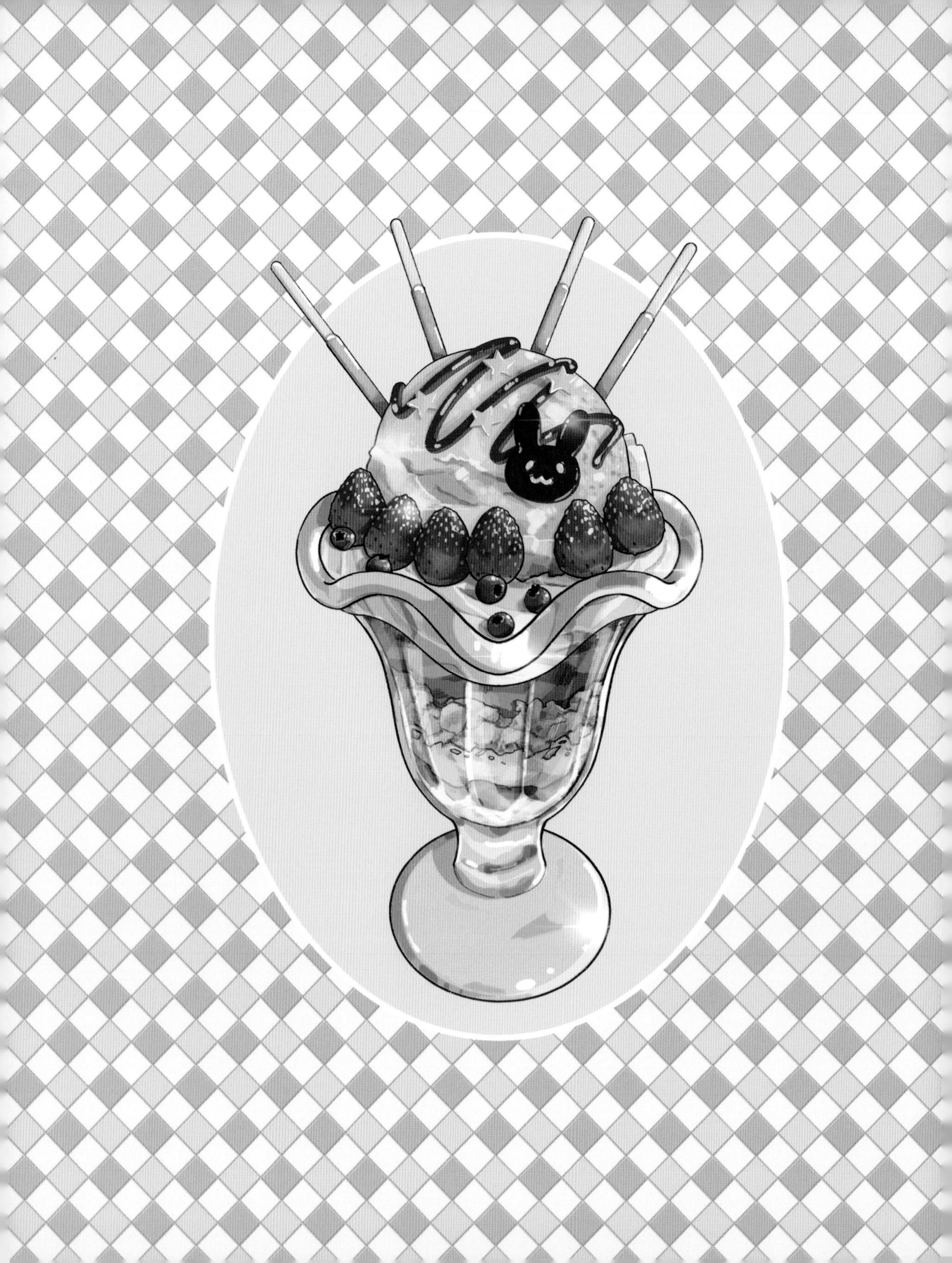

Cute

Café

ANYA AND BOND DUMPLINGS

ANIME

SPY X FAMILY

Twilight is a spy who needs a fake family as cover for his missions. Unbeknownst to him, the family he chooses has secrets of their own. His wife, Yor, is a secret assassin, and his adopted daughter, Anya, has telepathic abilities! Later, they adopt a dog named Bond, who can perceive the future. Here, I created dumplings in the likenesses of Anya and Bond, showcasing dumpling art techniques that can be useful in your cooking repertoire and that are sure to impress. Just don't cook like Yor—make sure you follow the recipe to a T!

MAKES	PREP TIME	COOK TIME	DECORATE TIME
10	**25**	**10**	**25**
dumplings	minutes	minutes	minutes

SPECIAL TOOLS

2½-inch (6 cm) round cookie cutter (or small bowl or glass)

VEGGIE FILLING

3½ ounces (100 g) firm tofu (about ¼ container), pressed (see Note on page 60) and finely minced

¼ cup (20 g) finely minced Napa cabbage

1 shiitake mushroom, finely minced

1 green onion, finely chopped

2 cloves garlic, grated

1 piece (¼ inch, or 6 mm) fresh ginger, peeled and grated

1 teaspoon soy sauce

2 teaspoons oyster sauce

¼ teaspoon sugar

1 pinch black pepper

WHITE DUMPLING WRAPPERS

1 cup (120 g) all-purpose flour

1 pinch salt

PINK DUMPLING DETAILS

¼ cup (30 g) all-purpose flour

1 drop pink gel food coloring

1 pinch salt

BLACK DUMPLING DETAILS

¼ cup (30 g) all-purpose flour

1 drop black gel food coloring

1 pinch salt

FOR SERVING

Dumpling sauce or soy sauce

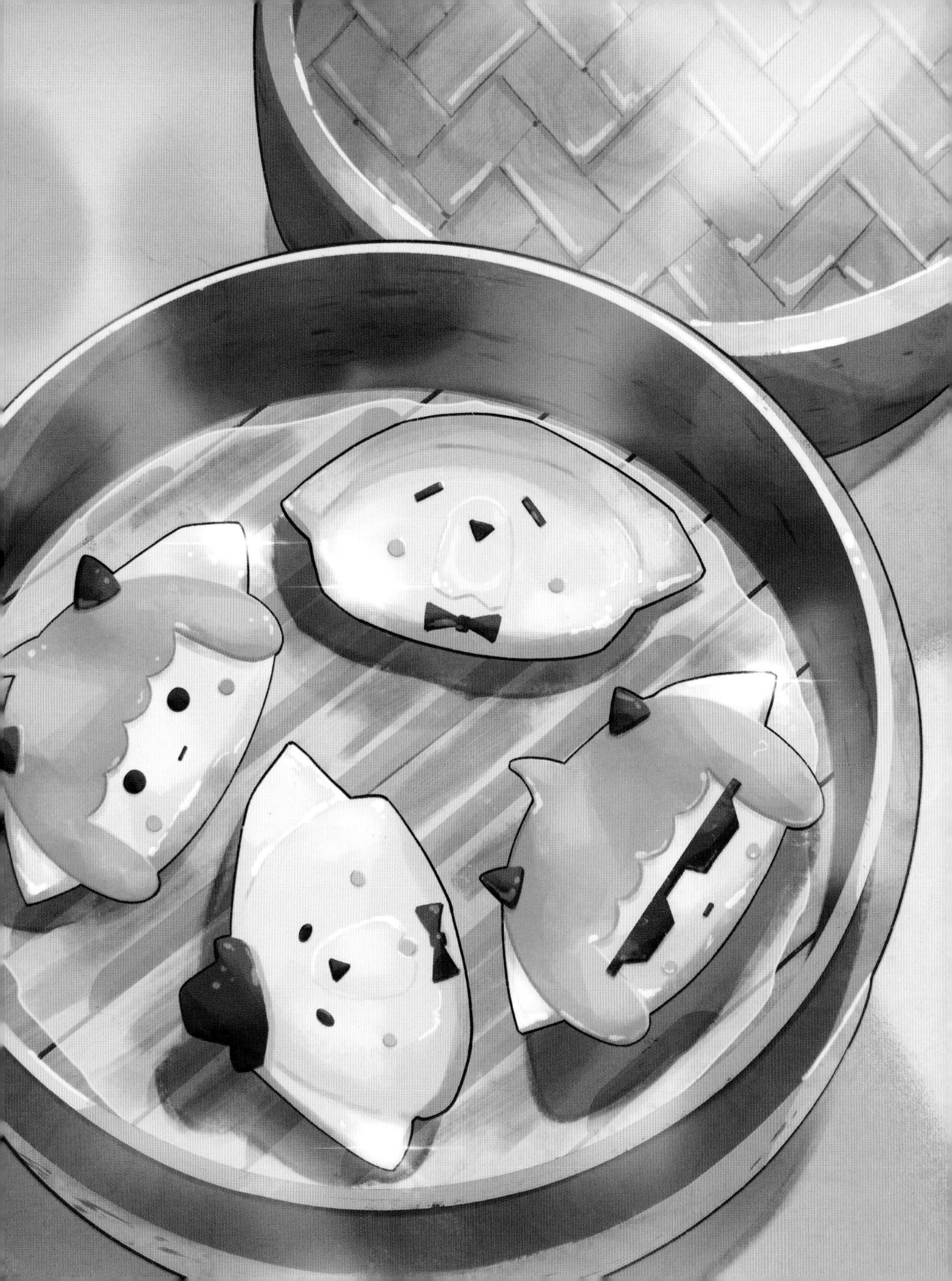

STEPS

1. **To make the veggie filling:** In a medium bowl, mix all the filling ingredients until well combined.

2. **To make the white dumpling wrappers:** In a small bowl, use chopsticks to stir together the 1 cup (120 g) flour and salt with ¼ cup (60 ml) of water until a shaggy dough forms. Transfer the dough to a clean work surface and knead until it comes together as a soft dough, about 7 minutes. Place the dough back into the bowl, wrap the bowl with plastic wrap, and let the dough rest, allowing the gluten to relax, 5 minutes. Once the dough has softened, knead again until smooth, about 2 minutes.

3. Using a rolling pin, roll out the dough ⅛ inch (3 mm) thick, then use a 2½-inch (6 cm) round cookie cutter (or trace a small bowl or glass with a knife) to cut out 10 white dumpling wrappers. Place parchment between each wrapper to prevent sticking. (You may store these dumpling wrappers by separating them with parchment and placing them in an airtight container—use within 3 days.) Save leftover cutout dough for Bond's design in step 8 and cover with a slightly damp tea towel.

4. Fill a small bowl with water. Set 1½ tablespoons of filling on the center of each dumpling wrapper. Dip a finger in the bowl of water and spread water sparingly around the edge of the wrappers, then fold the wrapper over the filling and pleat the sides to seal. Cover the dumplings with another damp tea towel while working on the dumpling details.

5. **To make the pink and black dumpling details:** In a small bowl, use chopsticks to stir together the ¼ cup (30 g) flour, food coloring, and salt with 1 tablespoon of water until a shaggy dough forms. Transfer the shaggy dough to a clean work surface and knead until it comes together as a soft dough, about 5 minutes. Wrap the bowl with plastic wrap and let the dough rest, allowing the gluten to relax, 5 minutes. Knead again until soft and smooth, about 2 minutes. Using a rolling pin, roll out the dough to ⅛ inch (3 mm) thick. Place on a sheet of parchment paper, then cover with a tea towel to prevent drying. Repeat this step with the black dumpling details ingredients.

6. To create the Spy Anya designs for 5 dumplings, start with the pink details. Place a filled dumpling on top of the sheet of the pink dumpling dough to gauge the size of the hair to fit the dumpling—the hair should cover half the dumpling. Using a small knife or fondant decorating knife, trace a hair design around the filled dumpling in the shape of an upside-down U. Remove the filled dumpling from the pink dumpling dough. Refine the hair design by cutting out small triangular pieces from the bottom of the hair and the bangs to create a shaggy look. Complete Anya's hair by creating her cowlick: cut out a small triangular shape and use a small amount of water to stick it on the top center of the hair. Wet both sides of the dumpling with a small amount of water, center the hair over the smooth end of the dumpling, and

attach the hair. Next, create Anya's blush: using a small, rounded piping tip, punch out 2 small circles from the pink dough, and adhere them to Anya's cheeks using dabs of water. Repeat the decorations with 4 more filled dumplings and cover them with a damp tea towel. Cover the leftover pink dough with a tea towel.

7. Create the rest of the Spy Anya details using the black dumpling dough. Using a small knife or fondant decorating knife, cut out 2 small triangles with rounded edges to make Anya's horn accessories. Adhere one onto each side of Anya's cowlicked hair with dabs of water. Use a small, rounded piping tip to cut out 2 small circles for Anya's eyes, then use the knife to cut out a small rectangle for the mouth. (Or, if you're feeling creative, make different expressions for Anya.) Repeat for the remaining 4 Anya dumplings.

8. To create the Spy Bond design for the remaining 5 dumplings, start with the pink details. Using a small, rounded piping tip, cut out 3 circles from the pink dough for the blush and tongue, then cut out 2 small circles from the black dough for the eyes. Using a small knife, cut a small triangle for the nose. To make Bond's tie, cut out a bow-tie shape (2 triangles connected at the tips). Cut out Bond's hat (a rounded top with a wider, bean-shaped base). Using the leftover white dumpling wrapper dough, make Bond's muzzle by cutting out a ⅛-inch (3 mm) circle, then cut out a small triangle at the base to indicate the mouth. Place the features accordingly on the rounded side of the dumpling using water sparingly to adhere. Repeat for the remaining 4 dumplings.

9. To steam the dumplings, fill a large pot a quarter full with water and bring to a boil. Line a steamer basket with parchment paper and arrange the dumplings so that they are not touching. Place the lid on the steamer and steam for 8 minutes, or until the dumpling wrappers are translucent.

10. Serve hot with dumpling sauce or soy sauce for dipping.

"It smells like . . . it's safe."

—Loid Forger

RAINBOW JELLY SELTZER

ANIME

FREE!: IWATOBI
SWIM CLUB

SEASON 1, EPISODE 6

"The Mermaid
of the Abyss"

When Hiyori was a young boy, he was often alone because his parents worked all the time. He spent his days reading his favorite story, "*The Little Mermaid*," and swimming. In the water, he felt at home and comfortable. One day, he meets Ikuya, who invites him to swim. Ikuya becomes his first childhood friend. The two go to university together, where they swim competitively. Ikuya reveals to Hiyori that their friend Haru saved Ikuya from drowning. But Haru left their group, which makes Ikuya sad. Hiyori goes to a book café alone and wonders how he can lift Ikuya's spirits. He thinks back on their past together, and swirls his beautiful jelly seltzer. It resembles the clear water of a swimming pool, and the fizz looks as if someone dove into the water. The colors of the jelly resemble the fish scales from his favorite childhood story. In this recipe, the frozen Jell-O cubes result in a fun, slushy consistency.

YIELD	PREP TIME	FREEZE TIME
4	**10**	**3**
servings	minutes	hours

SPECIAL TOOLS

4 mini ice silicone cube trays (40 cubes per tray)

INGREDIENTS

½ package (1½ ounces, or 43 g) blue gelatin dessert, (such as Berry Blue Jell-O)

½ package (1½ ounces, or 43 g) yellow gelatin dessert (such as Lemon Jell-O)

½ package (1½ ounces, or 43 g) green gelatin dessert (such as Lime Jell-O)

½ package (1½ ounces, 43 g) red gelatin dessert (such as Strawberry Jell-O)

4 cans (12 ounces, or 355 ml, each) strawberry seltzer, or any fruity clear-colored seltzer

STEPS

1 Mix each gelatin flavor according to the package directions, then carefully pour the liquid for each flavor into its own ice cube tray, one color per tray. Freeze the gelatin cubes until solid, 3 to 4 hours.

2 Pop the frozen cubes out of the molds and fill 4 large glasses with them, distributing the cubes evenly among the glasses for a mixture of colors in each. Pour a full can of seltzer into each glass, pop in a straw, and serve.

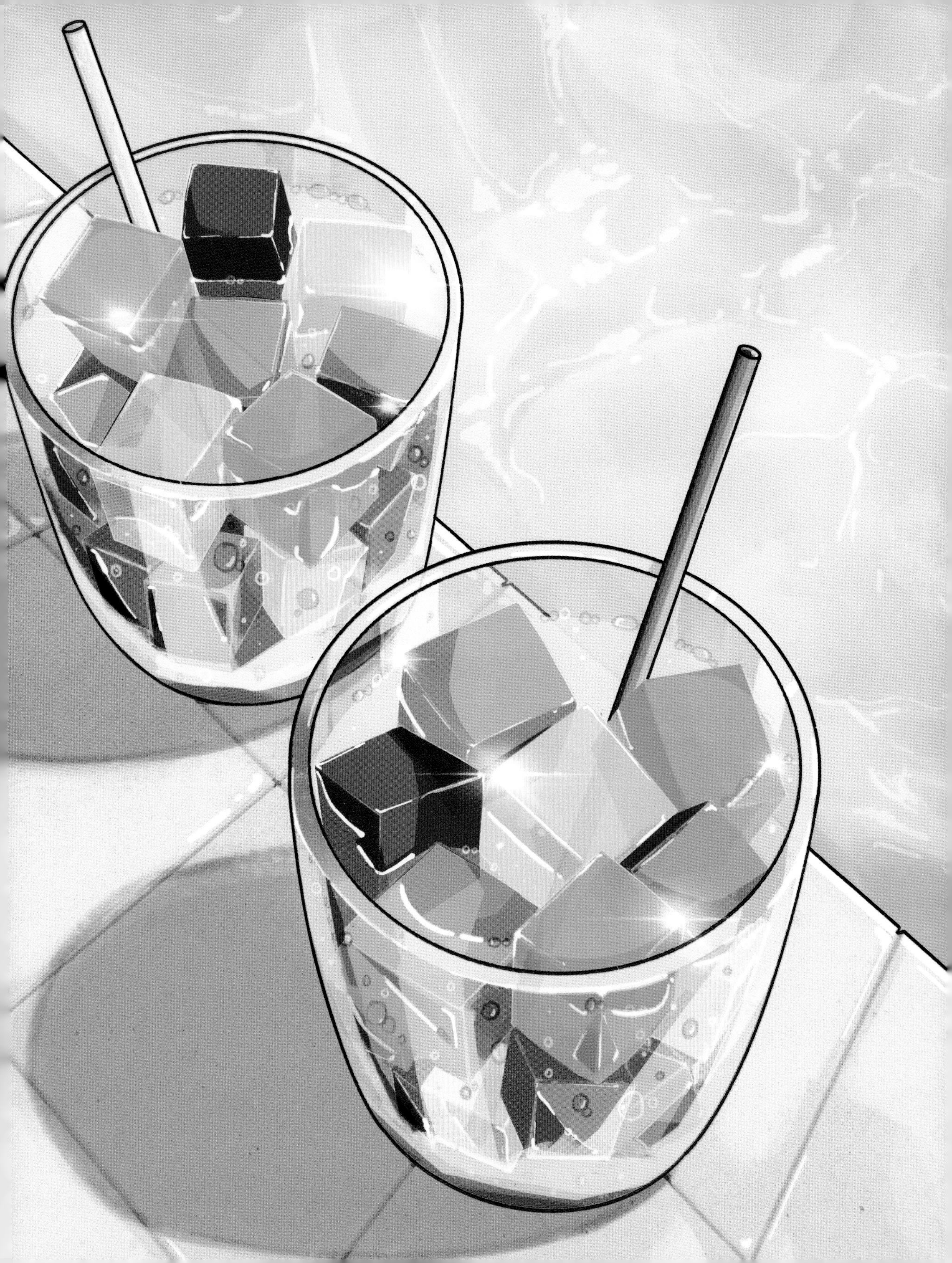

BUNNY APPLES

ANIME

CHAINSAW MAN

SEASON 1, EPISODE 4

"Rescue"

Denji is a rookie devil hunter who has fused with Pochita, a devil with a chainsaw nose. Together, they transform into "Chainsaw Man." In this episode, Denji is weakened from a fight, and his mentor, Aki, saves him. As the injured Denji recuperates in the hospital, Aki visits and cuts him these bunny-shaped apples—and his show of compassion is a new step in their relationship. Bunny apples are a simple design that will cheer anyone up. Add bunny apples to any bento or meal for a little fun for everyone.

MAKES

6

bunny apples

PREP TIME

5

minutes

INGREDIENTS

1 Cosmic Crisp apple (see Note)

1 teaspoon fresh lemon juice

NOTE

If you can't find Cosmic Crisp apples, you can use any red apple that has a crisp texture, such as Honeycrisp or Red Delicious.

STEPS

1. Cut the apple into 6 wedges, avoiding the seeds and core. To prevent browning, submerge the apple pieces in a bowl of water with the lemon juice.

2. Working with one apple wedge at a time, cut a shallow V into the apple's skin, starting from the cut side and ending in a point about ½ inch (1 cm) from the tip of one wedge. Cut out the piece of apple inside the V (about ⅛ inch, or 3 mm) to reveal bunny ears.

3. Repeat for the remaining apple wedges and serve.

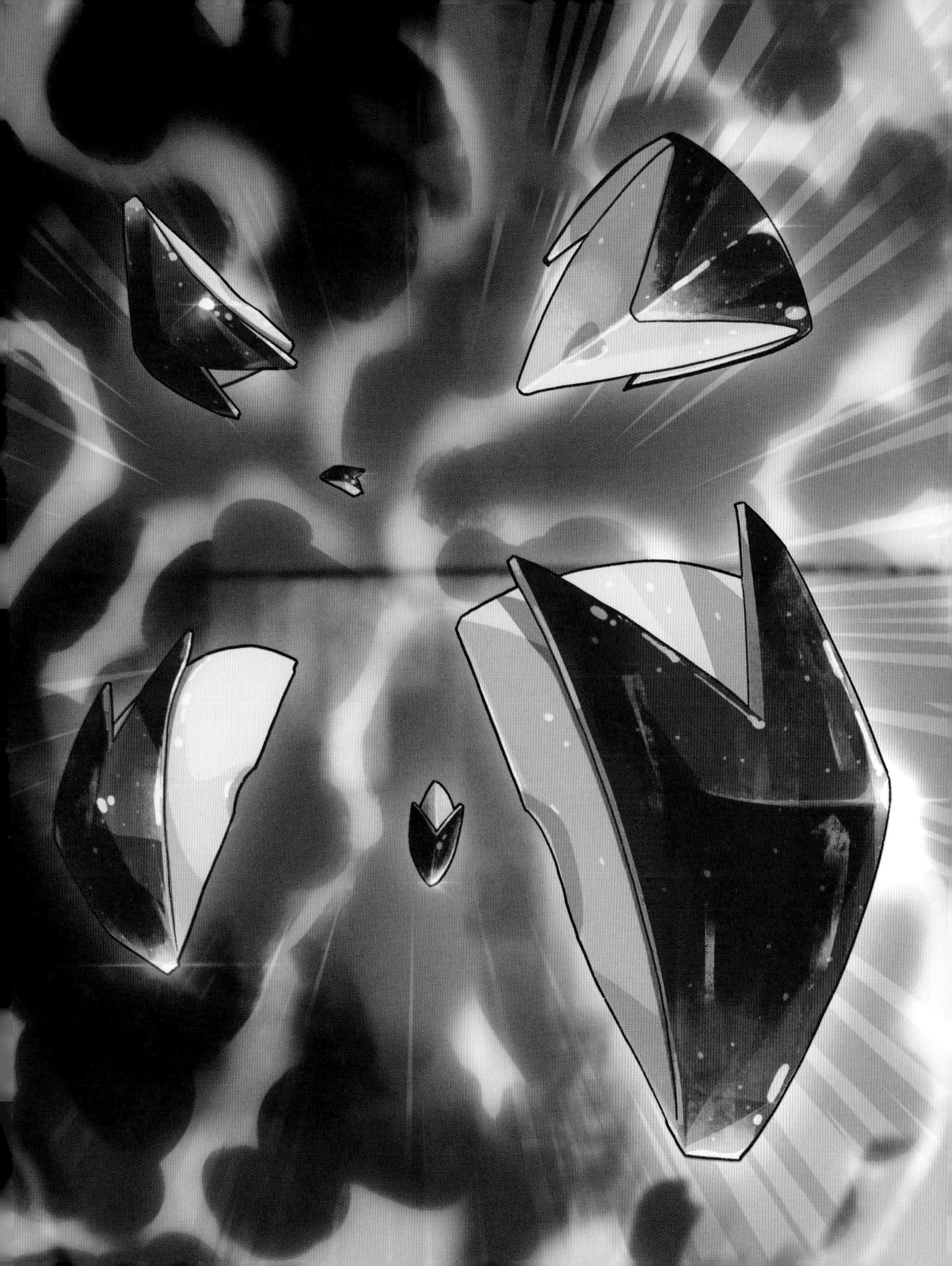

TRI-COLORED DANGO

Growing up, I watched this show with my brother. *Clannad*'s iconic dango outro song, "Dango Daikazoku," is so catchy and unforgettable. Here, I made regular dango with eyes—just like the outro song visual! It gives them life and character, and the simple addition of sesame seeds makes these dango unforgettably cute.

YIELD	PREP TIME	COOK TIME
3	**20**	**15**
skewers	minutes	minutes

SPECIAL TOOLS

3 bamboo skewers

1 toothpick

INGREDIENTS

1 cup (130 g) sweet rice flour (such as Mochiko; see Note on page 78)

4 ounces (115 g) silken tofu

2 tablespoons granulated sugar

1 teaspoon matcha powder

1 or 2 drops red gel food coloring

18 black sesame seeds

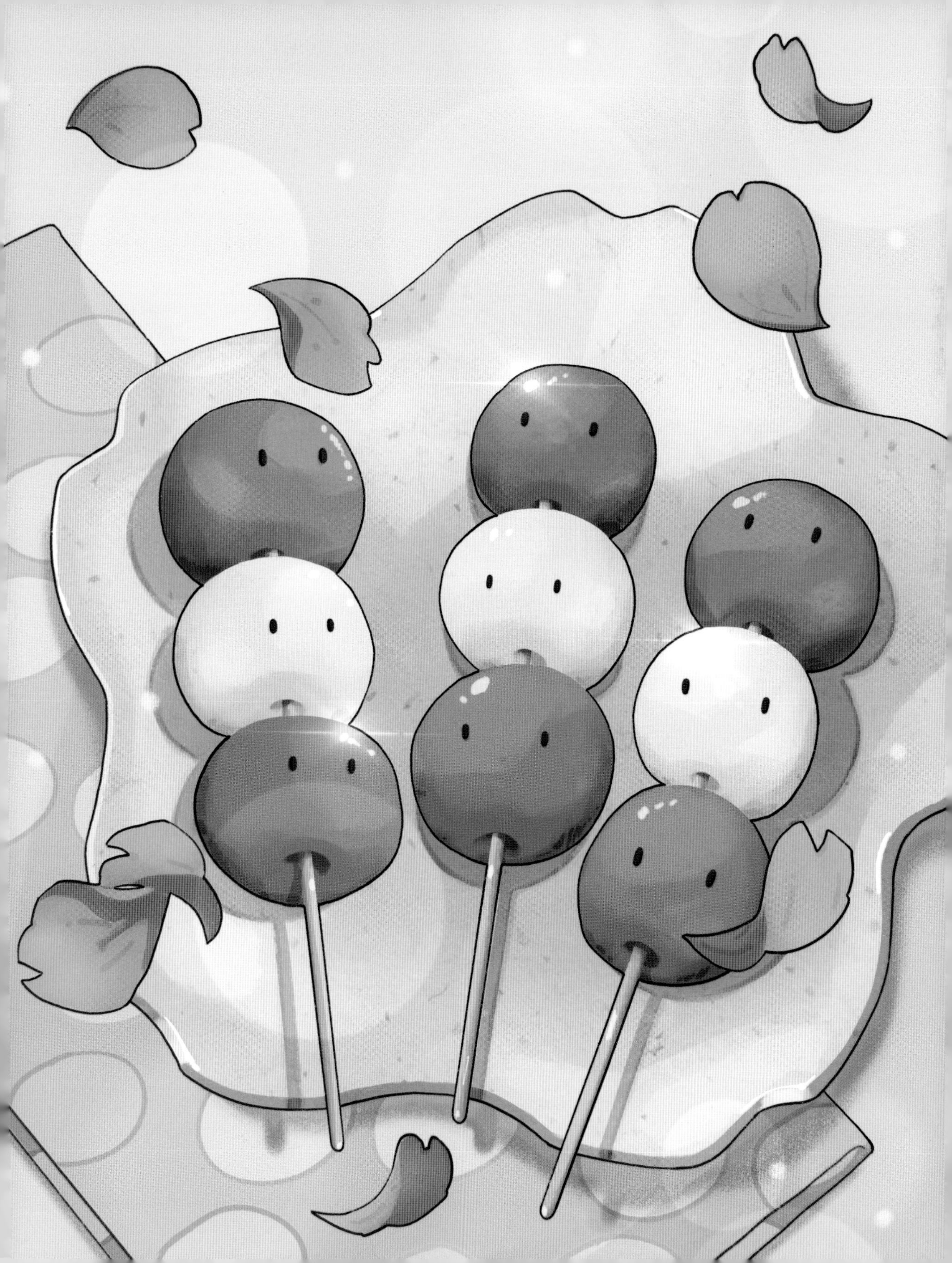

STEPS

1. In a medium bowl, combine the rice flour, silken tofu, and sugar. Knead for about 3 minutes, until a smooth and soft dough forms. Roll the dough into a log and divide it into 3 equal pieces.

2. To create green dango, add the matcha powder to one piece of dough and knead it until the color is fully and evenly incorporated. Divide the dough into 3 equal pieces and roll each piece into a ball.

3. To create pink dango, add the red gel food coloring to another piece of dough (use food-safe gloves, if needed, to prevent your hands from being dyed red) and knead it until the color is fully and evenly incorporated. Divide the dough into 3 equal pieces and roll each into a ball.

4. Divide the white dough into 3 equal pieces and roll each into a ball.

5. Fill a large pot halfway with water and bring to a boil over medium heat. Fill a large heatproof bowl with cold water. Carefully submerge the white dango balls into the boiling water, stir to prevent sticking, and cook for 15 minutes, or until the dough has cooked through and the dango floats to the top. Transfer the cooked dango to the cold water to stop cooking. (You can use the same cold water for all colors; the color won't transfer after cooking.) Repeat for the green and pink dango, working with one color at a time to prevent color transfer.

6. Wet your hands in the cold water to prevent sticking. Carefully skewer the dango onto a bamboo stick, adding green first, then white, and finally pink. Repeat for the remaining skewers and dango.

7. To create the eyes, use a toothpick to press divots for 2 eye placements in the center of each dango. Firmly push a black sesame seed into each divot using a toothpick or clean fingers.

NOTE

Mochiko rice flour is made from sweet rice. It's thick and sticky, and great for making sweet desserts like dango. It also makes for a great gluten-free thickener.

DUGTRIO SANDWICH WITH CREAMY ROASTED TOMATO SOUP

VIDEO GAME

POKÉMON CAFÉ REMIX

Pokémon Café Remix is a fun puzzle video game that features cute food in the shape of Pokémon. There's an ongoing discussion in the Pokémon world about whether they eat meat. No Dugtrios (or Digletts) were hurt in the making of this recipe; I kept it vegetarian. Make sure to buy sandwich loaves that have rounded tops, not squared!

YIELD	PREP TIME	COOK TIME	COOL TIME	DECORATE TIME
2	**10**	**40**	**10**	**10**
servings	minutes	minutes	minutes	minutes

SPECIAL TOOLS

Two 8-ounce (240 ml) soup ramekins

CREAMY ROASTED TOMATO SOUP

1 bulb garlic

3 tablespoons olive oil, divided

5 pinches salt, divided, plus more to taste

1 small onion, quartered

4 large whole tomatoes

4 pinches black pepper, plus more to taste

1 cup (240 ml) vegetable stock

¼ cup (25 g) grated Parmesan cheese

2 tablespoons unsalted butter

1 tablespoon honey

5 basil leaves

½ teaspoon red pepper flakes (optional)

¼ cup (60 ml) heavy whipping cream

2 pinches dried parsley, for serving

DUGTRIO SANDWICHES

12 slices rounded (not squared) sandwich bread

¼ cup (60 ml) Kewpie mayo

12 lettuce leaves

12 large tomato slices

Salt and black pepper

6 cherry tomatoes, cut in half crosswise

Black gel food coloring

STEPS

1. **To make the creamy roasted tomato soup:** Preheat the oven to 400°F (205°C). Line a sheet pan with parchment paper.

2. Cut off the tip of the garlic bulb to slightly expose the cloves. Drizzle 1 tablespoon of the olive oil on top of the bulb and season with 1 pinch of the salt. Wrap the bulb in aluminum foil and transfer it to the prepared sheet pan. Add the onion quarters and whole tomatoes to the prepared sheet pan, drizzle with the remaining 2 tablespoons olive oil and sprinkle with 4 pinches each of salt and pepper. Using a sharp knife, slice an X into each tomato to allow steam to escape during cooking.

3. Bake until the tomatoes and onion have softened and are slightly browned, about 40 minutes. When cool enough to handle, about 10 minutes, carefully unwrap the garlic and squeeze the contents into a blender. Add the roasted onions and tomatoes, vegetable stock, Parmesan, butter, honey, basil leaves, and red pepper flakes (if using). Leaving the lid of the blender slightly ajar and covering it with a towel to allow steam to escape, process until smooth.

4. Transfer the pureed soup to a medium pot and heat over medium-high heat until boiling. Reduce the heat to low. Stir in the whipping cream and season with salt and pepper. Keep warm until ready to serve.

5. **To make the Dugtrio sandwiches:** Lightly toast the sandwich slices. Spread the mayo on one side of each slice.

6. On top of one slice, mayo side up, stack 2 lettuce leaves, followed by 2 tomato slices. Sprinkle with salt and pepper, then add 2 more lettuce leaves and top with another slice of bread, mayo side down. Secure the sandwich by piercing a cherry tomato half with a toothpick, then piercing the sandwich with the toothpick about one-third from the rounded top to create Diglett's nose. Dip a small pastry brush into black gel food coloring and dab 2 oblong eyes above the nose. Repeat for the remaining ingredients to make 6 sandwiches total. Cut ¼ inch (6 mm) from the bottom of four sandwiches to create shorter Digletts.

7. **To serve:** For each serving, place the tallest, uncut, Diglett sandwich upright at the back of the plate. Stand the two smaller, cut, Diglett sandwiches in front of it to complete the Dugtrio evolution. Remove the soup from the heat and divide it between the ramekins. Serve immediately topped with a pinch of dried parsley.

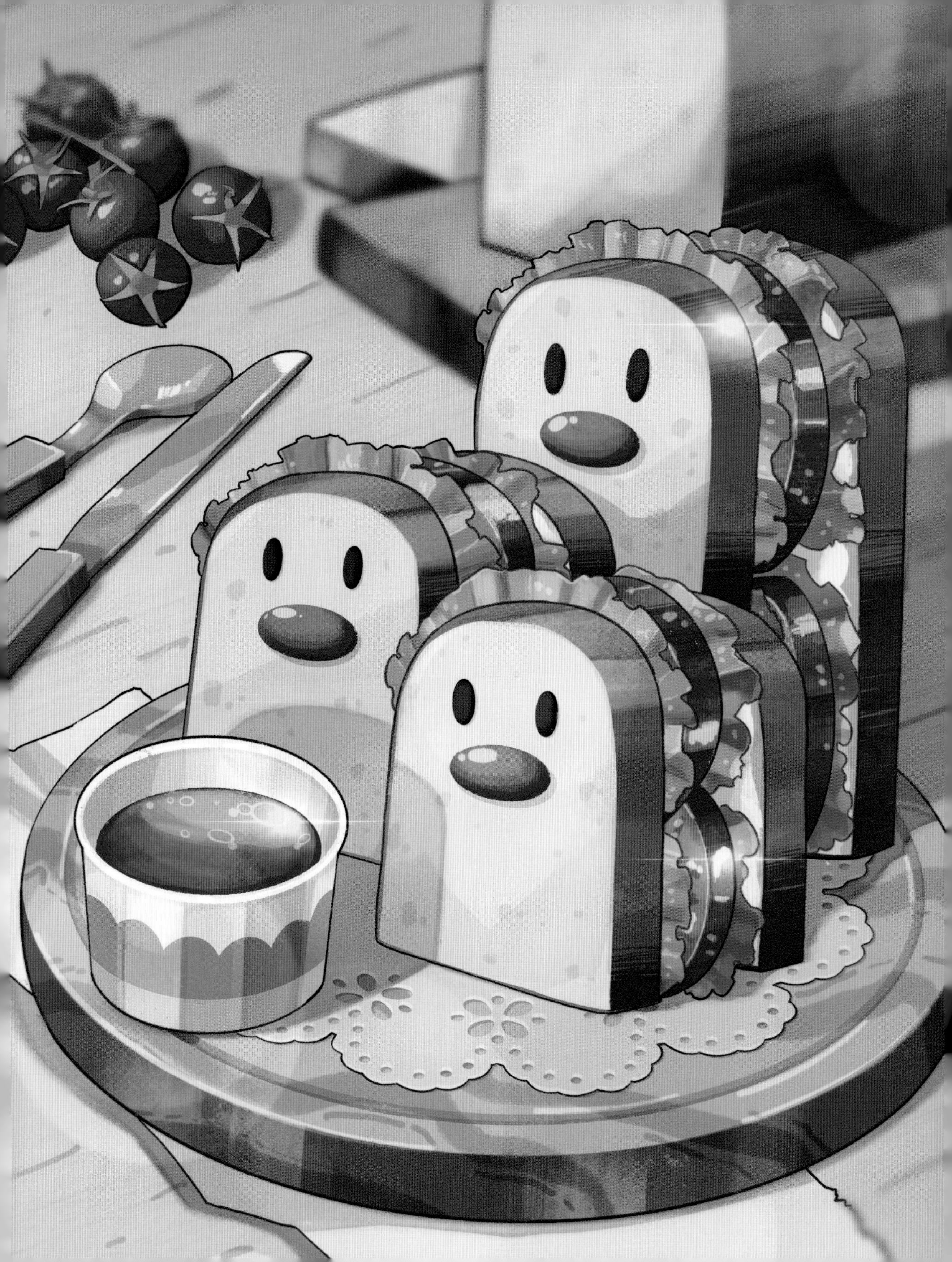

SADIST BUNNY PARFAIT

ANIME

BLEND S

EPISODE 2

"Sweets Without Honor"

To attract a wide range of customers, Café Stile employs waitresses with different personas. In this episode, the waitresses compete to create a new menu item. Maika and Mafuyu win the contest by making an unappetizing parfait that features a spicy sauce, which plays into Maika's sadistic persona. Parfaits are quintessential to anime cafés. I've chosen this one, in particular, because of its unique twist and funny story. Make this spicy parfait for your unexpecting friends—get into your sadistic character to really sell it!

YIELD	PREP TIME	COOK TIME
2	**40**	**20**
servings	minutes	minutes

STRAWBERRY SAUCE AND SPICY STRAWBERRY SAUCE

12 large strawberries (about 8 ounces, or 227 g), hulled and finely chopped

1 tablespoon granulated sugar, or to taste

1 pinch salt

¼ teaspoon cayenne pepper

BUNNY CHOCOLATE

4 tablespoons dark chocolate melts

1 tablespoon confectioners' sugar

WHIPPED CREAM

¼ cup (60 ml) heavy whipping cream

1 teaspoon confectioners' sugar

PARFAITS

1 cup (150 g) matcha ice cream

1 cup (150 g) vanilla ice cream

2 cups (52 g) cornflakes

1 cup (150 g) strawberry ice cream

1 cup (150 g) mango ice cream

6 mini strawberries, hulled and sliced in half lengthwise

2 banana slices (¼ inch, or 6 mm, thick)

10 blueberries

Blue star sprinkles

8 strawberry Pocky biscuit sticks

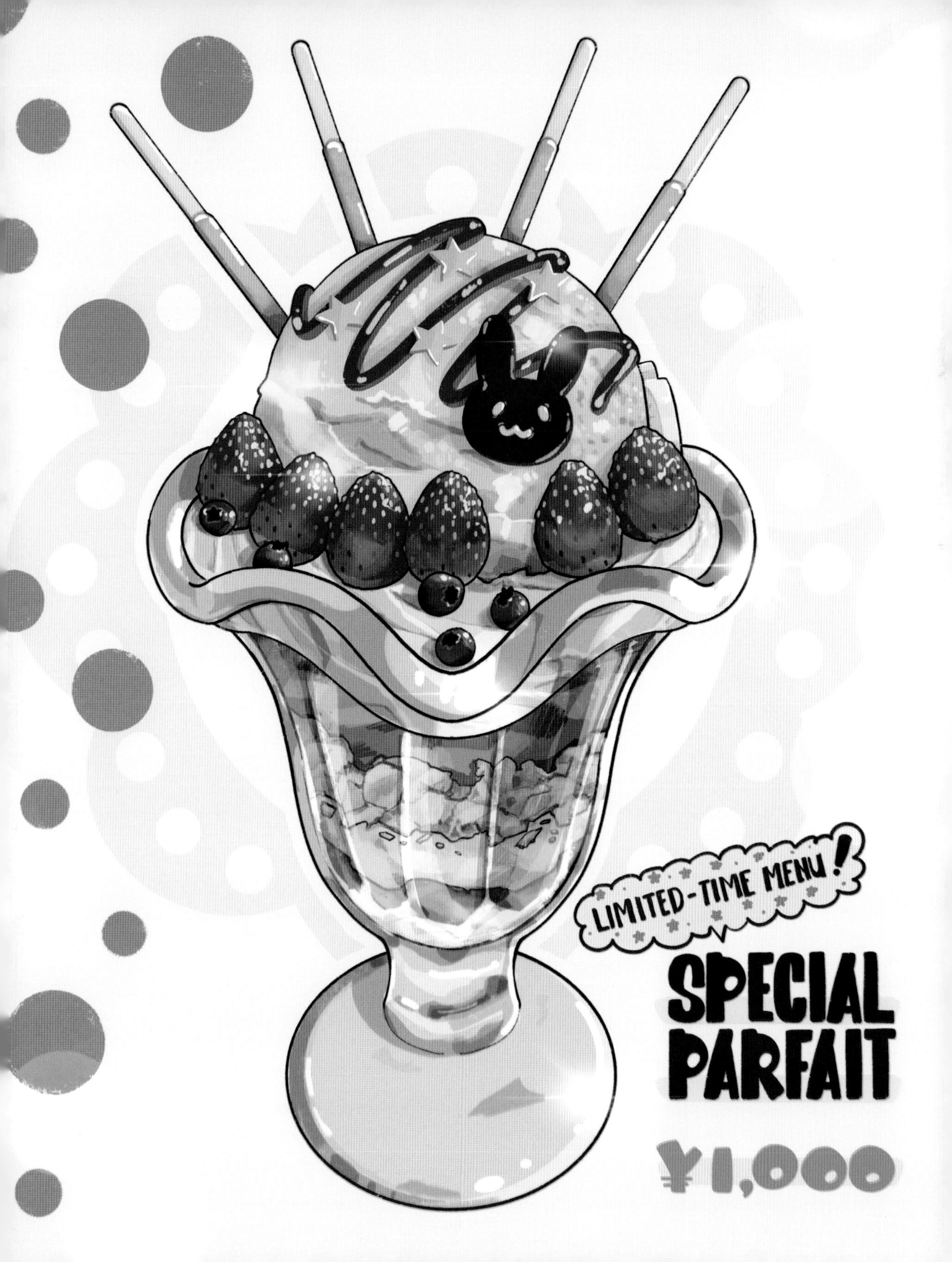
LIMITED-TIME MENU!
SPECIAL PARFAIT
¥1,000

STEPS

1. **To make the strawberry sauce:** In a medium saucepan over medium heat, combine the chopped strawberries, granulated sugar, and salt with ½ cup (120 ml) of water. Bring to a boil, then reduce the heat to medium-low and cook, stirring occasionally, until the strawberries soften and the sauce thickens, about 15 minutes. Remove from the heat.

2. **To make the spicy strawberry sauce:** Using a fine-mesh strainer, strain the strawberry sauce into a small bowl until you have 2 tablespoons of liquid. Return the strained strawberries to the saucepan. Stir the cayenne pepper into the liquid in the small bowl. Transfer to a piping bag and set aside.

3. **To make the bunny chocolate:** Line a plate or small sheet pan with parchment paper. In a microwave-safe bowl, microwave the dark chocolate melts for 30 seconds, or until almost fully melted. Remove the chocolate from the microwave and stir with a fork until it is smooth and fully melted. Carefully transfer the melted chocolate to a piping bag and let cool until warm. Cut a small opening at the tip of the piping bag and pipe a bunny onto the parchment, starting with a ½-inch (1 cm) solid circle for the face connected to two ½-inch-long (1 cm) solid, oblong ears at the top of the head. Repeat drawing bunny faces until all the chocolate has been used.

4. To draw the bunny's face, in a small bowl, combine 1 teaspoon of water with the 1 tablespoon confectioners' sugar and mix until smooth. Dip a toothpick into the icing, then use it to draw 2 elongated dots for eyes and a sideways number 3 for the mouth. Repeat for the remaining bunny chocolates.

5. **To make the whipped cream:** In a medium bowl, add the whipping cream and 1 teaspoon confectioners' sugar. Using a handheld electric mixer with a whisk attachment on medium speed, whip until peaks form, 2 to 3 minutes. Transfer the whipped cream to a piping bag fitted with a large star tip.

6. **To assemble the parfaits:** Working carefully to create neat, defined layers, scoop 2 tablespoons of strawberry sauce into the bottom of one parfait glass and top with ½ cup (75 g) of the matcha ice cream, followed by ½ cup (75 g) of the vanilla ice cream, 1 cup (28 g) of the cornflakes, and ½ cup (75 g) of the strawberry ice cream. Pipe a layer of whipped cream around the inside perimeter of the glass and place ½ cup (75 g) of the mango ice cream in the center. Cut a small opening in the spicy strawberry sauce piping bag, then drizzle it in a zigzag over the top of the mango ice cream. Sprinkle 5 blueberries on the whipped cream and top the mango ice cream with some blue star sprinkles. Gently push a chocolate bunny into the mango ice cream and stick 4 of the strawberry Pocky behind the ice cream. Place 4 small strawberries around the mango ice cream on the bunny's left side, then place 2 strawberries and a single slice of banana on the right side. Repeat the step for the second parfait. Servie with dessert spoons.

7. Make an intimidating face, put on your sadist maid persona, and serve immediately!

BEAR PANCAKES

ANIME

KIRA KIRA ☆ PRECURE A LA MODE

SEASON 1, EPISODE 20

"Wanting to Mix It Up! Ichika and Ciel!"

"PreCure," or pretty cure, is a Japanese series where pretty cute girls cure people with their abilities. In this case KiraKira PreCure is about pretty girls curing people with baked sweets! Middle schooler Ichika loves sweets. She lives in the real world with a magical team of Legendary Pâtissiers and a fairy named Pekorin. Together, they protect sweets from villains that turn desserts colorless and flavorless. Ichika asks the young celebrity prodigy pâtissier Ciel to be her teacher. To convince her, she makes pancakes with her inspired by fresh honey they've tasted. Ichika makes a three-stack of bear pancakes inspired by one of her favorite childhood books about three little bears eating honey. I wanted to include this recipe to show how everyday foods can easily be shaped into cute characters for simple joys in your home kitchen. Whoever you make this for is guaranteed to smile.

YIELD	PREP TIME	COOK TIME	DECORATE TIME
2	**5**	**15**	**10**
servings	minutes	minutes	minutes

PANCAKES

1¼ cups (150 g) all-purpose flour

1 teaspoon baking powder

2 pinches salt

1 large egg

¾ cup (180 ml) milk

2 tablespoons honey

WHIPPED CREAM

¼ cup (60 ml) heavy whipping cream

½ tablespoon granulated sugar

1 teaspoon vanilla extract

DECORATIONS

2 pink sprinkles

2 green star sprinkles

4 teaspoons chocolate hazelnut spread (such as Nutella)

4 fresh raspberries

Syrup or honey, for serving

STEPS

1. **To make the pancakes:** In a medium bowl, sift together the flour, baking powder, and salt, then whisk with a wire whisk to combine. In a separate medium bowl, whisk the egg, then add the milk and honey and whisk until combined.

2. Pour the wet ingredients into the dry ingredients, and stir until a thick, smooth batter forms. Transfer the mixture to a pouring vessel.

3. Wet a hand towel, wring out the excess water, and set aside by the stove. Heat a medium nonstick skillet over medium heat and add 1 teaspoon of the oil. Carefully wipe the pan with a paper towel to remove excess oil and prevent the pancakes from becoming blotchy, then turn the heat to medium-low.

4. To create bear ears, pour a 1-inch (2.5 cm) circle of the batter in the top left of the pan and repeat in the top right of the pan, then pour a 4-inch (10 cm) circle of batter in the center of the pan and also overlapping about a quarter of the ears for the head. Cook for 2 minutes, or until bubbles appear on the surface of the larger pancake. Flip with a spatula and cook for 2 minutes more, or until golden brown on both sides. Remove the pan from the heat and set the bottom of the pan on the wet towel to prevent it from overheating. Transfer the bear pancake to a plate. Repeat steps 3 and 4 to create 5 more bear pancakes.

5. **To make the whipped cream:** In a medium bowl, combine the whipping cream, 1 tablespoon sugar, and vanilla. Using a handheld electric mixer with a whisk attachment, whip on medium speed, gradually increasing to high speed, until stiff peaks form, about 2 minutes. Transfer the whipped cream to a piping bag and snip the tip to create a ½-inch (1 cm) hole.

6. **To decorate:** Squeeze about ½ teaspoon of the whipped cream onto the center of one plate to prevent the pancakes from slipping. Place a bear pancake on top and cover with whipped cream on the center, leaving a ½-inch (1 cm) border around the edge of the pancake. Use an offset spatula to spread the whipped cream flat. Set another pancake on top and repeat. Top with the third pancake and pipe a large mound of whipped cream on the bottom center of the pancake to create the nose. Pipe a smaller mound of whipped cream on the top-right side by the bear ear to make a headpiece. Place a pink sprinkle on top of the nose and a star sprinkle on the headpiece. Scoop 1 teaspoon of chocolate hazelnut spread on the upper left of the nose to create an eye and repeat for the upper-right side. Place 2 raspberries on the left side of the plate. Repeat this step for the second plate, then serve with syrup or honey.

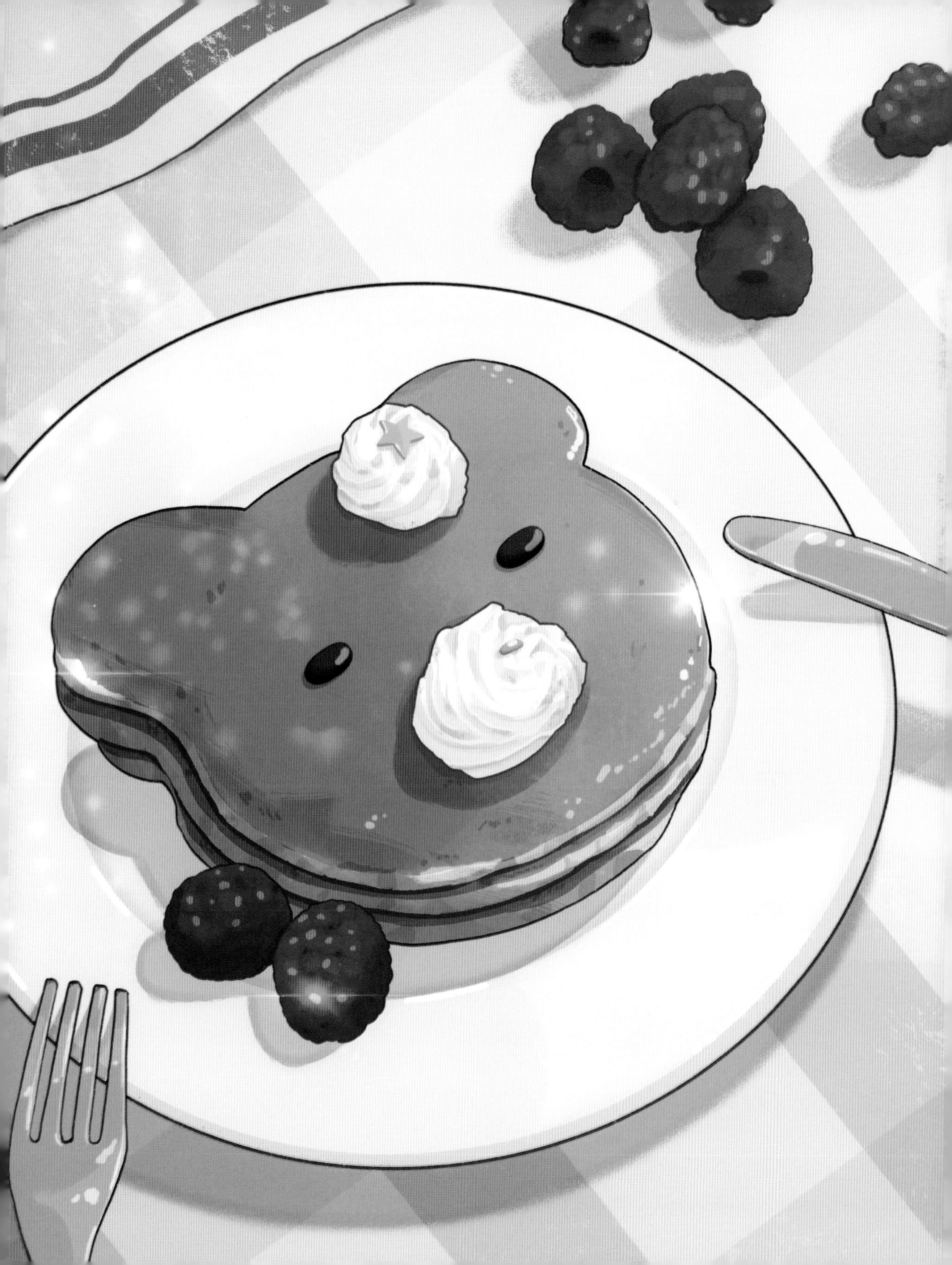

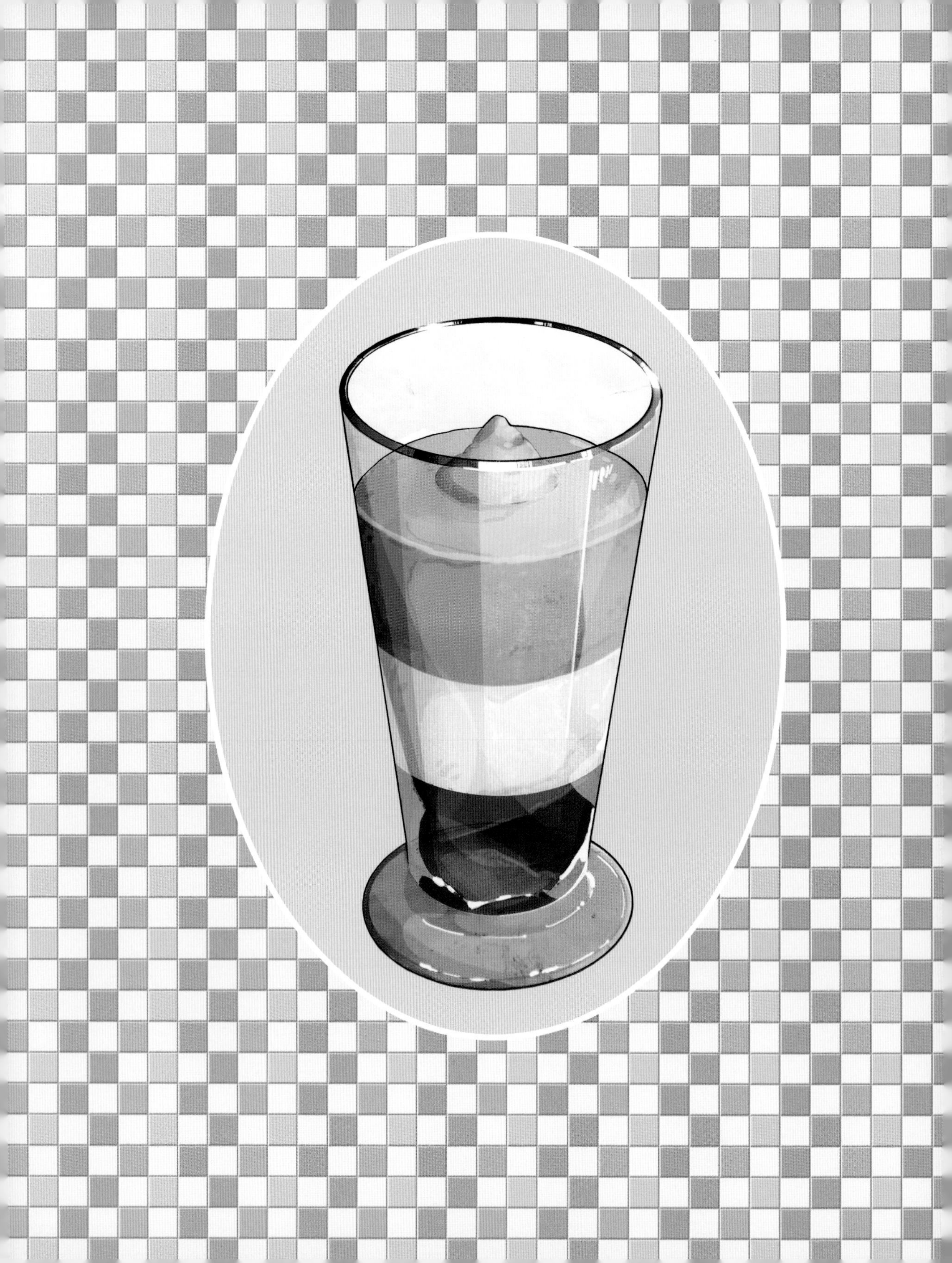

Modern

Café

CARROT ELIXIR

ANIME

I GOT A CHEAT SKILL IN ANOTHER WORLD AND BECAME UNRIVALED IN THE REAL WORLD, TOO

SEASON 1, EPISODE 10

"Master and Apprentice"

Yuuya has been bullied since he was in kindergarten. After he moves into his grandfather's home, he finds a magical portal door that leads him to another world, where he learns powerful skills that help him in real life. While adventuring in this other world, Yuuya meets a powerful rabbit named Usagi (*"rabbit"* in Japanese) who trains him to be his successor. After training, they discuss Usagi's divine background as Usagi drinks this refreshing carrot elixir. In anime, most drinks are either water or sweetened and colored drinks. That's why I wanted to include this healthy one—because it's so rare! I've also never seen such a theatrical garnish. This elixir will definitely be memorable for anyone who drinks it.

YIELD

2 servings

PREP TIME

15 minutes

SPECIAL TOOLS

Two 10-ounce (300 ml) wooden drinking cups

INGREDIENTS

6 carrots (1 pound, or 454 g), 4 peeled and roughly chopped, plus 2 left whole and unpeeled for garnishing

½ cup (120 ml) cold water

1 large Fuji apple, peeled, cored, and roughly chopped

1 large navel orange, peeled, separated, and pith removed

1 piece (½ inch, or 1 cm) fresh ginger, peeled

1 small clementine, peeled and pith removed

Ice cubes

STEPS

1. Add the chopped carrots, cold water, apple, navel orange, ginger and clementine to a blender, then process until a smooth mixture. Strain through a fine-mesh strainer or cheesecloth into a jug. Use a rubber spatula to press down on the pulp to squeeze out excess juice.

2. Add ice to two wooden drinking cups, then divide the carrot elixir between each cup.

3. To serve, make a 1½-inch (4-cm) cut from the top down the center of each whole carrot. Slide a carrot, cut side down, over the rim of each wooden drinking cup.

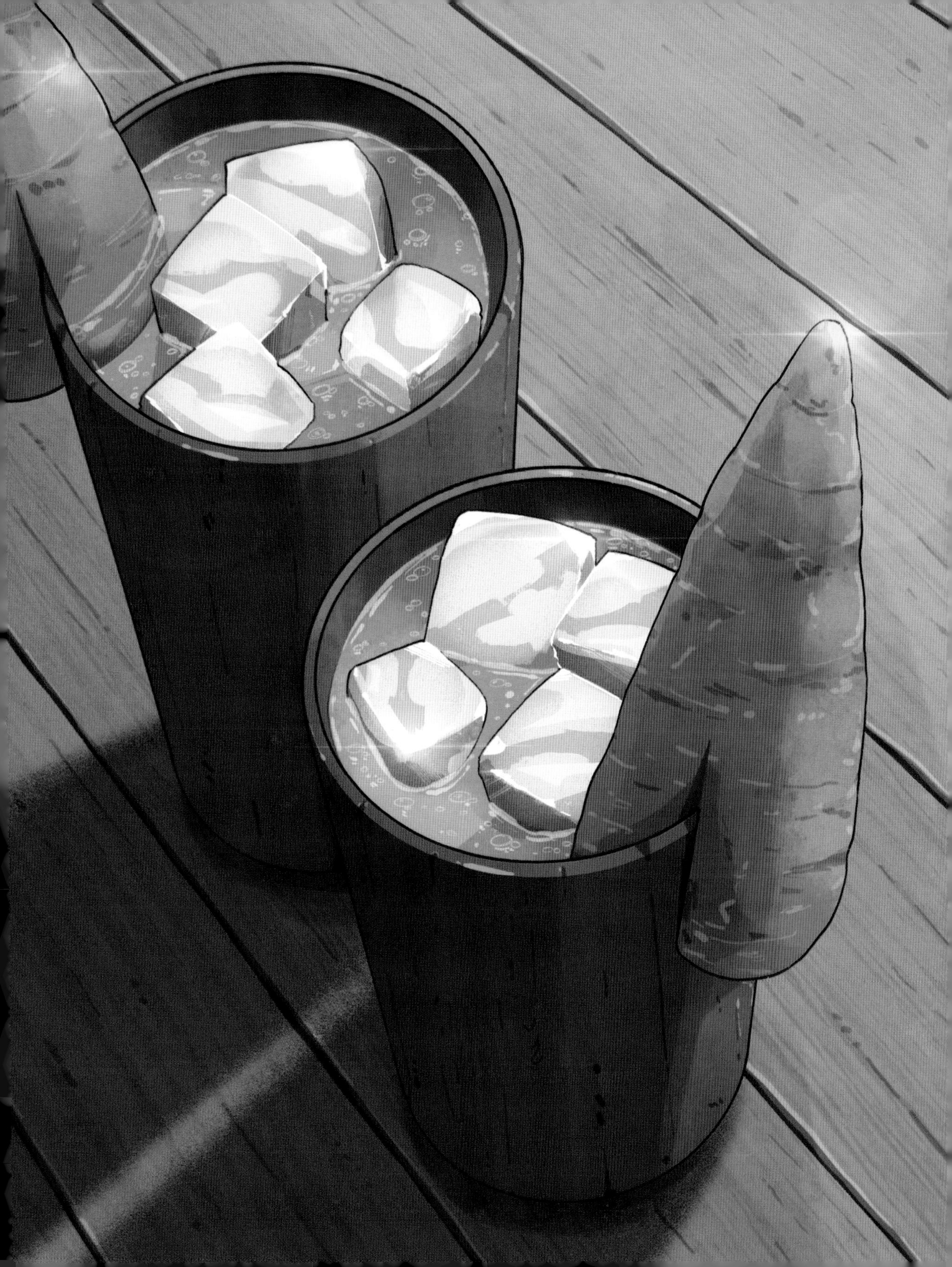

STRAWBERRY SELTZER

ANIME

BUDDY DADDIES

SEASON 1, EPISODE 5

"Crunch Time"

Kazuki and Rei recently took in four-year-old Miri. To cover their increased family spending, they've been working late nights—secretly employed as assassins. Because they're so exhausted, they don't realize that Miri slipped out of the house and ended up at their employer's bar. There, owner and seasoned bartender Kyutaro crafted this strawberry seltzer especially for Miri. It comes together in a pinch. Add a fancy bendy straw, and one sip will bring back childhood memories.

MAKES	PREP TIME	COOK TIME	COOL TIME
1	**5**	**8**	**15**
drink	minutes	minutes	minutes

SPECIAL TOOLS

Cocktail shaker

1 bendy straw

SIMPLE SYRUP

¼ cup (100 g) granulated sugar

STRAWBERRY PUREE

3 large strawberries, hulled

½ cup small ice cubes (120 ml)

FOR SERVING

3 large ice cubes

1 cup (240 ml) seltzer

STEPS

1. **To make the simple syrup:** In a small pot, combine the sugar and ¼ cup (60 ml) of water and bring to a boil over high heat. Once boiling, reduce the heat to medium-low and let simmer until the syrup thickens, about 2 minutes. Remove the pot from the heat and let the syrup cool to room temperature.

2. **To make the strawberry puree:** In a blender, combine the strawberries with 1 tablespoon of the simple syrup, or to taste, and blend until smooth. Transfer the puree to a cocktail shaker and shake with the small ice cubes until cold, about 2 minutes.

3. **To serve:** Fill a fancy glass with the large ice cubes. Using a fine-mesh strainer, strain the strawberry puree into the glass, then pour in the seltzer. Add a bendy straw, stir, and serve.

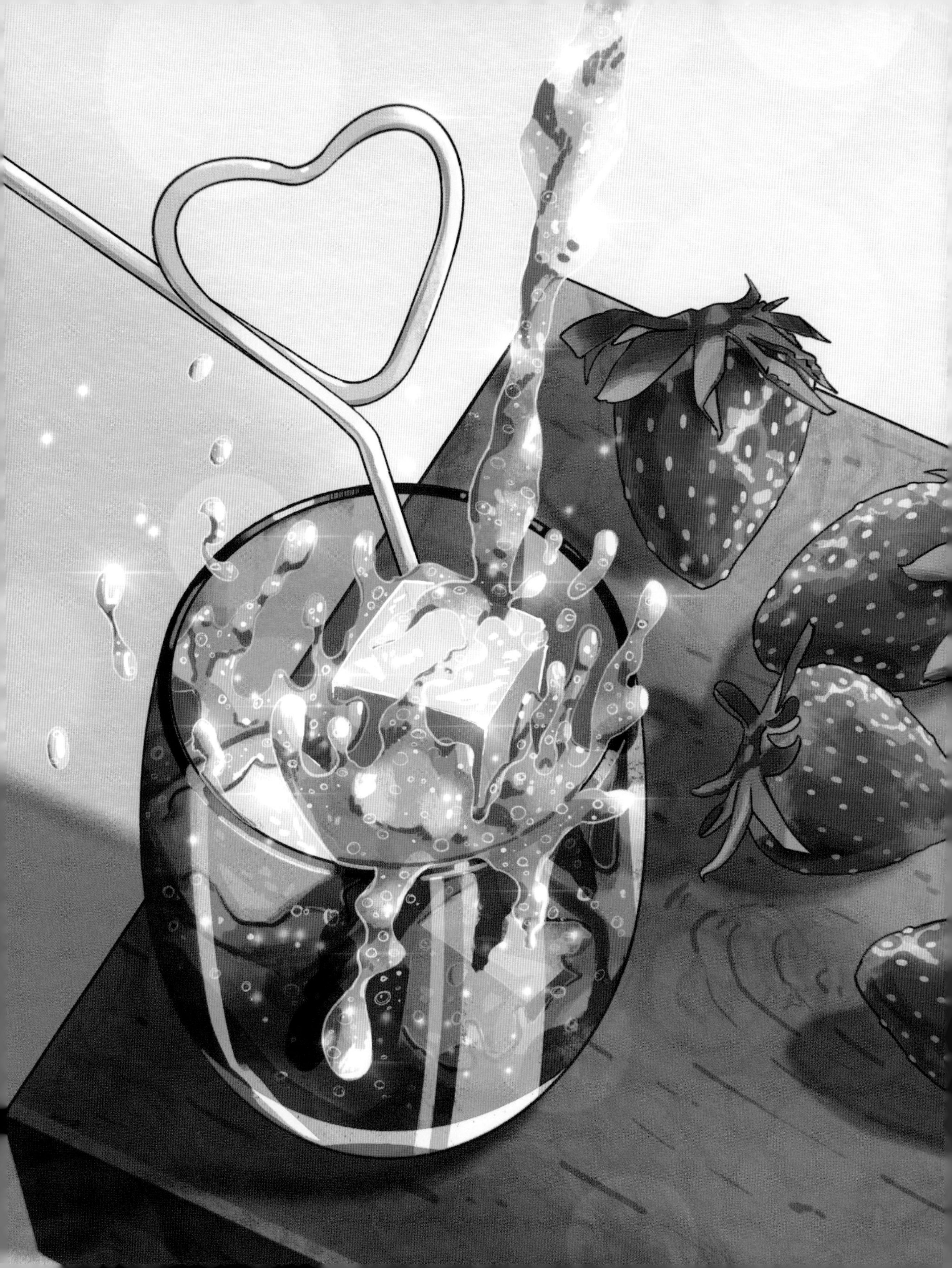

TOFU MOCHI DONUTS

ANIME

BEASTARS

SEASON 1, EPISODE 2

"The Academy's Top Dogs"

Beastars focuses on the students of Cherryton Academy, where the anthropomorphic animal characters go to school. Here, carnivores and herbivores coexist peacefully—until an herbivore is killed. Here's a delicious vegetarian option for donuts, inspired by the herbivore menu in the Cherryton Academy cafeteria.

This is one of my favorite recipes in this book: it's easy, it doesn't require kneading, and it's highly satisfying. I urge everyone to try it. Be ready to eat more than one!

YIELD	PREP TIME	COOK TIME
4	**15**	**5**
donuts	minutes	minutes

TOFU MOCHI DONUTS

1 ounce (30 g) silken tofu

½ cup (65 g) cake flour

¾ cup (90 g) sweet rice flour (such as Mochiko)

1 tablespoon granulated sugar

1 tablespoon baking powder

1 pinch salt

¼ cup (60 ml) soy milk or another milk alternative (such as hazelnut milk)

Oil (such as canola), for frying

VANILLA GLAZE

½ cup (60 g) confectioners' sugar

2 tablespoons soy milk, or another milk alternative (such as hazelnut milk)

1 teaspoon vanilla

1 pinch salt

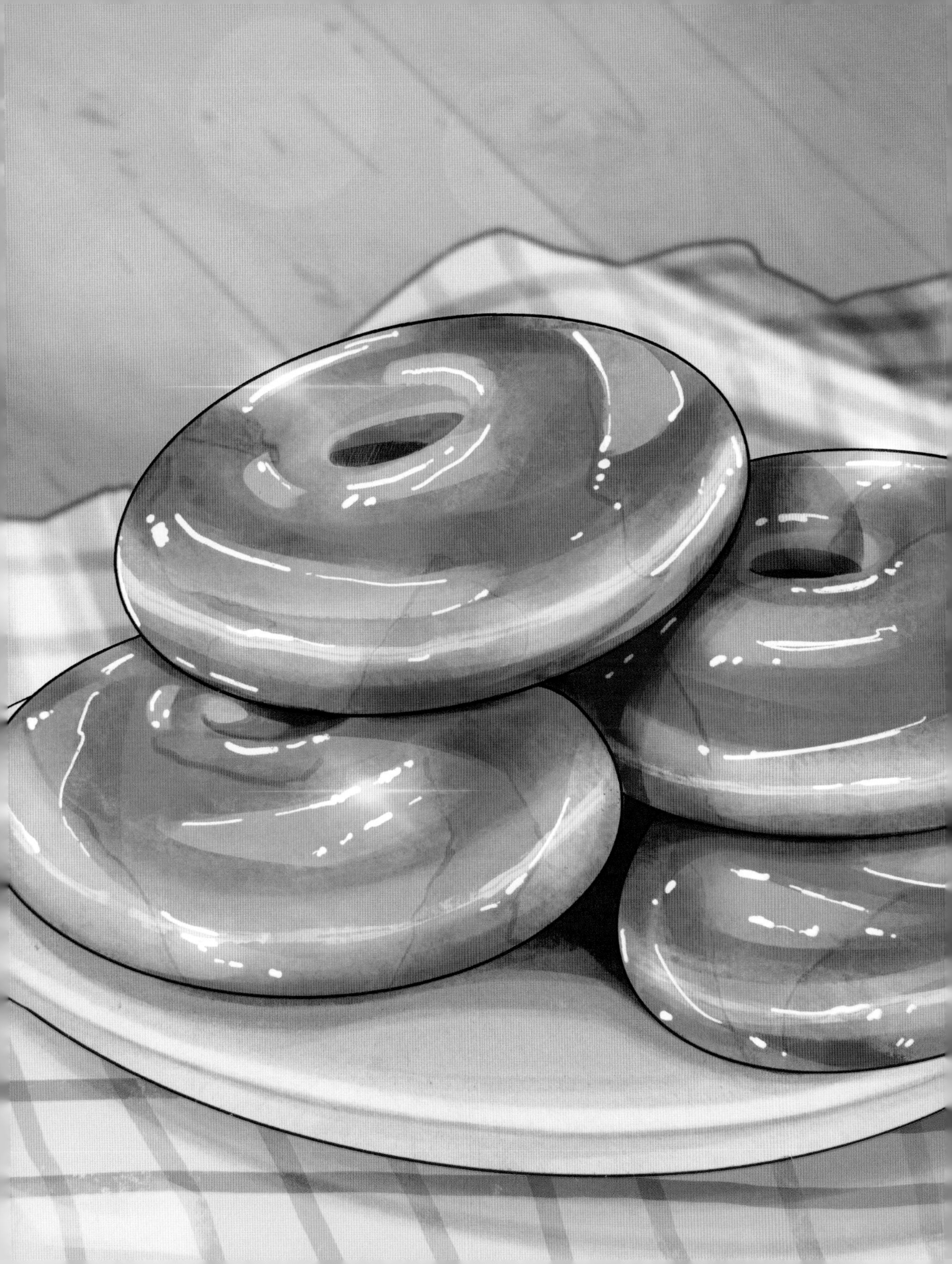

STEPS

1. **To make the tofu mochi donuts:** Cut four 5-inch (13 cm) squares of parchment paper and arrange them in a single layer on a baking sheet.

2. In a medium bowl, combine the silken tofu, cake flour, sweet rice flour, granulated sugar, baking powder, salt, and milk. Knead the mixture with your hands for 4 minutes, or until all the sweet rice flour is incorporated and becomes saturated and a dough forms. Transfer to a piping bag and cut a 1¼-inch (3 cm) hole in the tip. Pipe a 3-inch (8 cm) donut ring onto one of the parchment squares. Repeat for the 3 remaining donuts.

3. Fill a large, heavy-bottomed pot with at least 2½ inches (6 cm) of the oil and heat the oil to 350°F (180°C), measuring with a thermometer, or until a small piece of dough sizzles when it hits the hot oil. Working in batches as needed, carefully lower the donuts and the parchment paper squares into the oil using a spatula. Let the donuts cook for 2 minutes, then use tongs to carefully pull the parchment paper out of the oil and discard. Flip and cook the donuts until golden brown, another 2 minutes. Transfer the cooked donuts to a cooling rack in a single layer to cool.

4. **To make the vanilla glaze:** In a small bowl, stir together the confectioners' sugar, milk, vanilla extract, and salt until smooth and glossy. Drizzle the glaze over the mochi donuts in a thin layer while the donuts are still warm. Serve and enjoy!

"The menus are carefully devised in terms of nutrition and taste to satisfy all animals."

—Jack

CHOCOLATE PISTACHIO FROZEN CAPPUCCINO

ANIME

KOMI CAN'T COMMUNICATE

SEASON 1, EPISODE 2

"It's Just a Childhood Friend"

Komi shows her appreciation for her friend Najimi by stepping out of her comfort zone to order this drink from Standbakes Coffee, the anime's riff on Starbucks. But Komi has extreme anxiety and can't communicate the drink order properly. The fifteen-year-veteran barista feels it is their destiny to make a perfect drink just by looking at Komi. The result is a hilarious scene of deep ambition and effort, all to get the order wrong. I channeled that barista when creating this recipe.

MAKES	PREP TIME	COOK TIME
2	**15**	**25**
frozen cappuccinos	minutes	minutes

SPECIAL TOOLS

2 squeeze bottles

CHOCOLATE SYRUP

2 tablespoons condensed milk

2 teaspoons unsweetened cocoa powder

1 pinch salt

PISTACHIO CREAM

⅓ cup (50 g) shelled pistachios

3 tablespoons milk

1 tablespoon confectioners' sugar

½ tablespoon unsalted butter, melted

1 pinch salt

FROZEN CAPPUCCINO

⅓ cup (80 ml) boiling water

3 tablespoons instant coffee

¼ cup (30 g) confectioners' sugar

1 cup (240 ml) ice cubes

½ cup (120 ml) milk

2 tablespoons semisweet chocolate chips

2 tablespoons roasted walnuts (optional)

WHIPPED CREAM

½ cup (120 ml) heavy whipping cream

1 teaspoon granulated sugar (optional)

TOPPING

1 tablespoon shaved orange chocolate

1 tablespoon shaved white chocolate

STEPS

1. **To make the chocolate syrup:** In a small bowl, whisk together the milk, cocoa powder, and salt until smooth. Transfer to a squeeze bottle.

2. **To make the pistachio cream:** In a small pot, bring 1 cup (240 ml) of water to a boil over high heat. Once boiling, add the pistachios and boil for 1 minute, then remove the pot from the heat and let the pistachios sit in the water for 5 minutes. Drain the pistachios, transfer to a clean tea towel, and rub with the towel to remove the peels. (This will help keep the final pistachio cream a vibrant green.) Discard the peels. Transfer the prepared pistachios to a food processor and add 3 tablespoons milk, powdered sugar, melted butter, and salt. Process until a smooth and creamy mixture. Transfer to a second squeeze bottle.

3. **To make the frozen cappuccino:** In a small bowl, pour in the boiling water, add the instant coffee and ¼ cup (30 g) confectioners' sugar and stir until dissolved. Transfer to a blender and add the ice, milk, chocolate chips and roasted walnuts (if using) and blend until the ice is smooth in texture.

4. **To make the whipped cream:** In a medium bowl, combine the whipping cream and 1 teaspoon sugar (if using). Using a handheld electric mixer with a whisk attachment, whip the cream, starting on low and gradually increasing to medium-high, until stiff peaks form, about 3 minutes.

5. **To assemble:** Using a squeeze bottle, drizzle chocolate syrup in random swirls inside the glasses. Pour the frozen cappuccino equally between the glasses, then top both drinks with a dollop of whipped cream and a drizzle of chocolate syrup and pistachio cream to taste. Garnish with a sprinkle of orange and white chocolate shavings. Add a straw and serve immediately.

NOTE

Leftover chocolate syrup and pistachio cream will keep in airtight containers in the refrigerator for up to 1 week. Besides drinks, the chocolate syrup is delicious on waffles and ice cream, and the pistachio cream is amazing on toast—use it just like peanut butter.

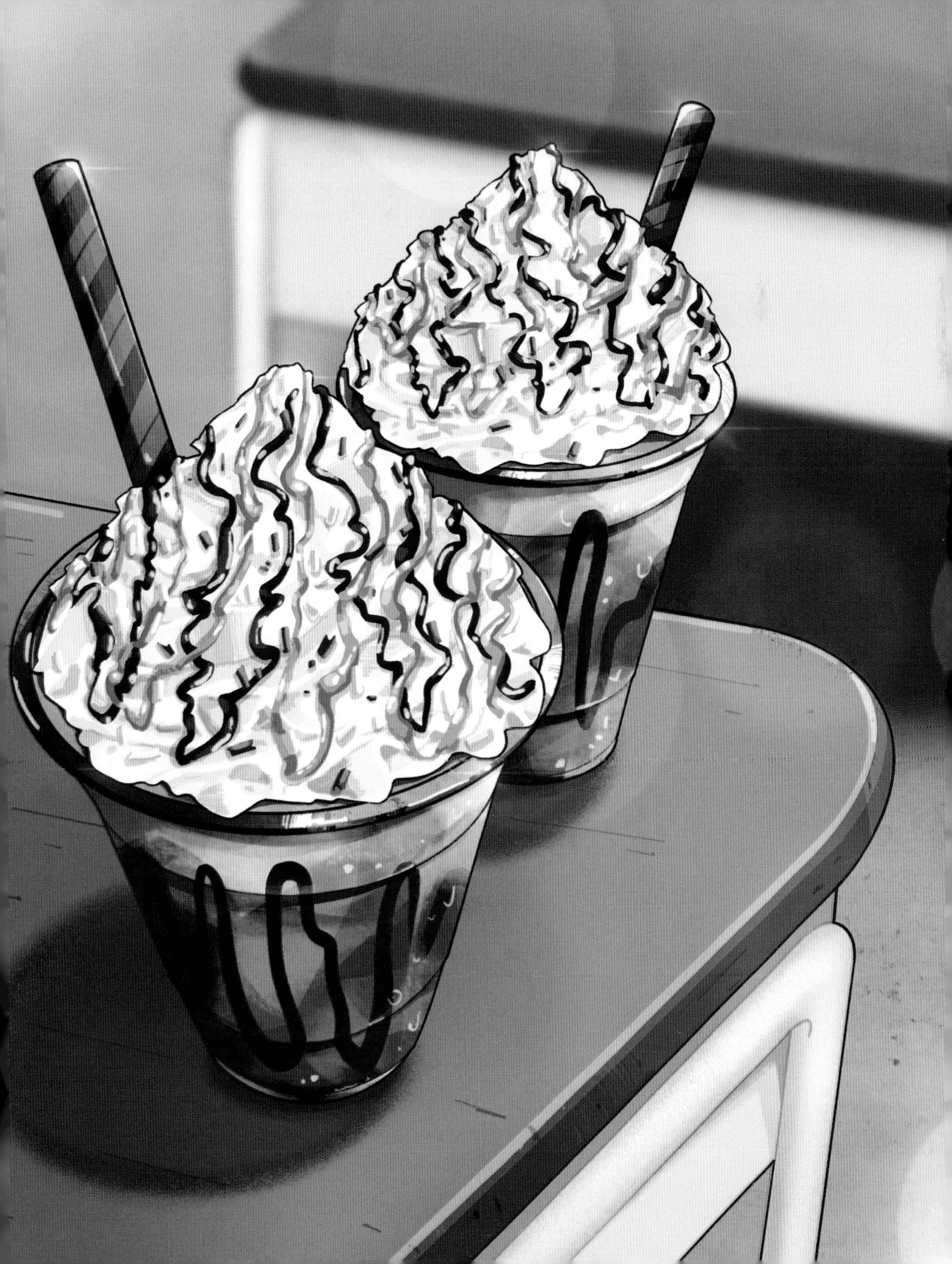

BUNNY CREAM PAN (CUSTARD BREAD)

ANIME

RASCAL DOES NOT DREAM OF BUNNY GIRL SENPAI

SEASON 1, EPISODE 1

"My Senpai Is a Bunny Girl"

Sakuta meets Mai in a library. Mai is dressed in a bunny girl costume, but no one appears to notice her except for Sakuta. Mai is starting to disappear—people can't see or hear her. It's as if she is being slowly erased from existence. Sakuta is one of the few who can still see and hear her. At the train station, Mai tries to order this custard-filled bun from the bakery, but she's invisible to the shopkeeper. Sakuta orders for her. Mai says how tragic it is not to be able to order and eat custard-filled buns. I sympathize with her because these soft, glossy buns filled with creamy custard are delicious! This Japanese pastry's iconic appearance is a classic moon shape with cut lines, modernized with Mai's pink bunny hairpin for extra cuteness.

YIELD	PREP TIME	PROOF TIME	COOK TIME
6	**30**	**90**	**30**
buns	minutes	minutes	minutes

SPECIAL TOOLS

2-inch (5 cm) bunny cookie cutter

CUSTARD

3 egg yolks

2½ tablespoons granulated sugar

1 pinch salt

2½ tablespoons cornstarch

1¼ cups (300 ml) milk

1 tablespoon unsalted butter

1 teaspoon vanilla extract

SOFT BREAD BUNS

½ cup (120 ml) milk

2 tablespoons granulated sugar

1 teaspoon active dry yeast

1½ cups (205 g) bread flour

1 large egg, beaten and divided

½ teaspoon salt

3 tablespoons unsalted butter, 2 tablespoons at room temperature and 1 tablespoon melted, divided

Oil, for greasing

BUNNY CLIP DECORATIONS

2 drops pink gel food coloring

¼ cup (35 g) bread flour

1 pinch salt

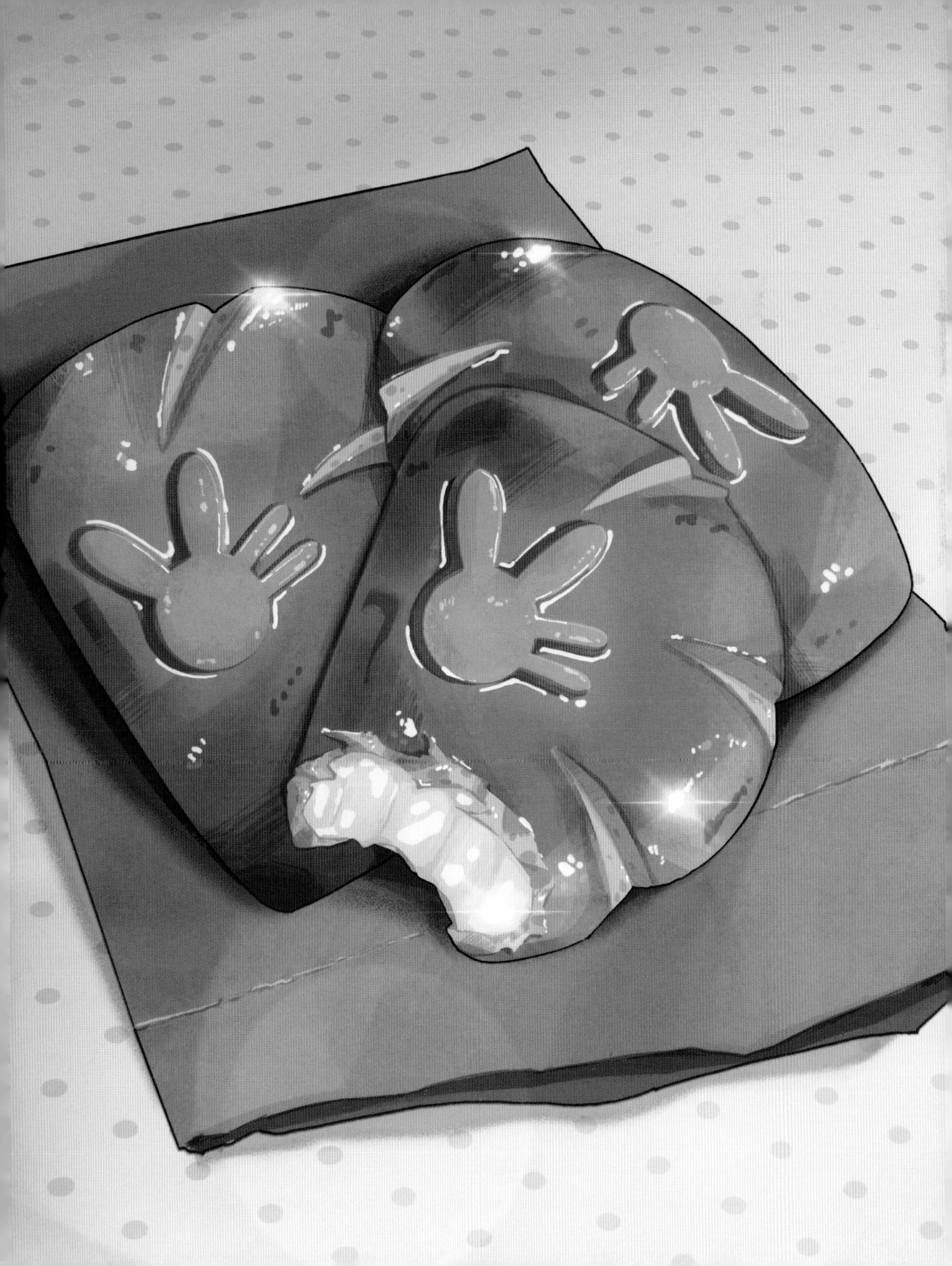

STEPS

1 **To make the custard:** In a small heatproof bowl, whisk together the egg yolks, granulated sugar, pinch of salt, and cornstarch until smooth. In a medium saucepan over medium heat, bring the milk, 1 tablespoon butter, and vanilla extract to a rapid simmer, then remove it from the heat. Temper the egg yolks by slowly pouring one-third of the heated milk into the egg yolk mixture and whisking until fully combined. Add the remaining two-thirds of the milk and whisk until fully combined. Pour the mixture back into the saucepan and turn the heat to medium. Continuously stir the mixture until it thickens and coats the back of a spatula, about 8 minutes. Remove the pan from the heat and pour the mixture into a clean medium bowl. Cover the bowl with plastic wrap, making sure that the plastic wrap touches the surface to prevent a skin from forming. Refrigerate until set, about 30 minutes. Once solidified, whisk to reconstitute and transfer to a piping bag. Snip the end to create a ½-inch (1 cm) hole for assembly.

2 **Meanwhile, make the soft bread buns:** In a heatproof bowl, microwave the milk for 40 to 60 seconds until warm. In the bowl of a stand mixer, stir together the warm milk, sugar, and active dry yeast and mix until the yeast becomes saturated. Cover the bowl with plastic wrap and let rest until the yeast bubbles and blooms, about 5 minutes, then add the bread flour, half of the beaten egg (about 2 tablespoons), and salt to the bowl. Using the dough hook attachment, set the mixer to low and mix, gradually bringing the mixer to medium-high speed. Knead for 10 minutes, or until the dough is smooth and not sticky. Add the 2 tablespoons

room-temperature butter and continue to mix until fully incorporated, about 5 minutes. Stop the mixer and test the dough: You should be able to stretch a small piece of the dough into a layer thin enough to see light through it without the dough ripping. If you can do this without any tears, continue to the next step. If not, continue to knead the dough for another 2 minutes before testing it again. Repeat until the dough passes the test.

3 When the dough is ready, remove it from the bowl and hand-knead it into a ball. Lightly oil the bowl before returning the dough ball to it. Cover the bowl with plastic wrap and proof at room temperature until the ball doubles in size and holds its shape when poked in the center, about 1 hour. If the dough returns to its original shape, then it is not ready and must be proofed further. Keep testing it every 5 minutes. Be careful not to over-proof, as that will result in collapsed buns.

4 Line a baking tray with parchment paper. Punch down the dough and transfer it to a lightly floured work surface. Knead the dough by hand for 2 minutes to get rid of large air bubbles, then shape it into a log. Divide the dough into 6 equal pieces (about 80 g each). Wrap all but one of the pieces in plastic wrap. Working with one piece at a time, roll the dough into a tight smooth ball, then use a rolling pin to roll out the dough into an oval about 5½ inches (14 cm) long by 3 inches (8 cm) wide. Squeeze about 2 tablespoons of custard in the center. Fold the dough over the custard lengthwise and firmly pinch the seams of the dough to close. Carefully transfer the custard bread onto the prepared baking sheet and repeat for the rest of the dough.

5. Once all buns are formed, use a knife or a bench scraper to cut through the dough's folded edges to create the unique and distinguished cream pan design: Starting in the middle, create a 1-inch (2.5 cm) cut from the middle of the pinched edge lengthwise toward the center of the bread. Then make one cut above and one below the middle cut, about 1 inch (2.5 cm) apart. (It's okay if you see some custard when you cut through—if it has been cooked correctly it should not leak out).

6. Cover the cream pans with plastic wrap and proof until risen and doubled in size, about 20 minutes, or until when poked it springs back 80 percent of the way. If it springs back all the way, it is not ready, and if it does not spring back, it means it is overproofed and the dough will not be tasty. If that happens, check every 5 minutes after the 20-minute mark. Preheat the oven to 400°F (205°C). While waiting for the second proof of the cream pan, make the bunny clip decoration.

7. **Meanwhile, make the bunny clip decorations:** In a small bowl, make a dead dough (without yeast) by combining 1½ tablespoons of water with the pink gel food coloring. Add the bread flour and salt, and mix until it comes together into a shaggy dough. Place the shaggy dough onto a work surface and knead with your hands (you may use gloves to prevent color transfer to your skin) for 2 minutes, or until the dough comes together and is soft and uniformly pink. Wrap the dough in plastic wrap and let rest for 10 minutes to relax the gluten and make it soft enough to roll out. Remove the plastic wrap and roll the dough into a ¼-inch (6 mm) thickness. Cut out 6 small bunnies with a bunny cookie cutter. With the remaining dough, use a knife to cut out twelve ½-inch-long (1 cm) by ⅛-inch-wide (3 mm) rectangles to represent the bobby pins for the clips.

8. Once the cream pans have completed their second rise, create the egg wash by adding 1 tablespoon of water to the remaining beaten egg, and mix. Brush the egg wash onto the surface of all the cream pans. Place 2 rectangles in the center of each bun, leaving a ¼-inch (6 mm) space in between, then place the bunny cutout slightly overlapping on top (overlapping helps to keep the pieces together while the bun expands during baking) to complete the bunny clip design.

9. Bake for 15 minutes, or until the tops have turned golden brown. Remove from the heat and brush on the 1 tablespoon melted butter while hot to add a glossy sheen. Let cool before serving. **Warning: Do not eat right away as the custard will be extremely hot!**

"Not being able to eat the custard-filled buns here is a problem."

—Mai Sakurajima

SENKU'S THREE-LAYER TEA LATTE

MANGA

DR. STONE

(CHAPTER 145)

When Bar Francois opens up for the crew on their journey to the United States via boat, Francois aims to create nonalcoholic drinks personalized for the crew members. For Senku, Francois makes this drink, which consists of three different densities of liquids.

MAKES

2 lattes

PREP TIME

15 minutes

SPECIAL TOOLS

Handheld milk frother

HOJICHA LAYER

3 teaspoons hojicha (Japanese roasted green tea powder)

1 cup (240 ml) boiling water

2 teaspoons honey, or to taste

MILK LAYER

1 cup (240 ml) milk

MATCHA WHIPPED CREAM

3 teaspoons matcha powder

½ tablespoon granulated sugar

1 teaspoon vanilla extract

½ cup (120 ml) heavy whipping cream

STEPS

1. **To make the hojicha layer:** In a heatproof mug, combine the hojicha, boiling water, and honey. Let steep for 2 minutes, then strain the hojicha using a fine-mesh strainer into a bowl or pitcher.

2. **To make the milk layer:** In a microwave-safe mug, microwave the milk until hot, about 1 minute and 15 seconds. (Alternatively, heat the milk in a small pot over medium heat until simmering.) Using a handheld milk frother, froth the milk until it doubles in size.

3. **To make the matcha whipped cream:** In a medium bowl, combine the matcha powder and sugar, then whisk with a wire whisk until combined. Add the vanilla and whipping cream. Using the handheld milk frother, mix until the mixture becomes uniform in color and stiff peaks form. Transfer to a piping bag and cut 1 inch (2.5 cm) from the tip.

4. **To assemble:** Divide the hojicha layer evenly between two glasses. Divide the milk layer between the glasses, slowly and gently pouring the milk over the back of a spoon so it drips on top of the hojicha layers. Gently pipe the matcha whipped cream on top of the milk layers, making a slight swirl at the top. Serve immediately.

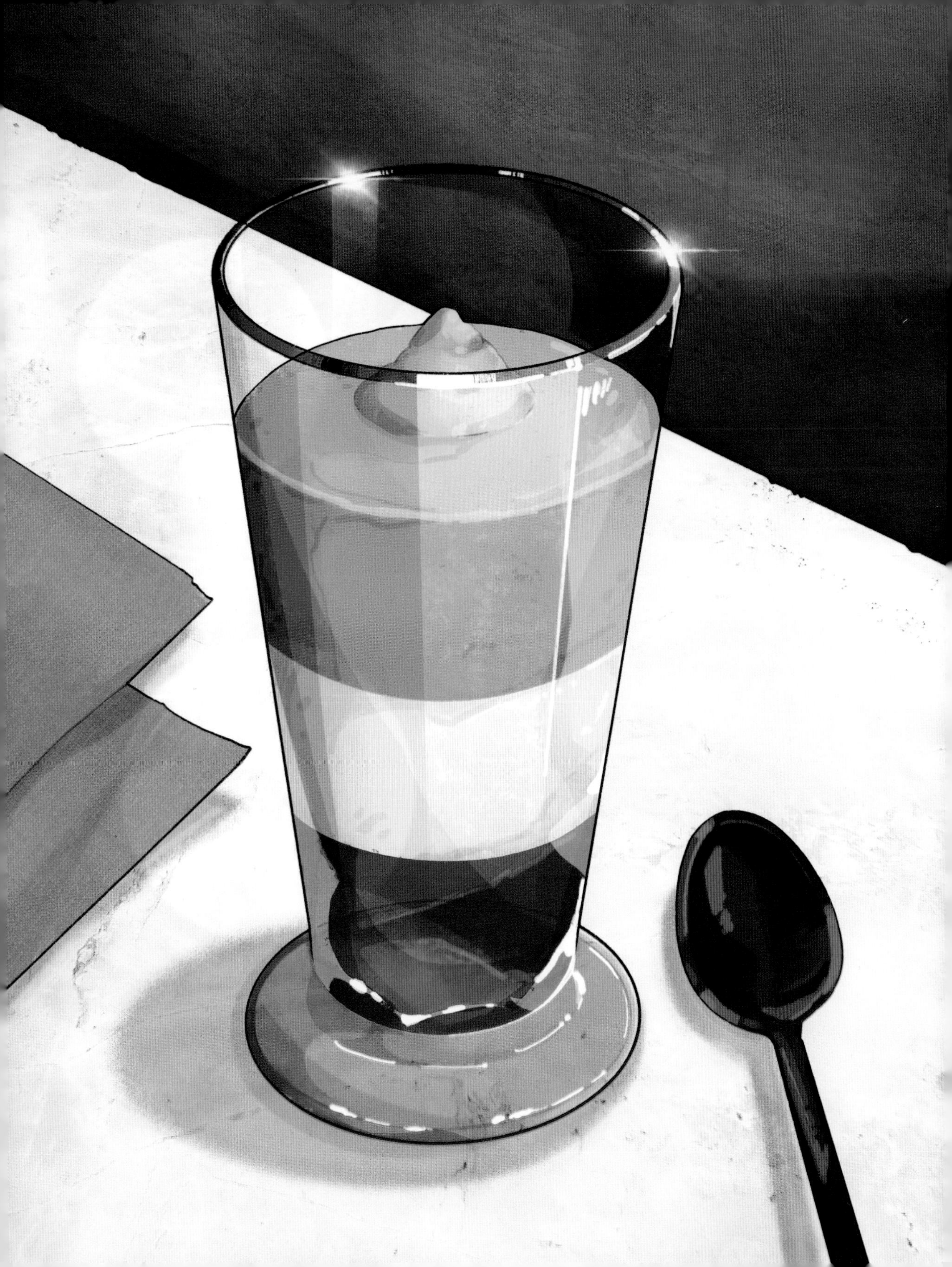

COFFEE JELLY

ANIME

THE DISASTROUS LIFE OF SAIKI K.

SEASON 1, EPISODE 6

"Hot-Blooded! Dodgeball!: Part 1"

Throughout the series, Saiki can be seen eating coffee jelly. Coffee jelly is just what it sounds like: a gelatinous coffee treat that's a perfect mix of bitter coffee and sweet sugar. I fine-tuned the ingredients here for the perfect ratio to create a flavorful and very jiggly coffee jelly. It's a simple and delicious dish that might be too precious to eat.

YIELD	PREP TIME	COOK TIME	CHILL TIME
6	**10**	**5**	**4**
servings	minutes	minutes	hours

SPECIAL TOOLS

6 small canelé molds (see Note on page 108) or small pudding molds

6 small glass stemmed dessert cups

COFFEE JELLY

1 packet (0.25 ounces, or 7 g) gelatin powder

½ cup (120 ml) cold water

4 teaspoons granulated sugar

4 teaspoons instant coffee

1 teaspoon vanilla extract

VANILLA WHIPPED CREAM

½ cup (120 ml) heavy whipping cream

2 teaspoons granulated sugar

1 teaspoon vanilla extract

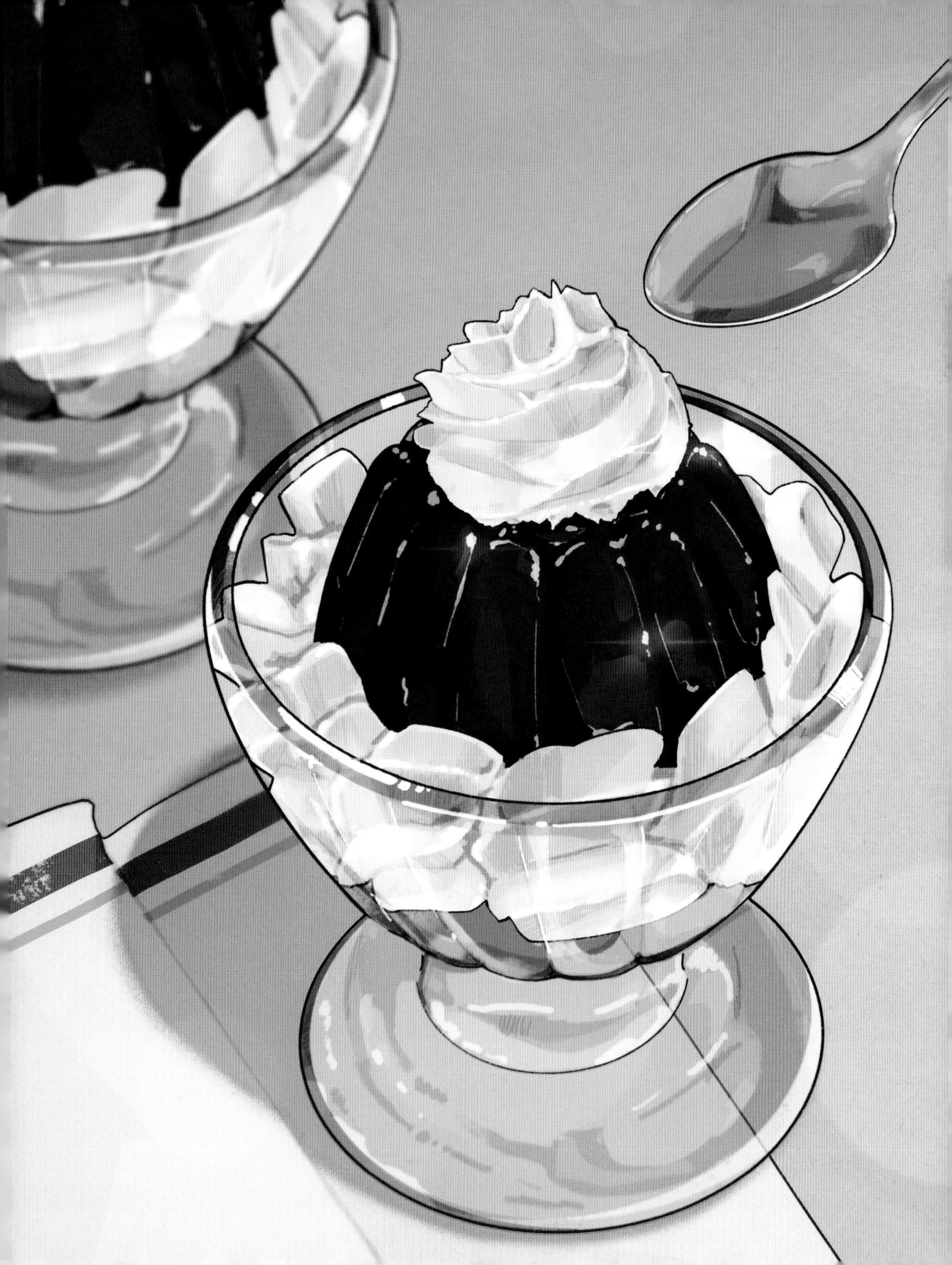

STEPS

1. **To make the coffee jelly:** In a small bowl, mix the gelatin and cold water together and set aside.

2. In a small pot over medium heat, combine 1½ cups (360 ml) of water with the 4 teaspoons sugar and instant coffee and bring to a boil. Once boiling, add the rehydrated gelatin and use a wire whisk to whisk constantly for 1 minute. Remove the pot from the heat and whisk in the vanilla.

3. Divide the coffee mixture evenly among 6 canelé molds. Place the molds on a small tray and cover the tray with plastic wrap. Refrigerate until the gelatin is set, at least 4 hours, or overnight.

4. **To make the vanilla whipped cream:** In a medium bowl, combine the whipping cream, 2 teaspoons sugar, and vanilla. Using a handheld electric mixer with the whisk attachment on low speed and gradually increasing to medium-high, whip the mixture until soft peaks form, about 2 minutes. Transfer the whipped cream to a piping bag fitted with a star tip.

5. **To assemble:** Unmold one coffee jelly by carefully submerging the canelé mold in warm water for about 30 seconds. (Make sure not to get any water inside the mold.) Wipe the canelé mold with a tea towel, then place a dessert glass on top, centering the mold. Flip the canelé mold and the dessert glass and, firmly holding the two together, shake until you hear a suction sound; that is the sound of the coffee jelly releasing from the mold. Set the dessert glass down and gently slide the mold from the jelly. Pipe the vanilla whipped cream in small mounds around the ring of the coffee jelly by squeezing and lifting the piping bag. Pipe a larger mound of cream at the center of the coffee jelly. Repeat for the remaining coffee jellies and vanilla whipped cream, then serve.

NOTE

Canelé molds are typically used to make canelés, which are little French pastries. But we repurpose the molds here. They have fluted sides that create a beautifully shaped jelly.

"A cup of coffee jelly for 2,950 yen?
That is so foolish. Who would buy that? Me."

—Saiki Kusuo

PUDDING À LA MODE

ANIME

DON'T TOY WITH ME, MISS NAGATORO

SEASON 2, EPISODE 4

"Why Don't You Come Inside, Senpai-kun?"

In this episode, Nagatoro's sister makes her a pudding à la mode as a pick-me-up for her high-school worries. It's a velvety custard made even more luxurious with a mix of fresh and creamy toppings. What an extravagant dessert!

YIELD	PREP TIME	COOK TIME
4	**20**	**75**
servings	minutes	minutes

SPECIAL TOOLS

Four 6-ounce ramekins

CARAMEL

¾ cup (150 g) granulated sugar

VANILLA PUDDING

2 large egg yolks

2 large eggs

¼ cup (50 g) granulated sugar

⅔ cup (160 ml) heavy whipping cream

1½ cups (360 ml) milk

1 pinch salt

1 teaspoon vanilla extract

About 4 cups (1 L) boiling water

VANILLA WHIPPED CREAM

½ cup (120 ml) heavy whipping cream

1 tablespoon granulated sugar

1 teaspoon vanilla extract

FOR ASSEMBLY

1 cup (150 g) vanilla ice cream

8 wedges (1 inch, or 2.5 cm, thick) honeydew melon, seeds removed and sliced in half lengthwise

1 banana, cut into 8 slices (½ inch, or 13 mm, thick)

1 red apple, cored and cut into 4 wedges (1 inch, or 2.5 cm, thick)

1 orange, cut into 8 wedges (1 inch, or 2.5 cm, thick)

4 Maraschino cherries

4 tall glasses freshly squeezed orange juice (optional)

STEPS

1. **To make the caramel:** Add the ¾ cup (150 g) sugar and ¼ cup (60 ml) of water to a medium pot over medium heat. Gently swirl the pan to cover the sugar with the water. (Do not mix the caramel with any utensils; swirling is the most efficient way to prevent crystallization.) Watch the caramel closely, swirling the pot as needed, until the mixture turns amber, 9 to 10 minutes. Let cook for 2 minutes more, or until it turns a deep caramel. Remove from the heat and quickly pour a ⅛-inch (3 mm) layer into each pudding cup. Lay a small cloth or towel in a deep baking dish to prevent the pudding cups from moving around. Once the pudding cups have cooled, transfer them to the prepared baking dish.

2. **To make the vanilla pudding:** Preheat the oven to 350°F (175°C). In a large heatproof bowl, use a balloon whisk to vigorously mix the egg yolks, eggs, and ¼ cup (50 g) sugar until fully combined; the mixture should be pale yellow, and there should be no visible egg-white lumps.

3. In a medium saucepan, add the ⅔ cup (160 ml) whipping cream, milk, and salt and bring to a simmer over medium heat. Pour one-quarter of the milk mixture into the bowl with the eggs and quickly whisk until fully combined. Pour in the rest of the milk mixture while whisking the egg mixture. Whisk in the vanilla extract. Using a fine-mesh strainer, strain the pudding mixture into a pouring vessel, then carefully pour or ladle it over the caramel in the pudding cups, filling each cup three-quarters full. Cover each pudding cup with aluminum foil.

4. Once the oven is at temperature, pour boiling water into the bottom of the baking dish to about halfway up the sides of the pudding cups. Carefully transfer the baking dish to the oven and bake for 1 hour, or until the tops are set, with just a slight jiggle. Remove from the water. Let cool to room temperature, then refrigerate until ready to serve.

5. **To make the vanilla whipped cream:** Right before serving, in a medium bowl, using a handheld electric mixer with a whisk attachment set to low and gradually increasing to medium-high, whip the ½ cup (120 ml) whipping cream, 1 tablespoon sugar, and vanilla until medium peaks form, about 2 minutes. Transfer the whipped cream to a piping bag and cut a ¼-inch (6 mm) hole at the tip.

6. **To assemble:** Place the vanilla ice cream in a separate piping bag and let it thaw until it becomes soft enough to pipe, about 5 minutes, then cut a ¼-inch (6 mm) hole at the tip of the bag. Meanwhile, remove the foil from the pudding cups. Fill a medium bowl with warm water and submerge the cups for about 1 minute. (Make sure not to get any water inside the molds.) Remove the cups from the warm water and wipe the exteriors dry with a tea towel.

7. Working with one pudding cup at a time, flip a serving bowl on top of the pudding cup, making sure to center the cup. Then flip both the serving bowl and cup together. Firmly holding the two together, shake until you hear a suction sound; that is the sound of the pudding releasing from the mold. Repeat for the remaining pudding cups.

8. Working on one pudding at a time, pipe a vanilla whipped cream swirl in the bowl on either side of the pudding, almost the height of the pudding, and pipe one vanilla ice cream swirl at the front. Fill in the empty spaces with fruit: place 2 honeydew slices on the left side of the pudding, 2 banana slices behind the pudding, 1 apple slice on the right side of the pudding, and 2 orange slices and 1 Maraschino cherry on the front of the pudding. Repeat for the remaining puddings. Serve with a dessert spoon and glasses of orange juice (if using)—just like the anime!

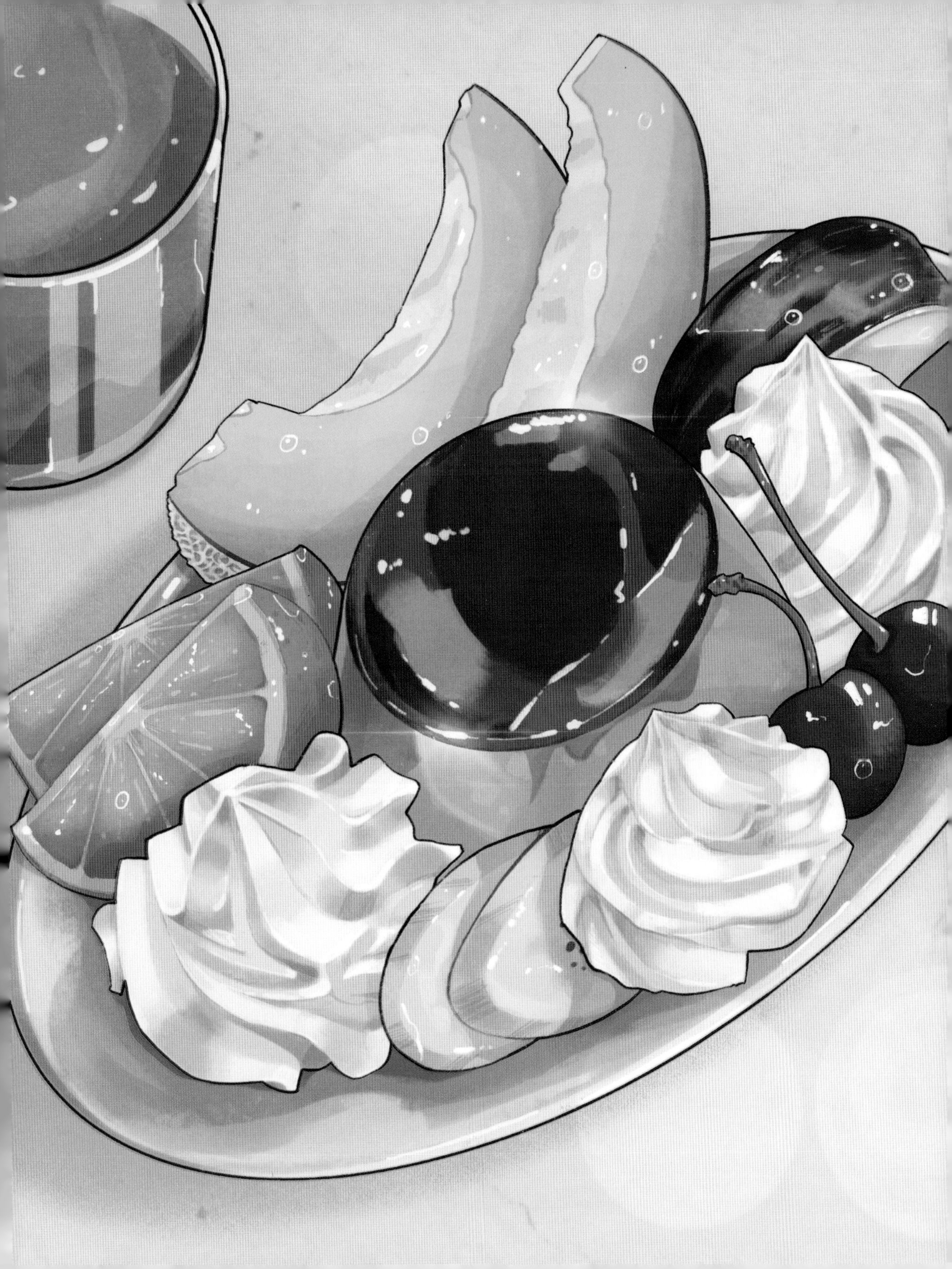

PEACH BUNS

In the spirit world, Chihiro ends up working at a bathhouse while trying to find a way to escape to the real world and save her parents, who have turned into pigs. At the bathhouse, she encounters No-Face, a lonely character who admires Chihiro. No-Face discovers that workers in the bathhouse will do anything for gold. Desperate for love and attention, he showers the workers with fake gold he created, and they, thinking it's real gold, shower him with gifts. Peach buns are just one of the delicious foods offered to No-Face during an incredible and iconic scene. In Chinese mythology, peach buns symbolize longevity. In modern society, these tasty treats are often served as gifts for birthdays, anniversaries, and New Year's.

YIELD	PREP TIME	REST TIME	COOK TIME	COOL TIME
8	**30**	**25**	**25**	**20**
steamed buns	minutes	minutes	minutes	minutes

SPECIAL TOOLS

Food-safe paintbrush

2 bamboo steamer baskets

INGREDIENTS

⅓ cup (80 ml) warm water

1 teaspoon cooking oil (such as vegetable or canola)

2 tablespoons granulated sugar

1 teaspoon active dry yeast

1⅓ cups (175 g) cake flour, plus more for dusting

1 pinch salt

Red Bean Paste (see page 19)

1 teaspoon beet powder or 2 drops pink gel food coloring

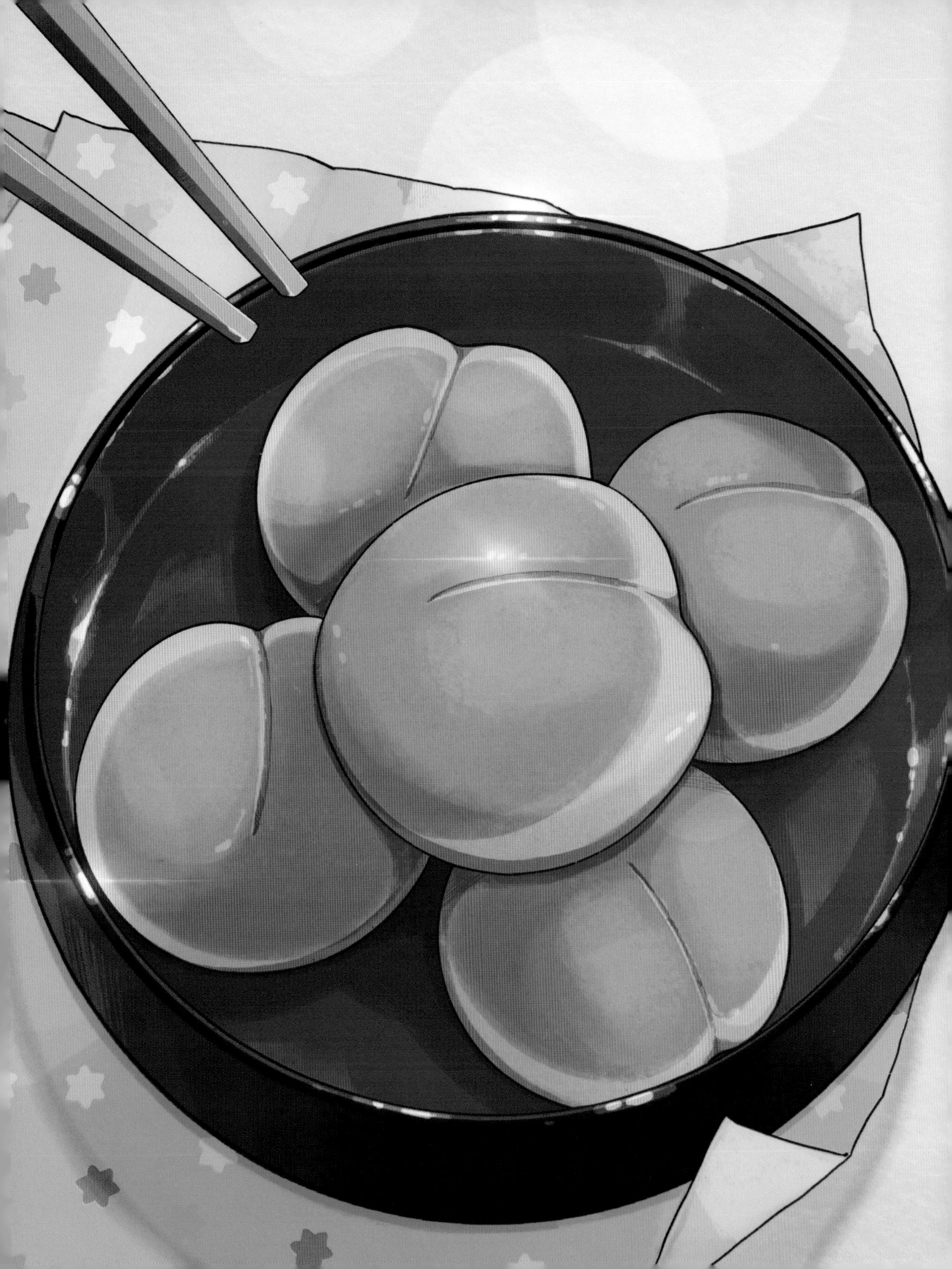

STEPS

1. In a small bowl, combine the warm water, oil, sugar, and yeast. Cover the bowl with plastic wrap and let the yeast bloom and become bubbly, about 5 minutes.

2. In a medium bowl, sift together the cake flour and salt. Whisk the dry ingredients until combined, then add the yeast mixture. Use your hands to roughly combine everything into a dough. Lightly dust a work surface with flour, then knead the dough on the work surface until the dough has softened and is smooth, about 8 minutes. Roll the dough into a log and divide it into 8 equal pieces (about 1½ ounces, or 35 g, per piece).

3. Cover the dough pieces with plastic wrap. Working with one dough piece at a time, use a rolling pin to flatten the ball to ⅛-inch (3 mm) thickness, then knead the dough back into a ball. Repeat this process 3 times. Finally, flatten just the edges and leave a small mound of dough in the center about 3 inches (8 cm) around. Place roughly 2 tablespoons of red bean paste on the center of the flattened dough, then close the edges of the dough around the red bean paste until it is covered. Pinch the seams together, then turn the bun, seam side down, and roll it into a neat ball before returning the dough to the plastic wrap. Repeat for the remaining dough pieces.

4. Cut out eight 4-inch (10 cm) squares of parchment paper. Fill a large pot with at least 3 inches (8 cm) of water and bring to a boil over high heat.

5. Decorate the buns by stirring together the beet powder and 2 tablespoons of water in a small bowl. Working with one bun at a time, use a food-safe paintbrush to draw a circle on top of each bun, leaving a ¼-inch (6 mm) border. Use the back of a knife to press a line indentation into the bun from the center to the perimeter. Be careful not to pierce through the bun. Rinse the knife with water and wipe off any food coloring with a paper towel. Press another line indent into the side of the bun, perpendicular to the center line, using the same technique. Set the peach bun on one of the prepared parchment squares then place the bun and paper in a bamboo steamer. Repeat for the rest of the buns. Stack the bamboo steamers and cover with the lid. Let the buns rise until they become 50 percent bigger, 15 to 20 minutes.

6. Reduce the heat to medium (and replenish water if some has evaporated), then place the bamboo steamers in the pot over the boiling water, making sure the bamboo steamers are suspended over the water. Steam for 15 minutes, or until the buns have almost doubled in size, are cooked through, and the tops are dry. Turn off the heat and carefully leave the lid slightly opened to release the steam slowly and prevent deflating the buns. Let sit for 5 minutes before transferring the buns to a wire rack to cool to room temperature.

7. Remove the parchment paper from the buns and serve stacked on a plate.

STRAWBERRY BRICK TOAST

ANIME

ATTACK ON TITAN

SEASON 4, EPISODE 9

"Brave Volunteers"

Food appears so rarely in *Attack on Titan*, and when it does, it's often European-style cuisine—like meat and potatoes or . . . you know, *other* meaty forms of protein. That's why I was surprised to see the brick toast in this episode. Brick toast is popular in Asia, though you can find it at some dessert tea shops in North America. It's a fun dessert that offers different tastes and textures: crunchy toast, soft ice cream, and sweet strawberries.

YIELD	PREP TIME	COOK TIME
2	**20**	**30**
servings	minutes	minutes

STRAWBERRY SAUCE

8 ounces (227 g) fresh strawberries, hulled and diced small

¼ cup (50 g) granulated sugar

BRICK TOAST

1 end piece of unsliced sandwich bread (see Note on page 116) (4 inches, or 10 cm, thick)

¼ cup (55 g) salted butter, melted

2 tablespoons granulated sugar

VANILLA WHIPPED CREAM

¼ cup (60 ml) heavy whipping cream

½ tablespoon granulated sugar

1 teaspoon vanilla extract

FOR ASSEMBLY

4 strawberries, hulled and thinly sliced

1 scoop vanilla ice cream

STEPS

1. **To make the strawberry sauce:** In a small pot over medium heat, combine the diced strawberries and ¼ cup (50 g) sugar with ¼ cup (60 ml) of water and bring to a boil. Reduce the heat to medium-low and let simmer, stirring occasionally, until the mixture thickens and becomes jammy, 18 to 20 minutes. Remove from the heat and let cool.

2. **Meanwhile, make the brick toast:** Preheat the oven to 350°F (175°C). Line a baking sheet with parchment paper.

3. Place the bread, crust side down, on a cutting board. Using a serrated knife, plunge the knife into the bread and trace a square, leaving a 1-inch (2.5 cm) border around the bread square. Remove the square bread innards by carefully pulling them from the base. Place the hollowed-out crust on the prepared baking sheet. Cut the bread innards into 1-inch (2.5 cm) cubes, then place on the prepared baking sheet.

4. In a small bowl, mix the melted butter and 2 tablespoons sugar until combined. Using a pastry brush, paint the inside of the hollowed crust and the cubed bread with sugary butter. Transfer to the oven and bake for 6 to 7 minutes, until the bread is lightly browned, with a slightly crunchy exterior and soft interior. Remove from the oven and let cool. Meanwhile, prepare the vanilla whipped cream.

5. **To make the vanilla whipped cream:** In a medium bowl, using a handheld electric mixer with a whisk attachment on low speed and gradually increasing to high, whip the whipping cream, ½ tablespoon sugar, and vanilla until stiff peaks form, 3 to 4 minutes. Transfer the vanilla whipped cream to a piping bag and snip a small ¼-inch (6 mm) opening at the tip.

6. **To assemble:** Layer 1 tablespoon of strawberry sauce into the toast box, followed by the sliced strawberries, some toasted bread cubes, vanilla whipped cream, and vanilla ice cream. Cover any visible gaps in the topping with vanilla whipped cream and leave ¼ inch (6 mm) of space at the top of the toast box. Spread strawberry sauce over the top and flatten it into the toast box using an offset spatula or the back of a knife, creating a smooth top. Pipe small mounds of whipped cream on each of the 4 edges of the toast, then serve.

NOTE

You can find uncut square sandwich bread bread in Asian markets in the bakery department or call ahead to local bakeries.

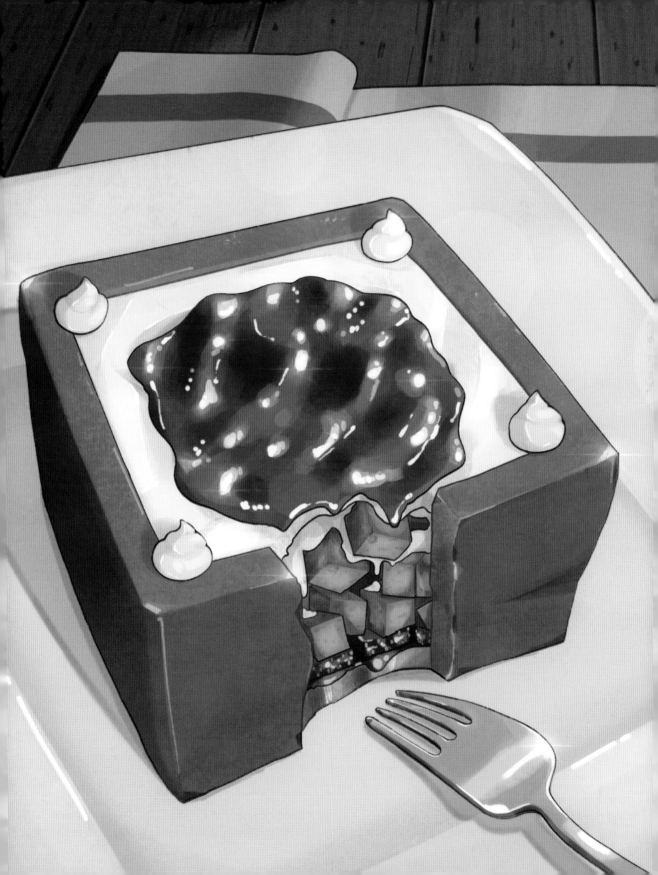

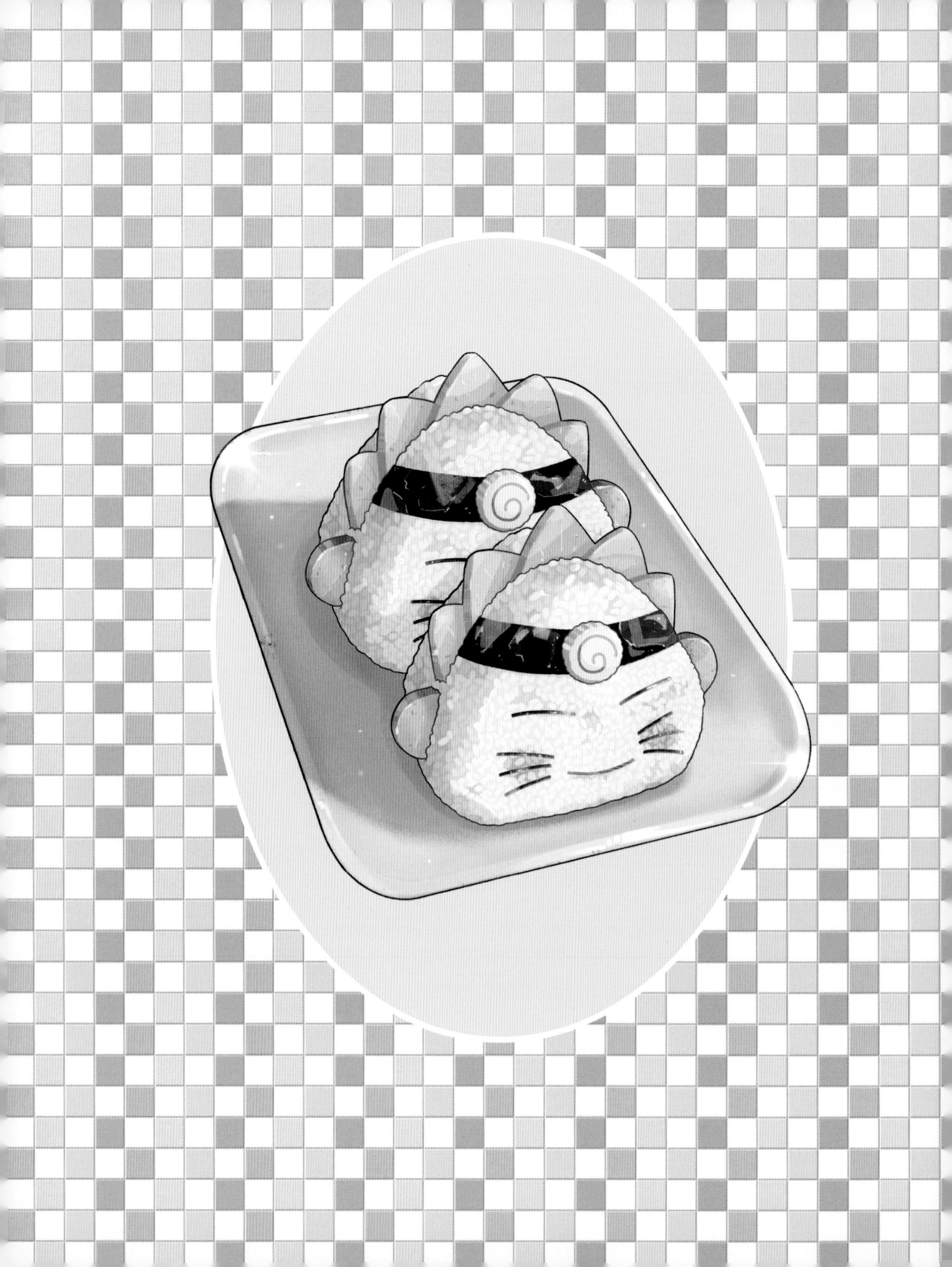

Outdoor

Café

HINATA'S NARUTO ONIGIRI

ANIME

NARUTO

SEASON 1, EPISODE 159

"The Bounty Hunter from the Wilderness"

Onigiri is a classic snack in Japan; they are rice balls that usually have savory fillings inside. In this episode, Hinata prepares Naruto a picnic in the park and presents him with a box lunch, which includes an onigiri shaped as Naruto's face. It's a gesture of thanks for allowing her to be part of his mission. Naruto is hesitant to eat it. He explains that it's hard to eat onigiri that looks like him, but once he does, he exclaims, "Hinata, you'd make a great wife!" (Which is funny because, well . . .) Follow the directions to create the special shape of Naruto's face, or let this recipe inspire you to create onigiri of your friends' faces to show your appreciation for them as well!

YIELD	PREP TIME	DECORATE TIME
2	**30**	**10**
servings	minutes	minutes

SPECIAL TOOLS

Kitchen scissors and/or a small cookie cutter

CREAMY CRAB FILLING

1 piece leg-style imitation crabmeat

1 green onion, both white and green parts, finely chopped

½ tablespoon Kewpie mayo

½ teaspoon soy sauce

1 pinch salt, plus more for dusting

1 pinch black pepper

DECORATIONS

Sheets of roasted nori

2 slices deli ham

1 piece (2 inches, or 5 cm) yellow pickled radish

1 narutomaki (fish cake)

½ teaspoon ketchup

3 cups (600 g) steamed short-grain white rice

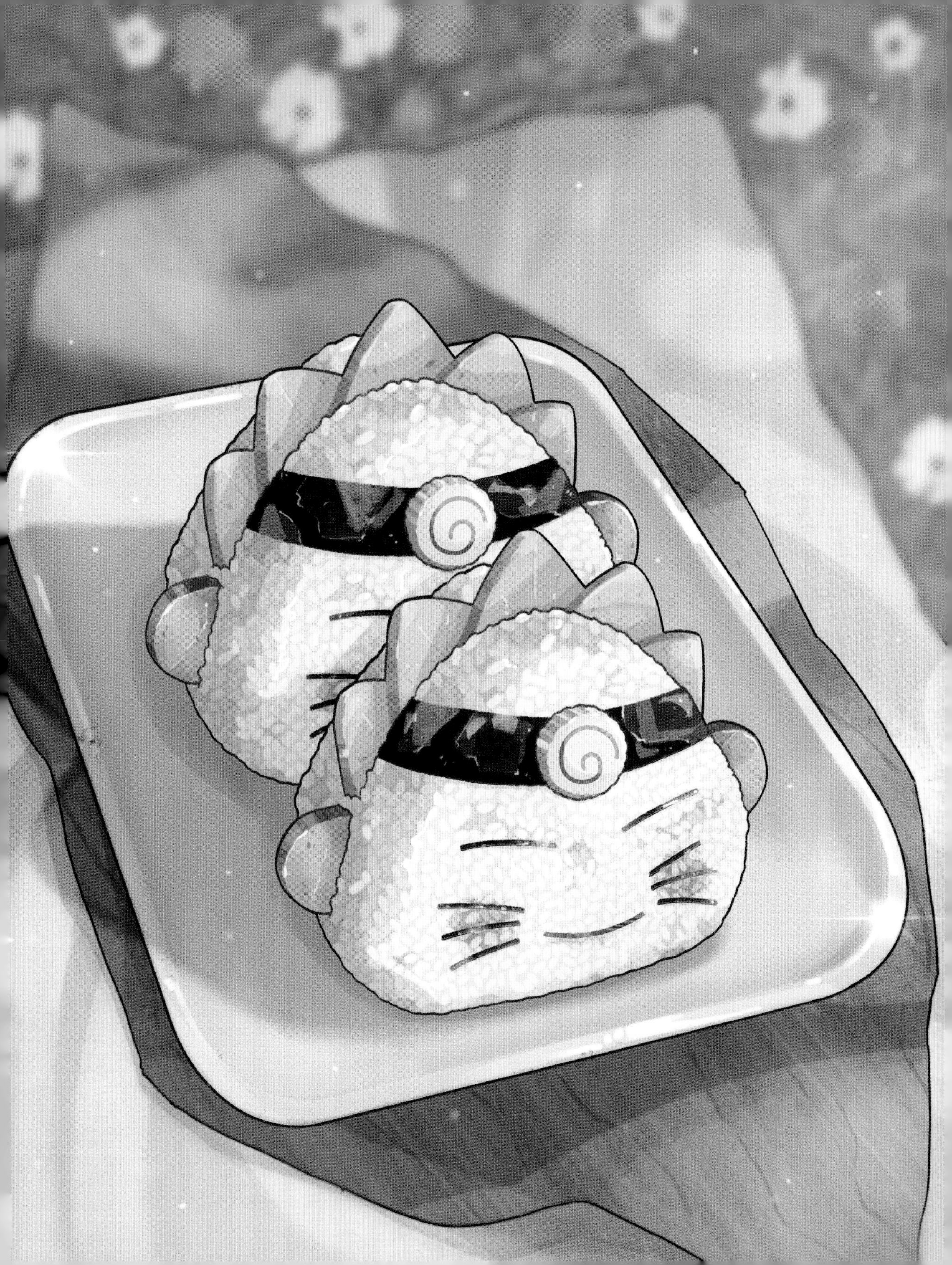

STEPS

1. **To make the creamy crab filling:** Place the imitation crabmeat on a cutting board and gently peel off 2 strips of the red skin. Set aside for creating Naruto's mouth details later. Mince the leftover imitation crab. In a small bowl, combine the minced crab, green onion, mayo, soy sauce, salt, and pepper and mix until combined.

2. **Prepare the decorations:** Using kitchen scissors, cut strips of roasted nori: twelve 1 x ⅛-inch (2.5 x 3 mm) strips for the whiskers, four 1 x ¼-inch (2.5 x -6 mm) strips for the eyes, and two 4 x ½-inch (10 x 1-cm) strips for the headband. Using the kitchen scissors or a small cookie cutter, cut the ham slices into four ½-inch (1 cm) circles for the ears. Slice the pickled radish into ten ⅛-inch (3 mm) rounds, then cut them into triangles for the hair. Slice two ⅛-inch (3 mm) rounds of narutomaki.

3. In a small bowl, combine the ketchup and 1 teaspoon of the steamed rice and mash together with a fork until a paste forms.

4. **To assemble and decorate:** Fill a small bowl with water. Wet your hands with water to prevent sticking, then dust them with a touch of salt. Rub your hands together. On a clean work surface, grab half a handful of cooked rice (about ¾ cup, or 150 g) and shape it into a triangle with rounded edges, then flatten it to ⅔-inch (2 cm) thickness; this piece will be the bottom of the onigiri and form the back of Naruto's head.

5. Arrange 5 triangles of pickled radish so that they hang over the pointed triangle of flattened rice, with 1 triangle in the top middle of the head and 2 triangles on each side to imitate Naruto's spiked hair. Position the ham circles as ears just below the pickled radish. Scoop 1 tablespoon of the creamy crab filling onto the center.

6. Wet your hands once more and dust another pinch of salt on them. Grab another handful of rice and shape it into an identical flattened, triangular head. Set the newly formed rice head on top of the filling, lining up the top and bottom pieces of rice and shaping and compressing carefully as you seal the corners.

7. To add the details of Naruto's face, place the nori headband at the top and add 2 nori eyes underneath. Smear some ketchup paste onto the center of the headband, then place one narutomaki on top and press gently to adhere. Smear more ketchup paste under each eye to create blush. Arrange 3 whiskers on each side of the face. Add a strip of the reserved imitation crabmeat and shape it into a curve to create Naruto's smile. Repeat steps 4 through 7 for the second onigiri, and serve.

BROWN SUGAR MILK TEA (BUBBLE TEA)

ANIME

MY TEEN ROMANTIC COMEDY SNAFU

SEASON 3, EPISODE 12

"My Teen Romantic Comedy is Wrong, As I Expected"

Hachiman and Yukino are a part of the Service Club that helps students achieve their goals and overcome problems that they have—which lands them in funny and dramatic incidents throughout the anime. Hachiman and Yukino are tasked to help plan their prom, but there are a few hurdles: a short timeline, low budget, and little manpower. They decide to scout Inage Seaside Park for the venue, and while there, they order bubble tea from the park's Bakery Café. Hachiman takes Instagram photos of his tea while Yukino enjoys hers. Hachiman offers Yukino his bubble tea for her own photos, since hers is already halfway gone. Yukino takes this opportunity to make a sly, flirty move: Instead of taking a photo of Hachiman's bubble tea on the table, she poses with his drink beside Hachiman—snapping a cute photo of them together alongside the drink. Brown sugar bubble tea is delicious: a cold, slightly bitter tea, with warm, sweet, chewy pearls!

YIELD	PREP TIME	REST TIME	COOK TIME
4	**20**	**40**	**40**
servings	minutes	minutes	minutes

SPECIAL TOOLS

4 wide bubble tea straws

MILK TEA

5½ cups (1.2 L) milk

10 black tea bags

TAPIOCA PEARLS

2 tablespoons packed muscavado or Taiwanese brown sugar (see Note on page 124)

½ cup (70 g) plus 1 tablespoon tapioca starch, divided

BROWN SUGAR SYRUP

½ cup (110 g) packed muscavado or Tawainese brown sugar (see Note on page 124)

ASSEMBLY

Ice cubes

STEPS

1. **To make the milk tea:** In a medium pot over medium heat, combine the milk and tea bags and let the mixture come to a slow simmer and cook for 3 minutes. Remove the pot from the heat and transfer the milk tea to a heat-proof pitcher along with the tea bags and continue steeping. Let cool to room temperature before transferring the pitcher to the refrigerator until cold, about 20 minutes. Discard the tea bags.

2. **To make the tapioca pearls:** Whisk together 2 tablespoons muscavado sugar, 1 tablespoon tapioca of the starch, and 2 tablespoons of water in a large shallow bowl until dissolved. Microwave on high heat until gelatinous and resembles slime, around 45 to 50 seconds. Mix with a spatula to combine (be careful as it is very hot). Add the remaining ½ cup (70 g) tapioca starch and mix for 2 minutes with the spatula, or until a dough forms that is cool enough to touch, but still warm. Knead on a surface until smooth, stretchy, free from lumps, and slightly sticky but does not leave residue, around 3 minutes. Roll the dough into a ¼-inch-wide (6 mm) log. Cut it into ¼-inch (6 mm) pieces, or slightly smaller than the width of your straw, then roll the pieces into balls between your hands. Dust the pearls lightly with more tapioca starch to prevent them from sticking to each other.

3. In a medium pot, bring at least 4 inches (10 cm) of water to a boil. Place the tapioca pearls in a ladle and gently lower them into the water. Bring the water to a boil again, then reduce the heat to medium-low. Using a spatula, occasionally agitate the water to separate the pearls and prevent sticking. Continue to boil for 30 minutes, or until the pearls become translucent and, when cut open, are cooked through and saturated (as opposed to the dry dough before cooking). While waiting, prepare a bowl filled with cold water to submerge the pearls. Scoop the cooked tapioca pearls using a small strainer into the bowl with cold water, and gently stir. Drain in a colander. Rinse the cooked tapioca balls in cold running water for 2 minutes, gently stirring occasionally with a spatula. (This step gives the pearls a chewier texture.)

4. **To make the brown sugar syrup:** In a medium pot, mix together the muscavado sugar and ¼ cup (60 ml) of water and cook on medium-low heat until the sugar has dissolved. Do not let the mixture boil, as it will turn to hard candy. Return the rinsed tapioca pearls to the pot and cook, stirring frequently, until a thick brown sugar syrup forms, about 2 minutes. Remove from the heat.

5. **To assemble:** Add ice to four glasses and divide the hot brown sugar tapioca pearls, and cold milk among them. Serve with wide bubble tea straws in each glass.

NOTE

It is best to use muscavado sugar or Taiwanese brown sugar, as it has a higher molasses content than regular brown sugar. It gives the tapioca pearls a more delicious flavor! You can find these specialty sugars in your grocery store or Asian markets.

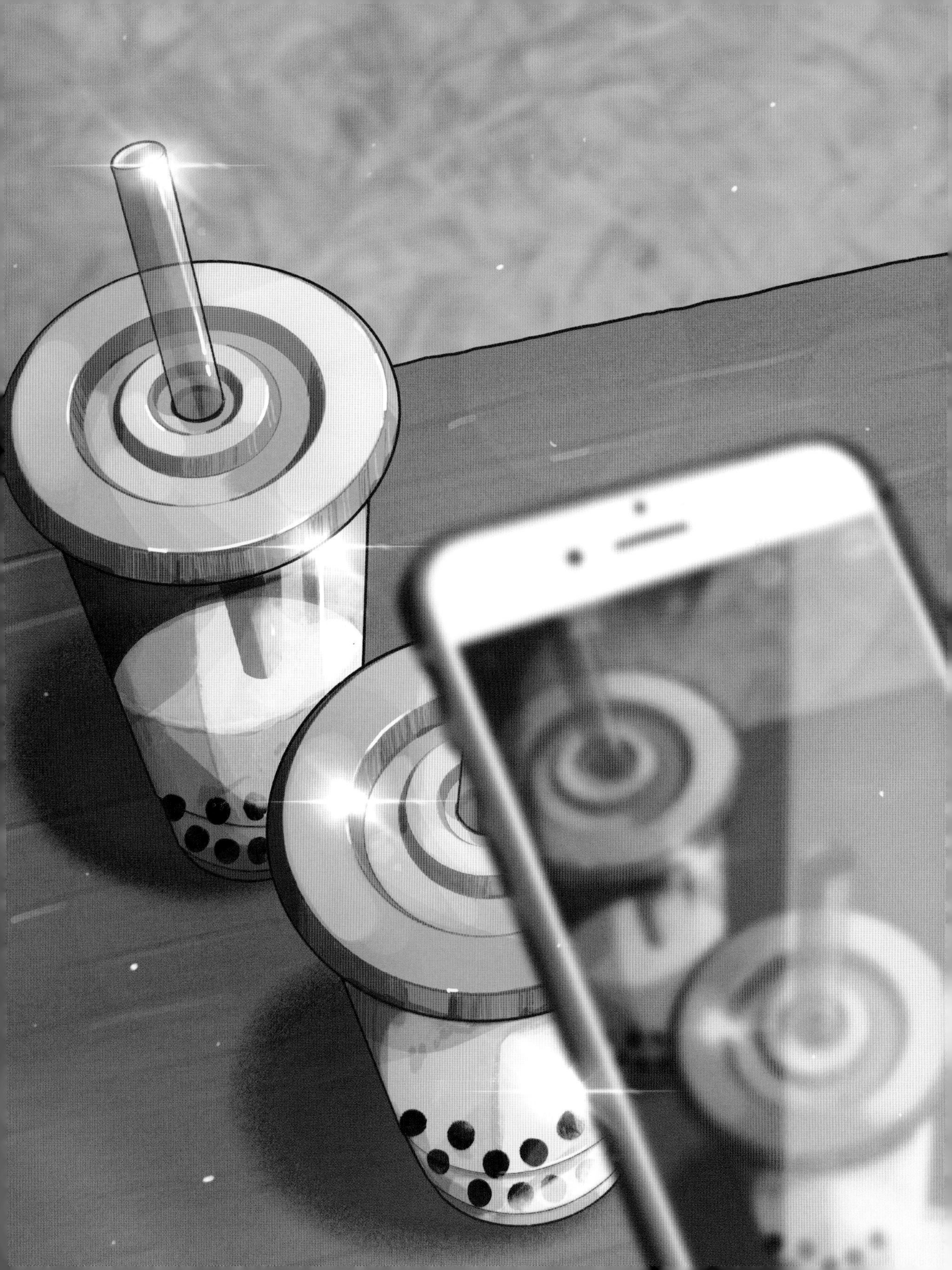

CAPRESE SALAD

ANIME

JOJO'S BIZARRE ADVENTURE

SEASON 3, EPISODE 10

"Let's Go Eat Some Italian Food"

Chef Tonio opens a new Italian restaurant named Trattoria that has no menus. Instead, he serves people based on what he perceives they would like or "according to the customer." Okuyasu and Josuke visit the restaurant. When they are sized up by Chef Tonio, he determines that they need a caprese salad. Once Josuke eats it, his stiff shoulder magically regenerates and feels much better!

YIELD
2
servings

PREP TIME
20
minutes

DRESSING

2 anchovies

½ sheet roasted nori, finely chopped

¼ cup (60 ml) lemon juice

3 tablespoons olive oil

2 tablespoons white wine vinegar

2 tablespoons balsamic vinegar

¼ teaspoon salt

⅛ teaspoon black pepper

SALAD

6 green lettuce leaves

2 large globe tomatoes, cut into ½-inch-thick (1 cm) slices

8 ounces (227 g) fresh mozzarella cheese, cut into ½-inch-thick (1 cm) slices

2 fresh basil leaves, chiffonade, plus 2 sprigs basil for garnishing

2 slices white bread, cut in half diagonally and lightly toasted

FOR SERVING

2 pinches dried basil

Pepper grinder for freshly cracked black pepper (optional)

STEPS

1. **To make the dressing:** In a medium bowl, crush the anchovies into fine pieces with a fork. Add the rest of the dressing ingredients and use a wire whisk to whisk until emulsified. (Alternatively, add all the ingredients to a blender and process until a smooth mixture.)

2. **To make the salad:** Prepare two serving plates by arranging 2 lettuce leaves on the top half of each plate and 1 lettuce leaf on the bottom half.

3. Alternate layers of tomato and mozzarella slices over the lettuce on the top of the plate. Drizzle the dressing and sprinkle the basil chiffonade evenly between the plates.

4. Stack a piece of toast on the bottom-right side of each plate. Garnish with a basil sprig on the top left of each plate, covering the mozzarella and tomato slices.

5. Sprinkle a pinch of dried basil on each plate, and serve with the option of tableside freshly cracked black pepper.

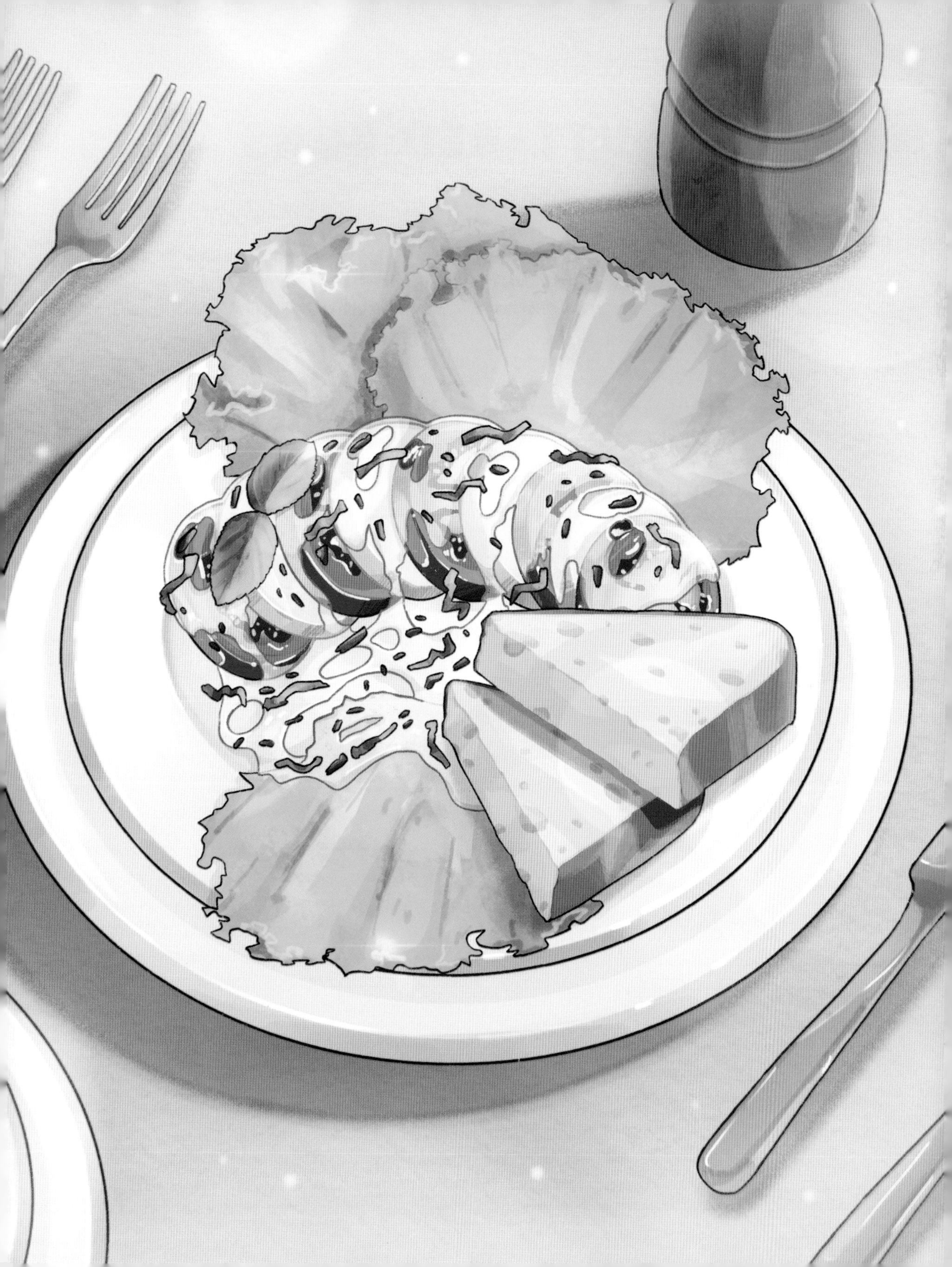

BUTTERED BUNS

ANIME

LAID-BACK CAMP

SEASON 1, EPISODE 10

"Clumsy Travelers and Camp Meetings"

Rin wakes up late for her solo camping trip, and it's already dark when she's close to arriving at the campground but encounters a roadblock. After informing her friends of the roadblock, Ohgaki calls Rin and guides her through it. Rin is a fan of quick meals when she camps, so these buttered buns made with steamed pork buns she bought from a convenience store are quick, easy, and hearty.

YIELD	PREP TIME	COOK TIME
2	**5**	**15**
servings	minutes	minutes

SPECIAL TOOLS

Single-burner camping stove (optional)

Stovetop sandwich press

BUTTERED BUNS

2 tablespoons butter, divided

2 prepared nikuman (steamed pork buns; see Note)

QUICK GYOZA SAUCE

2 tablespoons soy sauce

2 tablespoons apple cider

½ teaspoon sesame oil

¼ teaspoon granulated sugar

1 green onion, thinly sliced (optional)

STEPS

1. **To make the buttered buns:** Turn the single burner stove or a burner on a regular stove to medium heat and preheat the sandwich press.

2. Once warm, melt 1 tablespoon of the butter on one side of the press, close, and flip the sandwich press to butter the other side with the remaining 1 tablespoon butter.

3. Open the sandwich press and place one of the nikuman in the center. Securely close the sandwich press and cook for 3 minutes on one side, or until golden and crispy, then repeat for the other side. Cook for about 6 minutes total, or until golden, then remove from the heat and transfer to a cutting board. Slice the nikuman in half, then repeat this step for the second nikuman.

4. **To make the quick gyoza sauce:** Mix all the gyoza sauce ingredients in a small bowl until well combined.

5. Serve the gyoza sauce alongside the buttered buns for dipping.

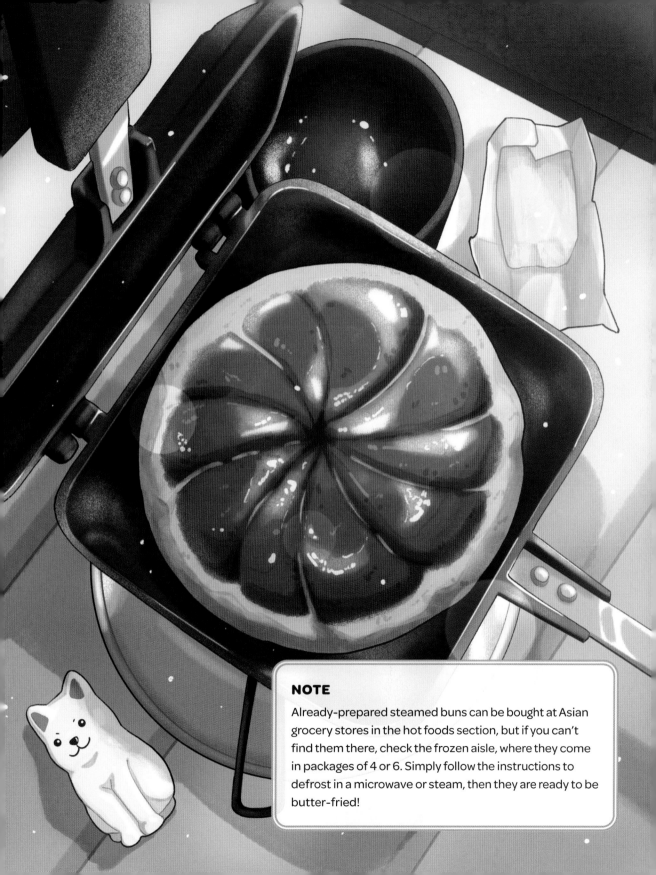

NOTE

Already-prepared steamed buns can be bought at Asian grocery stores in the hot foods section, but if you can't find them there, check the frozen aisle, where they come in packages of 4 or 6. Simply follow the instructions to defrost in a microwave or steam, then they are ready to be butter-fried!

LEMON GINGER CURE

ANIME

MARCH COMES IN LIKE A LION

SEASON 2, EPISODE 11

"Where the Sun Shines/Small World"

When Gakuto and Issa go mountaineering and encounter a snowstorm, they take shelter in a tent, where Issa falls ill. Gakuto makes this hot drink to help cure him. Unbeknownst to Issa, Gakuto often takes friends and rivals to experience "Sakurai 7th-Dan's mountain therapy," in which they run into inconveniences, and then Gakuto helps them through it in order to gain their trust. Though it sounds mischievous, this method is not done by Gakuto on purpose—it adds to his charm, as well as his status as the world's favorite shogi (Japanese chess) player.

YIELD	PREP TIME	COOK TIME
1	**5**	**5**
serving	minutes	minutes

INGREDIENTS

1½ cups (360 ml) boiling water

1 teaspoon grated fresh ginger

½ tablespoon honey

½ teaspoon lemon juice

1 lemon slice, seeds removed, for garnishing

STEPS

1. Carefully pour the boiling water into a mug. Stir in the grated ginger, honey, and lemon juice.

2. Place the lemon slice on top and serve.

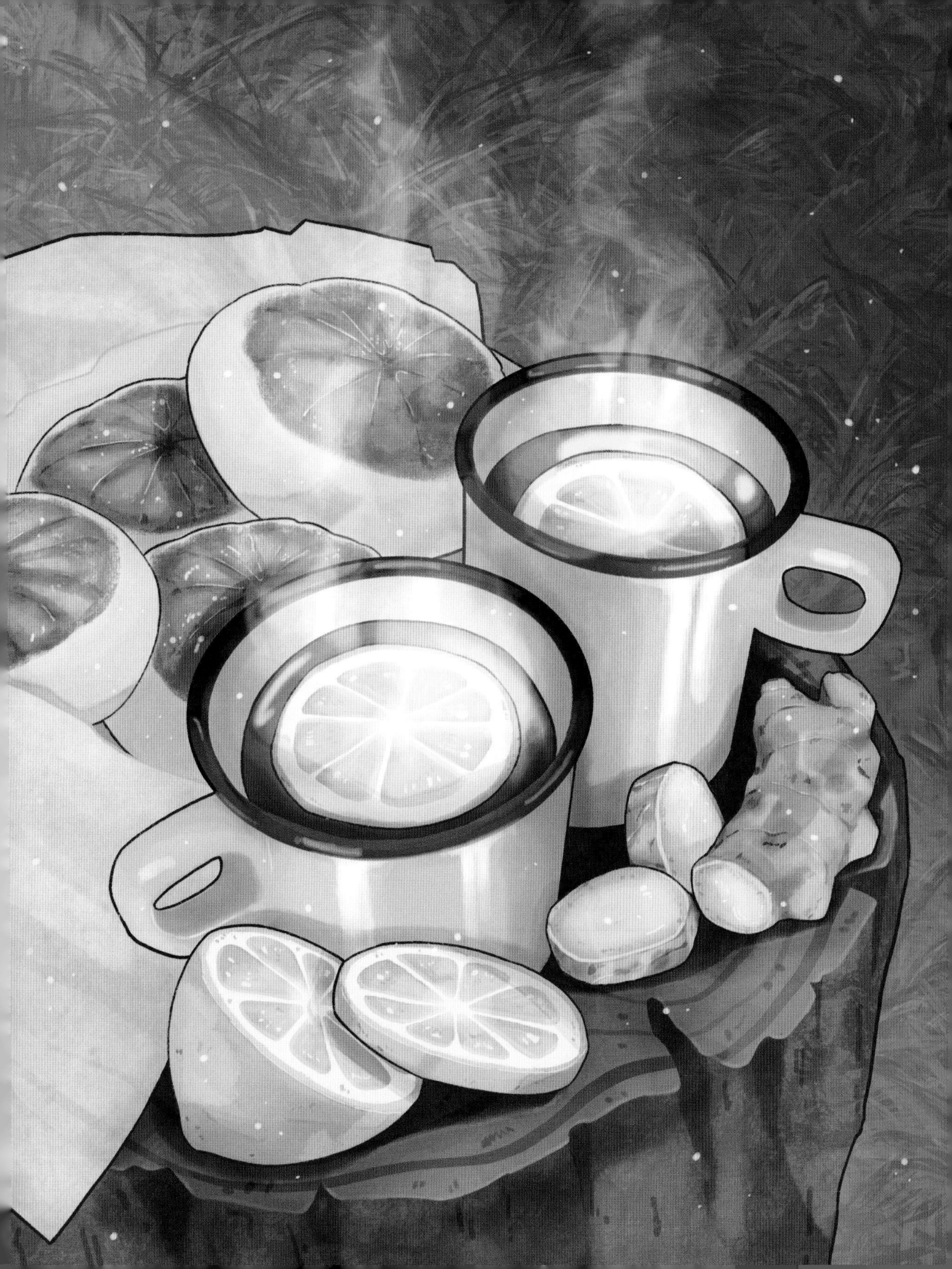

HOMEMADE LEMONADE

ANIME

CARDCAPTOR SAKURA: CLEAR CARD

SEASON 1, EPISODE 6

"Sakura, the Rabbit and the Song of the Moon"

Cardcaptor Sakura was one of the first animes to introduce me to cute anime food. It has plenty of scenes depicting home cooking. When Sakura and her friends have a picnic in the park, or as they call it, a "flower viewing party," to experience cherry blossom season, they all bring small handheld snacks and share this delicious lemonade. Lemonade is a staple, and everyone should have a solid recipe!

YIELD	PREP TIME	COOK TIME	COOL TIME
4	**10**	**10**	**15**
servings	minutes	minutes	minutes

LEMON SIMPLE SYRUP

1 cup (200 g) granulated sugar

Lemon zest from 6 or 7 lemons

LEMONADE

1 cup (240 ml) fresh lemon juice, from 6 or 7 lemons (use the zested lemons above)

6 cups (1.5 L) cold water

Ice cubes

1 lemon, sliced into ¼-inch-thick (6 mm) rounds, seeds removed

STEPS

1. **To make the lemon simple syrup:** Place the sugar and lemon zest into a small pot and mix with your fingers, lightly squeezing the lemon zest to release its aroma, about 30 seconds. Add 1 cup (240 ml) of water.

2. Transfer the pot to the stove over medium heat and bring to a boil. Once boiling, reduce the heat to low and let simmer until the sugar has dissolved. Remove from the heat, strain with a fine-mesh strainer, and set aside until cooled.

3. **To make the lemonade:** Add the lemon juice, 1 cup (240 ml) of the lemon simple syrup, and cold water to a clear pitcher and mix to combine well. Refrigerate until it is time to serve.

4. To serve, fill glasses with alternating layers of ice and lemon slices, then pour in the lemonade.

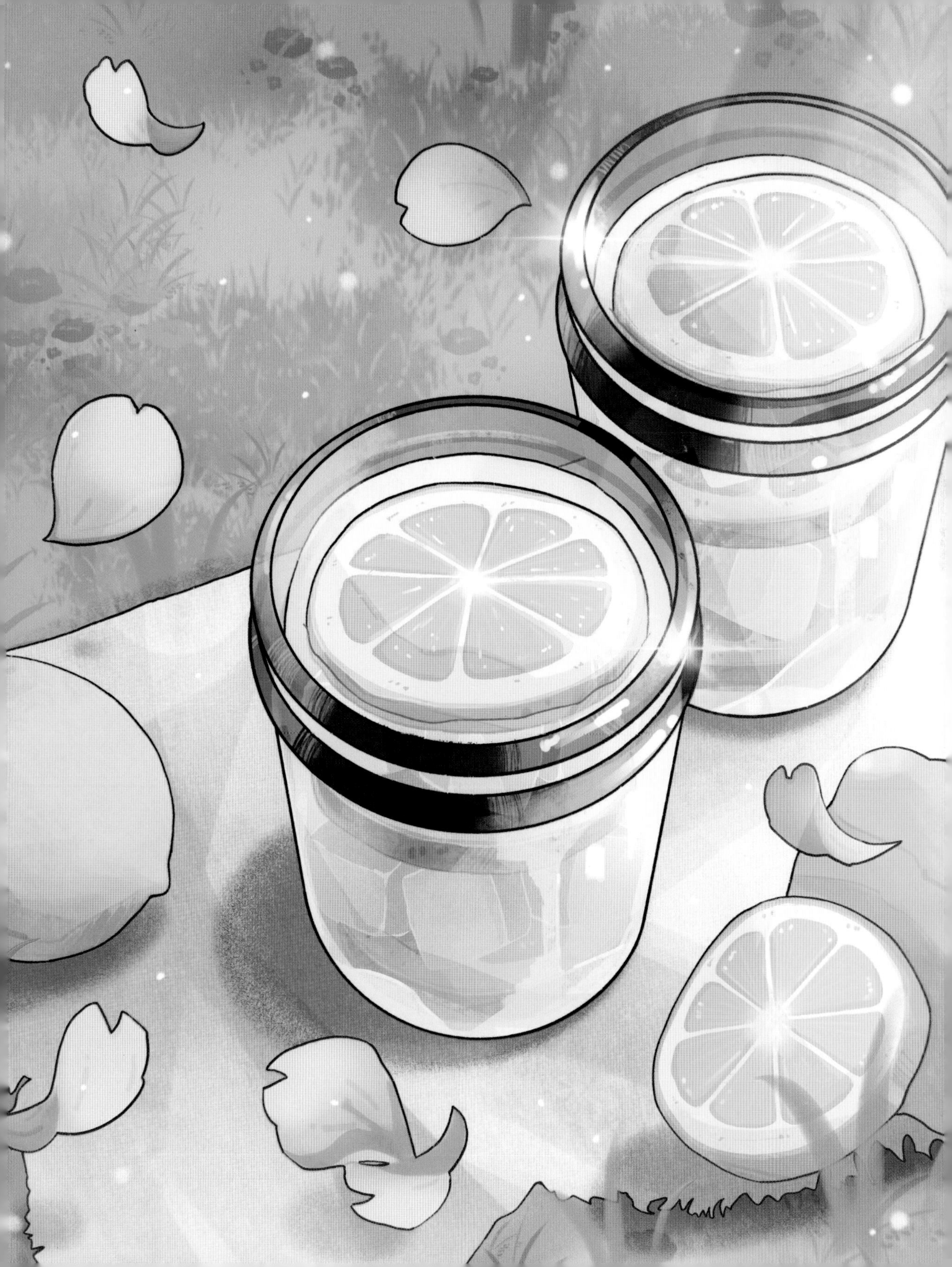

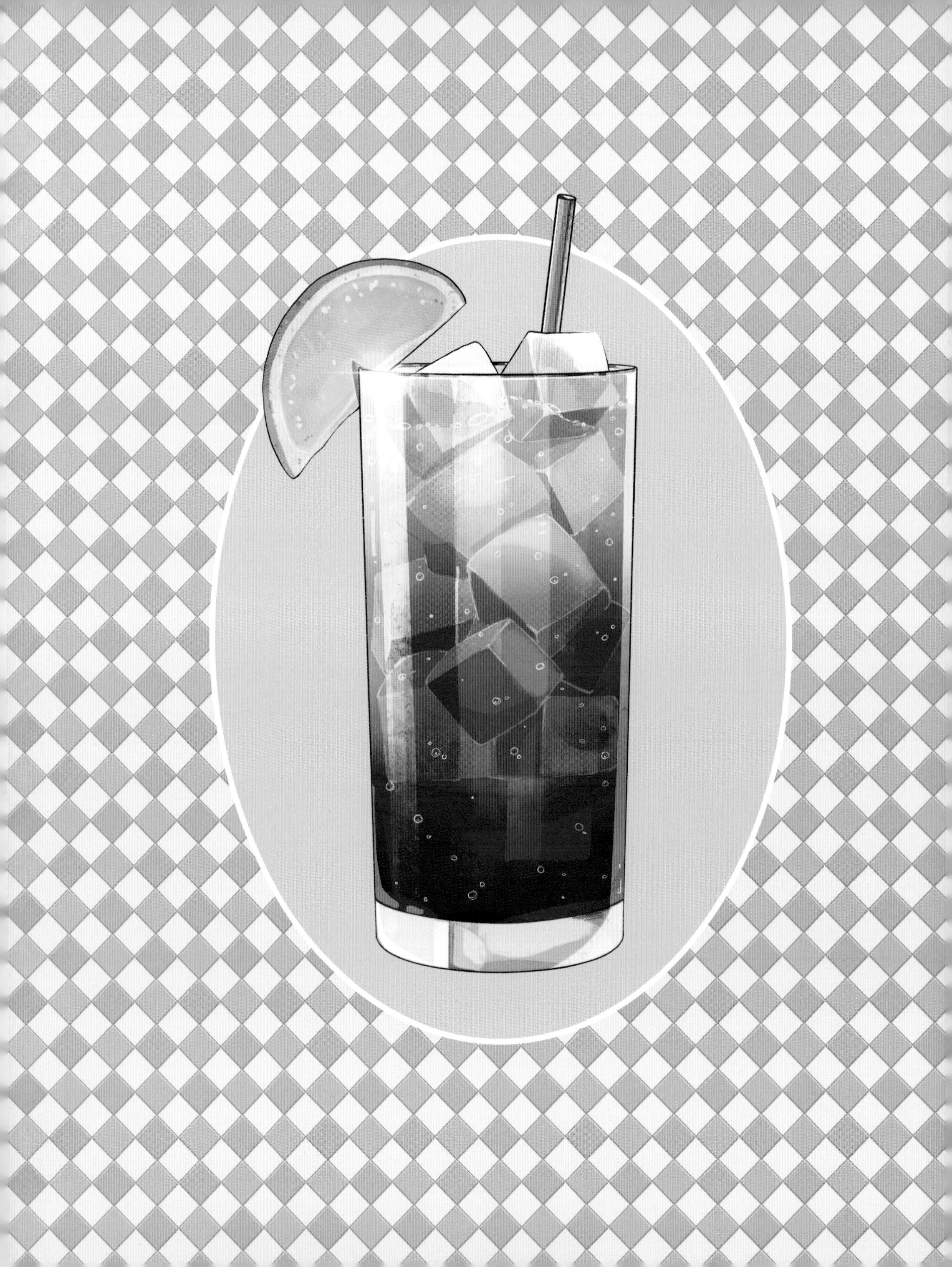

Bar

Café

SHANDYGAFF

ANIME

LOVE IS LIKE A COCKTAIL

SEASON 1, EPISODE 10

"Shandygaff"

The main characters of this anime include a wife-and-husband duo: Chisato, who loves drinks, and Sora, whose love language is creating drinks for Chisato. Sora makes Chi-chan a shandygaff, or "fake beer," for April Fools' Day! Notes from the anime also include using a nonalcoholic "fake beer" version that's equal parts ginger ale and pineapple juice for a sweet and spicy flavor.

MAKES	PREP TIME
2	**5**
drinks	minutes

INGREDIENTS

1 can (12 ounces, or 355 ml) pilsner or lager beer

1 can (12 ounces, or 355 ml) ginger ale

¼ cup (60 ml) pineapple juice (optional)

STEPS

1. Divide the beer between two tall glasses, followed by the ginger ale.

2. Add 2 tablespoons of pineapple juice (if using) to each glass to create a sweeter, refreshing flavor.

"It's infuriatingly good!"

—Chisato Mizusawa

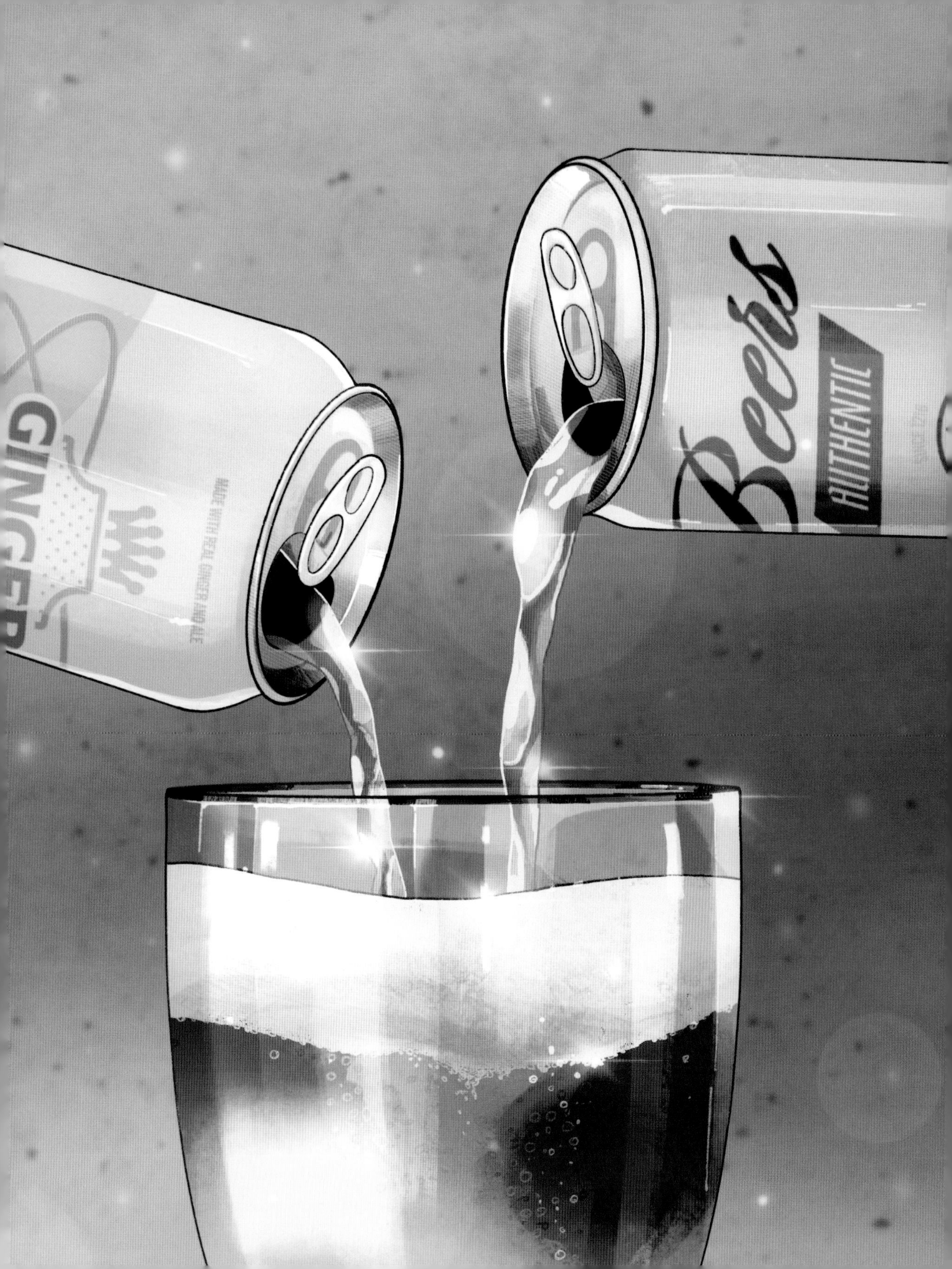
MADE WITH REAL GINGER AND ALE
Beers
AUTHENTIC

FIZZY HIBISCUS LEMONADE

ANIME

MY LOVE STORY WITH YAMADA-KUN AT LV999

SEASON 1, EPISODE 3

"I Wanna Have an Offline Meeting ♡"

Recovering from an embarrassing breakup, Akane agrees to go on a double date with her friend Momoko. At the bar, they order food and fizzy hibiscus lemonade drinks. When their dates arrive, Akane is completely bored and tries to give Momoko the hint that she is ready to leave with not-so-subtle expressions. This fizzy hibiscus lemonade is refreshingly sweet and sour, and it pairs perfectly with bar food like Creamy Yaki Udon (page 144) and Water-Water Meat Barbecue (page 147).

YIELD	PREP TIME	CHILL TIME
4	**10**	**30**
servings	minutes	minutes

INGREDIENTS

2 cups (480 ml) boiling water

2 hibiscus tea bags

¼ cup (60 ml) honey

1 tablespoon fresh lemon juice

Ice cubes

4 cups (1 L) seltzer

STEPS

1. In a large heatproof pitcher, pour in the boiling water and add the hibiscus tea bags. Let the tea bags steep for 10 minutes, then discard the bags.

2. Transfer the pitcher to the refrigerator until chilled, about 30 minutes.

3. Stir in the honey and lemon juice. Divide the hibiscus-honey-lemon mixture and ice among four glasses, then pour in the seltzer and fill to the rims of the glasses. Serve immediately.

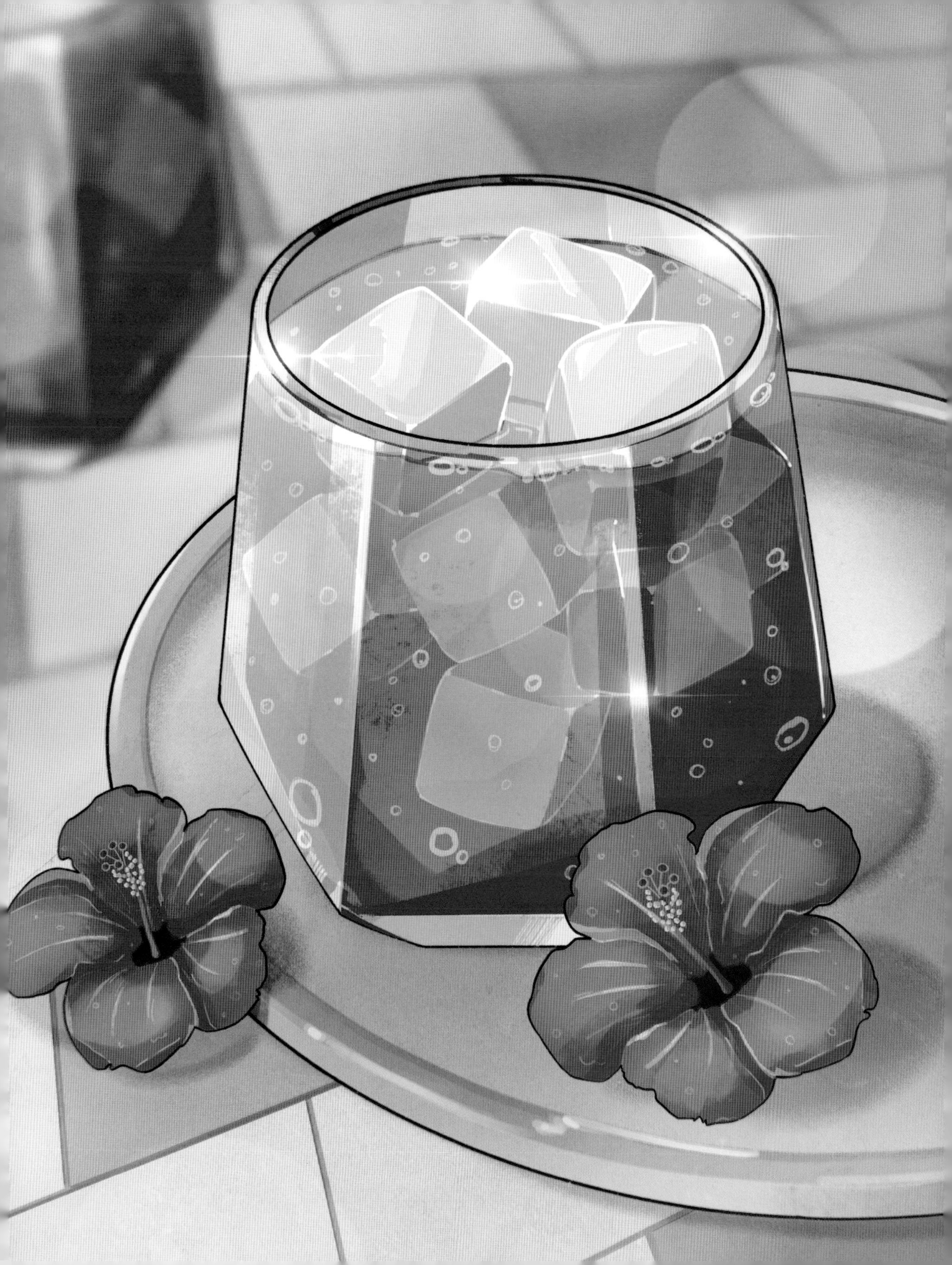

THREE-TIERED OTOKO UME SOUR

ANIME

TAKUNOMI

SEASON 1, EPISODE 9

"Otoko Ume Sour"

Takunomi is a sweet anime that involves women in different occupations living in the same house. At night, they unwind, share stories, and try different combinations of snacks and alcoholic drinks after a hard day's work. Nao is inspired to have a drink that embodies a snack. This pickled plum drink mimics a pickled plum candy. If you've never had one, it is sweet and tart! The beer and pickled plum flavor is a refreshing sip between bites of snacks.

YIELD

2

servings

PREP TIME

2

minutes

SPECIAL TOOLS

2 beer mugs

INGREDIENTS

2 tablespoons salt, or to taste

1 lime wedge

Ice cubes

2 cans (12 ounces, or 355 ml, each) Sapporo Otoko Ume Sour beer

2 umeboshi (pickled plums), pits removed, for garnish (see Note)

STEPS

1. Pour the salt onto a small plate. Rub the rim of two beer mugs with a lime wedge, then one mug at a time, turn each upside down and tap it into the salt for a salt rim.

2. Turn the mugs upright, then add enough ice to fill each 80 percent. Pour a can of beer into each mug.

3. Float a pickled plum on top of each drink and serve with salty snacks for the perfect pairing.

> **"That looks really salty . . . and really sour. H-huh? I'm drooling!"**
>
> —Michiru Amatsuki

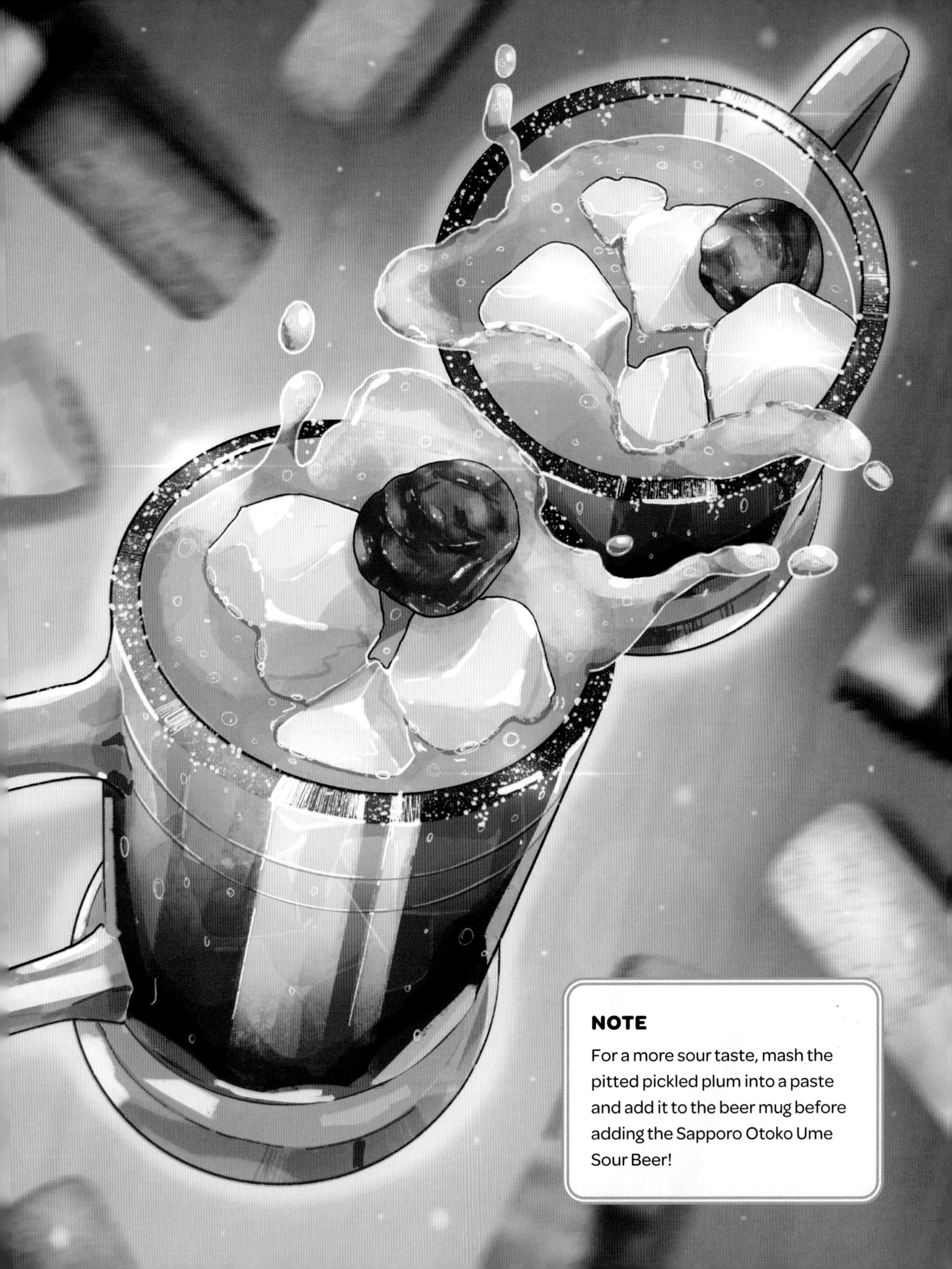

NOTE

For a more sour taste, mash the pitted pickled plum into a paste and add it to the beer mug before adding the Sapporo Otoko Ume Sour Beer!

SHIRLEY TEMPLE

ANIME

RENT-A-GIRLFRIEND

SEASON 1, EPISODE 2

"Ex-Girlfriend and Girlfriend"

Rent-a-Girlfriend is a comedic anime about college student Kazuya and Chizuru, the girlfriend he rents (pays) after being heartbroken by his ex-girlfriend. In this episode, Kazuya brings Chizuru to a restaurant to meet his friends, unaware that his ex-girlfriend is also there. This scene is hilariously uncomfortable as Kazuya tries to hide the fact that he now rents a girlfriend, all while his fake girlfriend defends him from his petty ex. Chizuru orders this Shirley Temple at the bar. It's a nonalcoholic drink that has pretty layers of colors. It's refreshing and delicious and often served with fried foods or grilled meats.

YIELD

2

servings

PREP TIME

5

minutes

SPECIAL TOOLS

2 straws

INGREDIENTS

Ice cubes

4 ounces (120 ml) grenadine

16 ounces (480 ml) lemon-lime soda

4 ounces (120 ml) orange juice

2 lime wedges

STEPS

1. Fill two tall glasses about 80 percent with ice.

2. Divide the grenadine, orange juice, and lemon-lime soda evenly and in this order between the glasses.

3. Garnish each glass with a lime wedge. Serve immediately with straws.

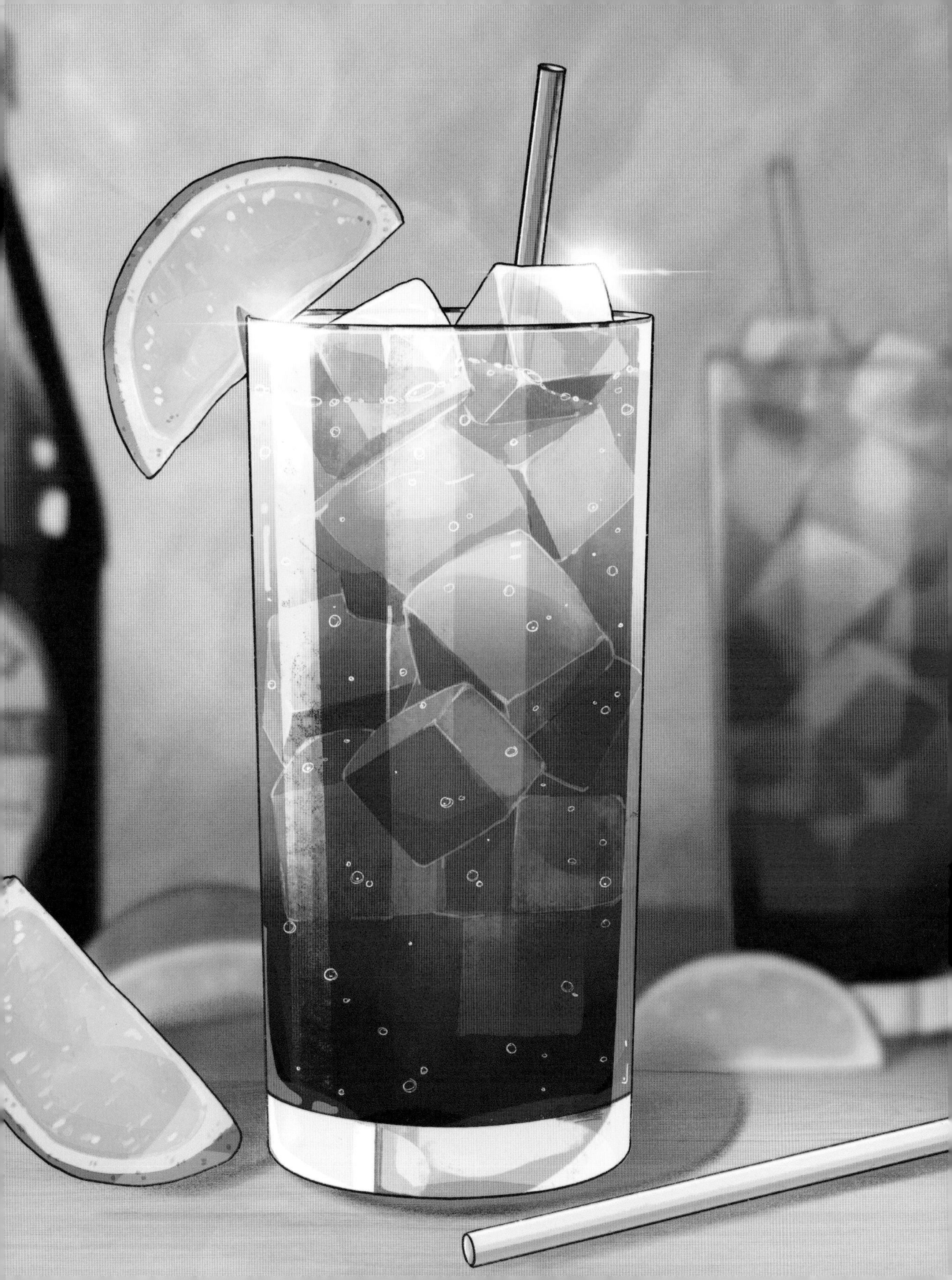

CREAMY YAKI UDON

MOVIE

SUZUME

The barkeepers offer to make yaki udon and mention that they like theirs with a sunny side-up egg and tuna mayo, while Suzume likes hers cooked with mashed potatoes! It sounds like a weird combination at first, but after tasting it, the bartenders are impressed. This yaki udon has addictive textures, from the chewiness of the udon noodles and the velvety creaminess of the mashed potatoes. The bartenders suggest drinking beer with this dish (see page 136 on how to make a Shandygaff).

YIELD
2-3
servings

PREP TIME
15
minutes

COOK TIME
1
hour

HOMESTYLE MASHED POTATOES

1 russet potato, peeled and quartered

½ small carrot, julienned

2 tablespoons salted butter

¼ teaspoon granulated sugar

2 tablespoons Kewpie mayo

Salt and black pepper

YAKI UDON

2 packages (9 ounces, or 255 g, each) udon
    (thawed if frozen; see Note on page 146)

1 teaspoon plus ½ tablespoon cooking oil
    (such as vegetable or canola), divided

3½ ounces (100 g) pork belly, sliced into batons

½ small onion, sliced

3 green onions, chopped and separated into
    white and green parts

¼ small cabbage, chopped into 1½-inch (4 cm) squares

2 tablespoons beni shoga (pickled red ginger)

UDON SAUCE

2 tablespoons soy sauce

1 tablespoon sake

1 tablespoon mirin

1 tablespoon Bull-Dog Sauce or
    Worcestershire sauce

½ tablespoon granulated sugar

FRIED EGGS

1 tablespoon cooking oil (such as
    vegetable or canola)

2 eggs

2 pinches salt

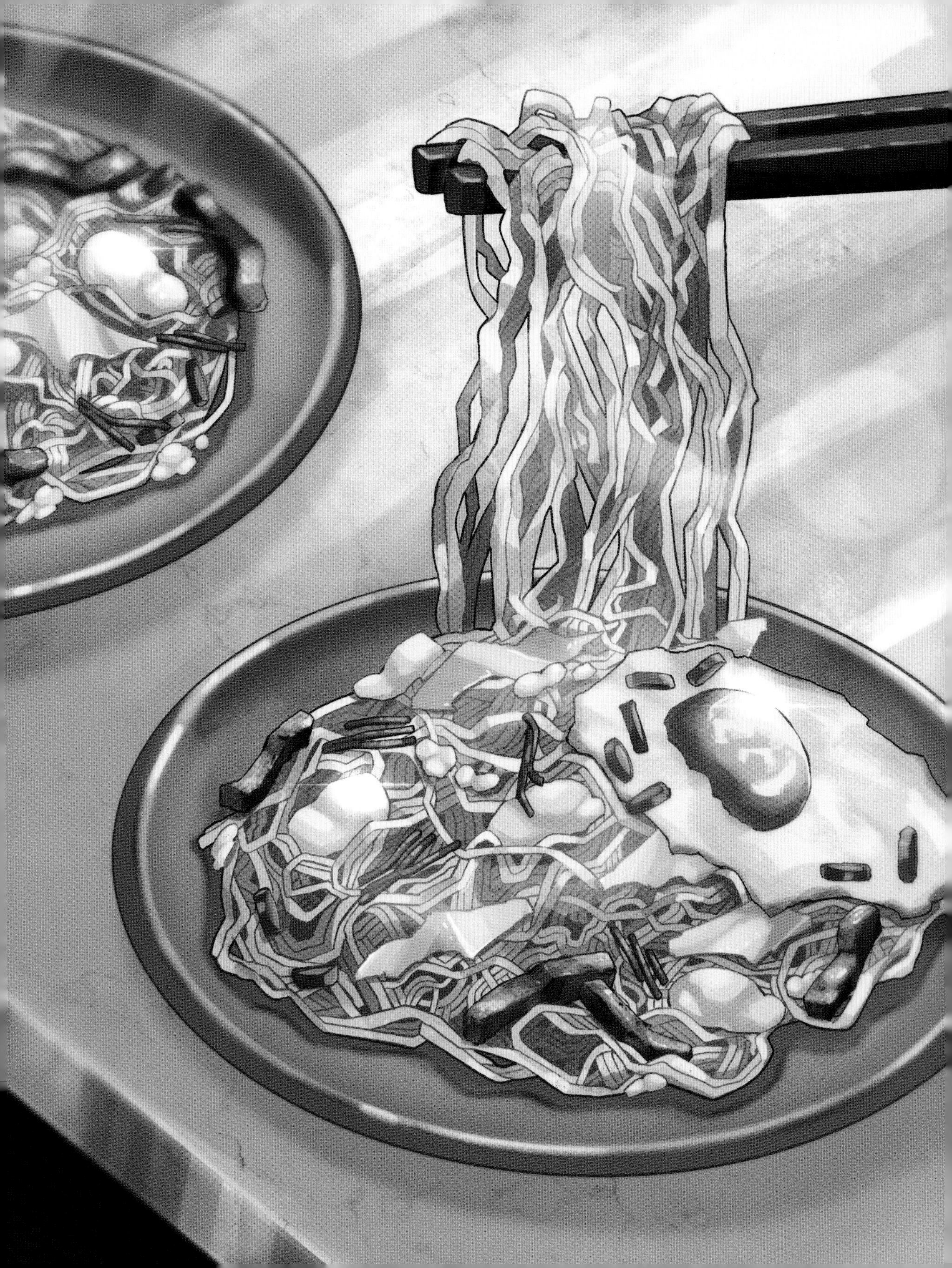

STEPS

1. **To make the homestyle mashed potatoes:** In a medium pot, add the potato and enough water to cover it by 1 inch (2.5 cm) and bring to a boil over medium-high heat. Reduce the heat to medium and cook until the potato is easy to pierce with a knife, about 20 minutes. Leave the pot on the heat, remove the potatoes with a slotted spoon., and transfer them to a medium bowl.

2. Raise the heat to medium-high and return the water in the pot to a boil. Quickly blanch the julienned carrots in the boiling water until slightly softened, about 1 minute. Remove from the heat.

3. In the bowl with the potatoes, add the butter and ¼ teaspoon sugar and mash until fully combined. Mix in the carrots. Let the mashed potato cool to room temperature, about 20 minutes, then stir in the mayo. Season with salt and pepper.

4. **To prepare the udon for the yaki udon:** Cook the udon noodles according to the package instructions. Drain the water and rinse the noodles in the pot with cold water until they reach room temperature. Drain the excess water, then add 1 teaspoon of the oil and toss with the noodles.

5. **While the udon cooks, make the udon sauce:** In a small bowl, combine the soy sauce, sake, mirin, Bull-Dog sauce, and ½ tablespoon sugar.

6. **To make the fried eggs:** Heat a medium nonstick skillet over medium heat. Add the 1 tablespoon oil. Crack in the eggs, leaving space in between. Reduce the heat to medium-low and add a pinch of salt to each egg. Cook for 3 to 4 minutes, until the egg whites are mostly set. Remove from the heat and transfer to a plate.

7. **To make the yaki udon:** In the same nonstick skillet, add the remaining ½ tablespoon oil and turn the heat to medium. Add the pork belly and cook until golden, about 3 minutes. Remove the pork with a slotted spoon and transfer to a paper towel–lined plate. Add the sliced onion and white parts of the green onions to the pan and cook until the onions are translucent, about 2 minutes. Add the cabbage and cook until slightly softened and vibrant in color, about 2 minutes. Add the cooked udon, the udon sauce, and the fried pork belly and stir to combine. Cook for about 1 minute, then reduce the heat to medium-low. Add the beni shoga, 3 heaping tablespoons of the mashed potatoes, and half of the chopped green parts of the green onions. Stir until combined, then remove from the heat.

8. To serve, divide the creamy yaki udon between two plates. Top with small dollops of mashed potato and then a fried egg. Sprinkle with the remaining green part of the green onions. Serve hot.

NOTE

You can find udon in most Asian supermarkets in the fresh noodle aisle, often near the tofu, or in the freezer section. Simply thaw and cook according to package instructions.

WATER-WATER MEAT BARBECUE

ANIME

ONE PIECE

EPISODE 315

"Its Name Is the New World! The Whereabouts of the Great Grand Line!"

Sanji is the Straw Hat Pirate's cook. When he makes his friends breakfast, he finds out one of his many love interests—Nami, the Straw Hat Pirate's navigator—is swimming in the pool. Urgently, he makes his way to the pool and cooks up Water-Water meat barbecue. (Water-Water is a trademarked name of food sold in the city of Water 7.) Sanji yells for Nami to try his food, but it is devoured quickly by everyone but Nami. Sanji cries, but he blames his tears on the smoke from the barbecue. When Luffy and Chopper bite into this meat skewer, it looks so soft; the anime mentions that the meat has been marinated well. So, after many iterations of this recipe, I used beef tenderloin and developed a flavorful marinade. *One Piece* is one of my favorite animes, and I am aware that Sanji's food is held to high standards! Please try this out—I think it's as delicious as Sanji's.

MAKES	PREP TIME	MARINATE TIME	COOK TIME
4	**10**	**30**	**15**
servings	minutes	minutes	minutes

SPECIAL TOOLS

Outdoor grill

Charcoal, for grilling (optional)

8 grilling skewers (if using wooden skewers, soak for 1 hour in cold water before placing on the grill)

INGREDIENTS

2 tablespoons soy sauce

2 tablespoons mirin

½ tablespoon fresh lemon juice

½ teaspoon granulated sugar

⅛ teaspoon black pepper

2 cloves garlic, grated

12 ounces (360 grams) beef tenderloin

1 small onion, quartered

1 small green bell pepper, seeded and sliced into 2 x 1½-inch (5 x 6 cm) rectangles

1 tablespoon cooking oil (such as vegetable or canola)

STEPS

1. In a large bowl, mix the soy sauce, mirin, lemon juice, sugar, black pepper, and grated garlic until well combined.

2. Slice the tenderloin against the grain into 1-inch-thick (2.5 cm) pieces, then cut those pieces into rectangles roughly the same dimensions as the bell pepper. Add the beef tenderloin to the marinade and marinate for 30 minutes max, flipping the beef pieces after 15 minutes. (Tenderloin is already soft, so marinating for longer will result in mushy meat.) While marinating the meat, heat the grill.

3. Remove the tenderloin from the marinade and set the marinade aside. Pierce a piece of meat with 2 skewers to prevent slipping, followed by 2 slices of onion, a piece of tenderloin, a slice of green bell pepper, and another slice of tenderloin. Repeat this step to make 3 more double skewers.

4. Once the grill is hot and registers about 350°F (180°C), oil the grates. When the oil begins to smoke, add the skewers and grill for 2 minutes. Baste with the marinade, then flip and cook for another 2 minutes. Baste with the marinade, then flip and cook for 5 minutes. Finally, baste, flip, and cook for 5 minutes more and to your desired doneness—140°F (60°C) for medium and 160°F (70°C) for well done, measuring with a thermometer.

5. Remove from the heat, remove a skewer from each set (optional), and serve immediately.

"If there's someone who's hungry, I'll feed them. If they're your enemies or not, everyone gets hungry. Then we'll talk!"

—Zeff and Sanji

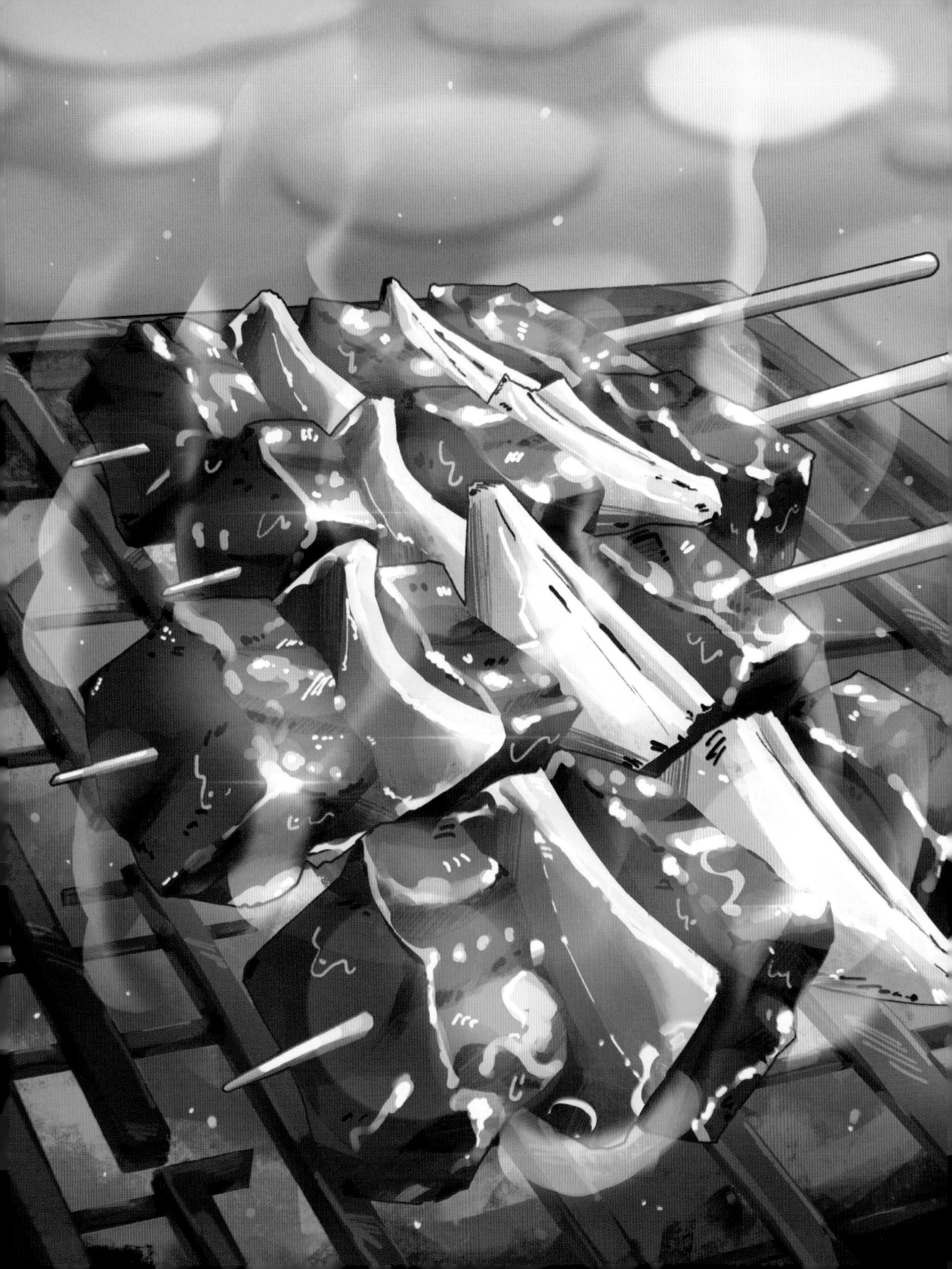

CHRYSANTHEMUM PEAR REFRESHER

ANIME

THE ANCIENT MAGUS' BRIDE

SEASON 1, EPISODE 10

"We Live and Learn"

This anime takes place in a European setting, which is why I love including it in my cookbooks as an example that anime food is not restricted to Japanese or Asian cuisine. It's also a classic anime that released its second season in 2023 after a six-year pause, making longtime fans very happy. In this episode, Elias sips a refreshing drink with his companions, a serene moment before Chise starts to seek a cure for Elias' condition.

YIELD	PREP TIME	COOK TIME	COOL TIME
4	**5**	**25**	**15**
servings	minutes	minutes	minutes

PEAR SIMPLE SYRUP

1 large Bosc pear, peeled, cored, and diced

1 cup (200 g) granulated sugar

CHRYSANTHEMUM TEA

1 tablespoon dried chrysanthemum flower buds

2 cups (480 ml) boiling water

FOR SERVING

Ice cubes

4 cups (1 L) cold water

4 sprigs fresh mint

STEPS

1. **To make the pear simple syrup:** In a small pot over medium-high heat, combine the diced pear and sugar with 1 cup (240 ml) of water and bring to a boil. Once boiling, reduce the heat to medium-low and let gently simmer for 20 minutes, or until the pears have softened and the syrup thickens. Strain the liquid through a fine-mesh strainer into a small bowl and set aside to cool to room temperature.

2. **Meanwhile, make the chrysanthemum tea:** In a heatproof bowl or mug, combine the dried chrysanthemum flower buds and boiling water. Let steep for 10 minutes, then strain the liquid through a fine-mesh strainer into a pouring vessel and let cool to room temperature, about 15 minutes.

3. **To serve:** Add ice to two glasses. To each glass, add 2 tablespoons of chrysanthemum tea and 1 tablespoon of pear simple syrup, or to taste. Fill the rest of the glasses with cold water and stir. Serve garnished with a sprig of mint.

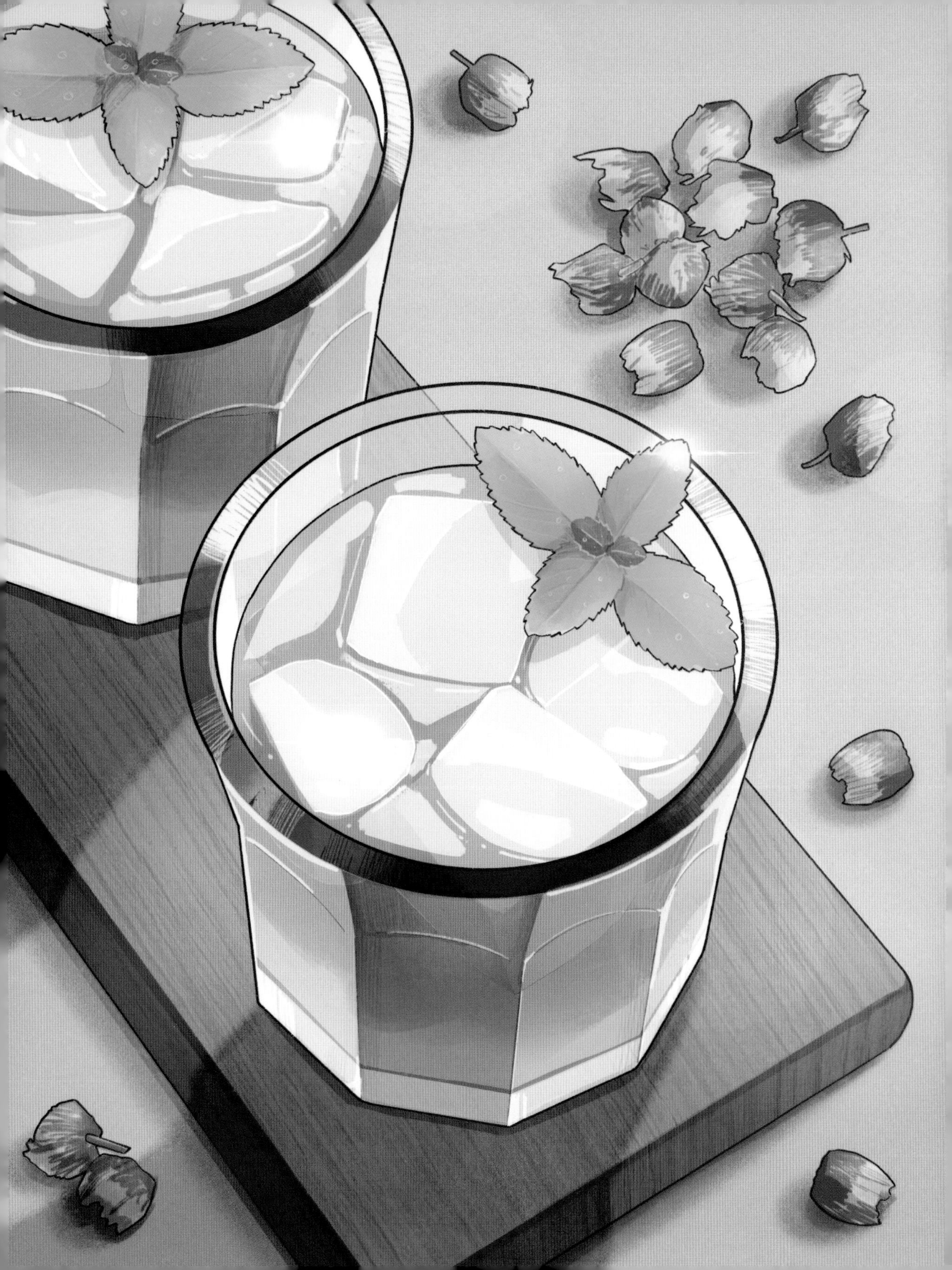

PINK PUNCH

MOVIE

DETECTIVE CONAN: THE TIME BOMBED SKYSCRAPER

Detective Conan is a successful classic anime that has been ongoing since 1996! A scene from Detective Conan's first movie is set at an exclusive garden tea party. There, only important, famous people are served cookies, scones, and this vibrant pink punch. The scene is straight out of the '90s, and I love how uniquely the food is portrayed. Who knows, maybe extravagant punch will become popular again, just like '90s fashion has!

YIELD	PREP TIME	FREEZE TIME
6-8	**10**	**4**
servings	minutes	hours

SPECIAL TOOLS

3 ice cube trays

Large punch bowl and ladle

FRUITY ICE CUBES

1 large orange, peeled, pith removed, and sliced into chunks

1 cup (165 g) pineapple chunks

1 cup (165 g) strawberries, hulled and diced medium

PINK PUNCH

4 cups (1 L) lemon-lime soda

2 cups (480 ml) cranberry juice cocktail

½ cup (120 ml) tequila (optional)

¼ cup (60 ml) fresh lime juice

2 cups (300 g) strawberry sherbet

STEPS

1. **To make the fruity ice cubes:** Pack the oranges into one of the ice cube trays and fill the rest of the space with water. Repeat for the pineapples and strawberries in separate ice cube trays. (Avoid squeezing the fruit; if they release juices, it may alter the color of the pink punch when the ice cubes melt.) Freeze completely, at least 4 hours, or overnight.

2. **To make the pink punch:** In a large punch bowl, stir together the lemon-lime soda, cranberry juice cocktail, tequila (if using), and fresh lime juice.

3. Right before serving, add the prepared fruity ice cubes to the punch bowl and float scoops of the strawberry sherbet on top.

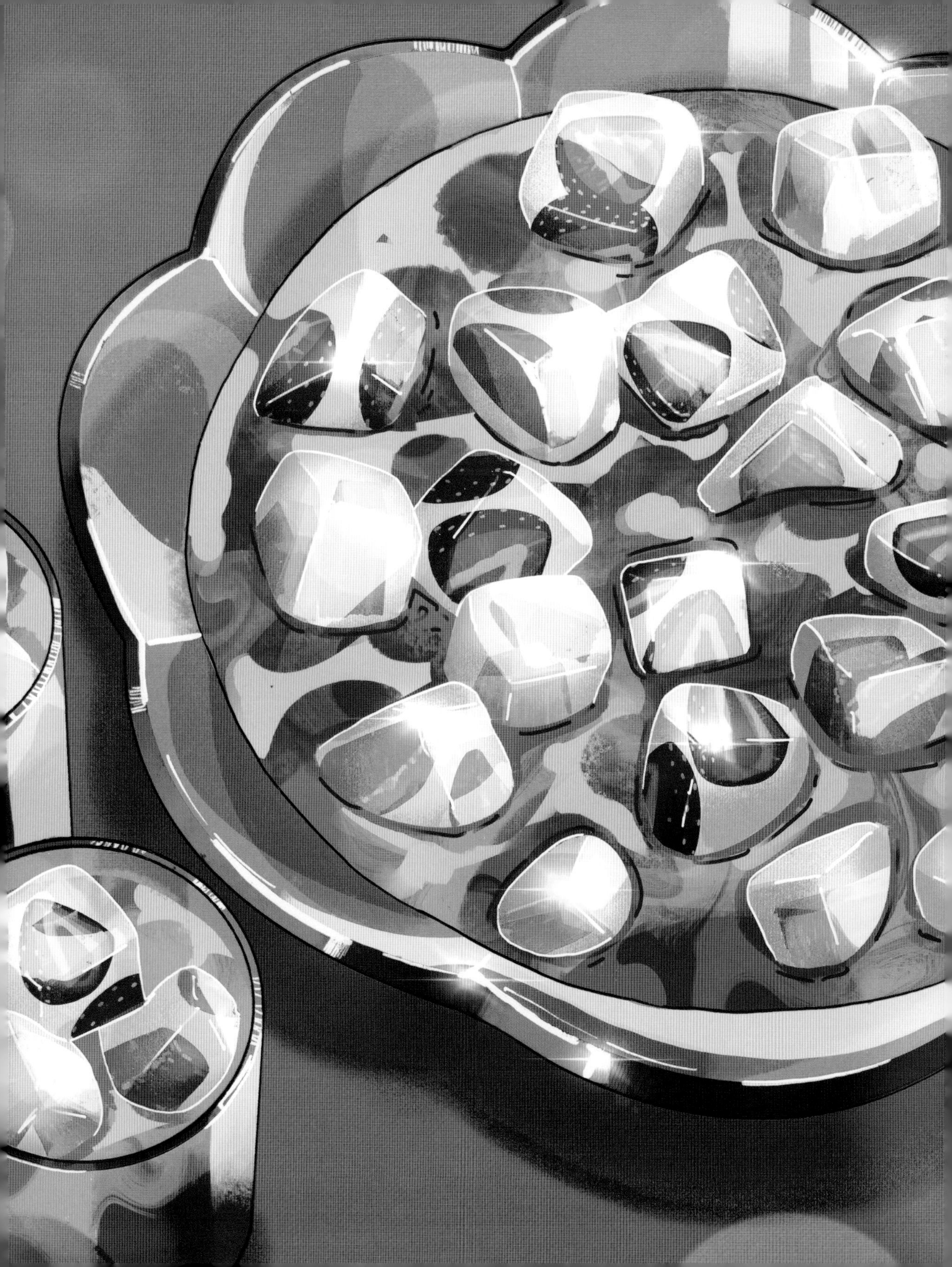

FRIEND-A-VERSARY KARAAGE, TWO WAYS!

ANIME

BOCCHI THE ROCK!

SEASON 1, EPISODE 7

"To Your House"

Hitori "Bocchi" has extreme anxiety and is shy. Her parents worry that she isn't making friends, so they are excited when Bocchi decides to bring her bandmates over. Bocchi's dad coins the term "Friend-a-versary" to celebrate and makes a feast for her newfound friends, serving two kinds of karaage: soy sauce and garlic and shio koji. Shio koji is fermented rice. It has a salty and sweet umami taste. You can find it online or in Japanese supermarkets.

YIELD	PREP TIME	MARINATE TIME	COOK TIME
4	**10**	**30**	**15**
servings	minutes	minutes	minutes

SOY SAUCE AND GARLIC KARAAGE

3 skin-on, boneless chicken thighs, cut into 1-inch (2.5 cm) pieces

1 tablespoon grated onion

1 tablespoon grated Fuji apple

3 cloves garlic, grated

1 tablespoon soy sauce

1 tablespoon mirin

1 teaspoon grated fresh ginger

2 pinches salt, divided

1 pinch black pepper

SHIO KOJI KARAAGE

3 skin-on, boneless chicken thighs, cut into 1-inch (2.5 cm) pieces

1 tablespoon shio koji

1 tablespoon mirin

1 clove garlic, grated

1 teaspoon grated fresh ginger

1 pinch black pepper

FOR FRYING

Canola oil, for frying

½ cup (95 g) potato starch

¼ teaspoon salt

FOR SERVING

2 lettuce leaves

4 lemon wedges

Shichimi togarashi

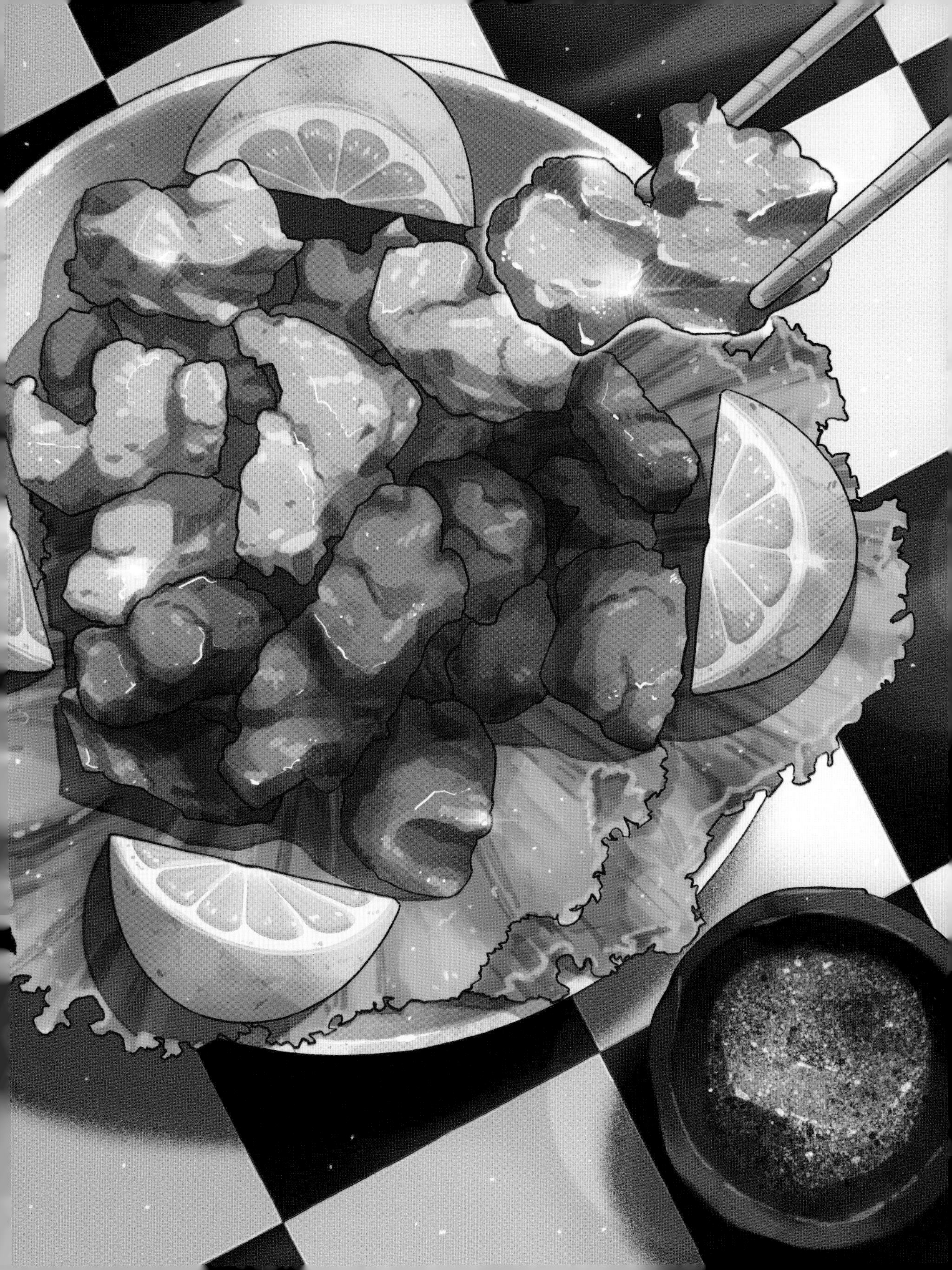

STEPS

1. **To make the soy sauce and garlic karaage:** In a large bowl, combine the chicken, onion, apple, 3 cloves grated garlic, soy sauce, mirin, ginger, 1 pinch of the salt, and the pepper and mix well. Marinate in the refrigerator for at least 30 minutes, or overnight (any longer will deteriorate the proteins too much and the meat will get mushy).

2. **To make the shio koji karaage:** In a separate large bowl, combine the chicken, shio koji, mirin, 1 clove grated garlic, ginger, and pepper and mix well. Marinate in the refrigerator for at least 30 minutes, or overnight (any longer will deteriorate the proteins too much and the meat will get mushy).

3. In a large heavy-bottomed pot, heat at least 3 inches (8 cm) of oil over medium heat to 350°F (180°C), measuring with a thermometer. Meanwhile, fill a shallow dish with the potato starch. Once the oil is hot, remove the soy sauce and garlic karaage from the refrigerator.

4. **To fry:** Working with one piece of soy sauce and garlic karaage at a time, remove the chicken from the marinade, letting the excess marinade drip off. Dredge the piece in the potato starch, pressing the chicken down to cover and shaking to remove the excess. Carefully transfer the chicken to the hot oil. Cook the chicken for 4 to 5 minutes, until cooked through and lightly browned. Transfer to a cooling rack. Repeat for the remaining soy sauce and garlic karaage.

5. Repeat step 4 for the shio koji karaage.

6. Increase the heat so that the oil reaches 355 to 360°F (180°C), then return the fried soy sauce and garlic karaage to the pot and cook until extra crispy and golden, about 2 minutes. Transfer to the cooling rack and sprinkle with the remaining pinch of salt while still hot. Repeat this step for the shio koji karaage, but skip the sprinkle of salt.

7. **To serve:** Arrange the lettuce leaves on a serving plate, then place the karaage on top. Add lemon wedges around the perimeter and serve with shichimi togarashi for topping.

"Eat your fill, all right?"

—Michiyo Gotoh

INDEX

ABOUT THE AUTHOR

NADINE ESTERO has always loved cooking and art, and she combines her interests by re-creating food from anime, video games, and shows and sharing her creations on social media (@IssaGrill) with over one million followers. Her work has been featured on Refinery29 and in the *New York Times* and *Philippine Star*. Her first cookbook, *The Anime Chef Cookbook: 75 Iconic Dishes from Your Favorite Anime*, made the *Globe and Mail's* best-seller list.

She used to watch a lot of action anime, like Dragon Ball, growing up, but now her favorite genre of anime is slice of life. Her current favorite character is Bond Forger from *Spy X Family*, who you can find in one of the creations in this book (page 68). Nadine lives in Vancouver, Canada.